THE LEGAL SYSTEM

OF NORTHERN IRELAND

The Servicing the Legal System Programme

This Programme was inaugurated in August 1980 in the Faculty of Law at Queen's University, Belfast to promote the publications of commentaries on various aspects of the law and the legal system of Northern Ireland. Generous financial and other support for the Programme has been provided by the Northern Ireland Court Service, the Inn of Court of Northern Ireland, the Bar Council of Northern Ireland, the Law Society of Northern Ireland and Queen's University. Details of all SLS publications may be obtained from the SLS Office, School of Law, Queen's University, Belfast BT7 1NN, Northern Ireland.

THE LEGAL SYSTEM OF
NOTHERN IRELAND

Brice Dickson

Professor of Law, University of Ulster

Belfast
1993

First edition published in 1984 by SLS Legal Publications (NI), Faculty of Law, Queen's University, Belfast, BT7 1NN.
Second Printing 1985
Third Printing 1986
Second Edition 1989
Second Printing 1991
Third Printing 1992
Third Edition 1993

ISBN 0 85389 474 4

Typeset by SLS Legal Publications (NI)
Printed by Dataplus, Belfast

To the memory of Jonathan Mallon
(1973 - 1993)

PREFACE

The main purpose of this book remains the supply of basic information about the legal system of Northern Ireland. It does not pretend to be a sophisticated critique of present arrangements or a scholarly examination of the actual substance of specific branches of the law. It simply describes in non-technical language what institutions and processes currently exist to put the law into operation in Northern Ireland.

In this third edition I have preserved the main features of the first two editions but have updated each section in the light of developments occurring and statistical information appearing since 1989. I have also sought to break up the text with a greater number of Tables. Tables of Cases and Legislation have been inserted at the start because it was becoming too cumbersome to include references to these in the general index.

Once again I would like to thank the many people, too numerous to mention by name, who dealt with my queries during the course of preparing this new edition. Without the co-operation of a great number of officials in a variety of bodies the book would simply not have appeared. The staff of the Northern Ireland Court Service deserve my special gratitude. For help with updating Chapters 7 and 8, and the Appendices, I am grateful to Ruth Hagan and Carole Sholdis. Mrs Sara Gamble and Mr Christopher Martin, of SLS Legal Publications, provided excellent assistance during the final stages of production. As ever the support of Patricia Mallon was invaluable.

The text is based on material which was available to me on 1st August 1993. Occasionally I have been able to anticipate events which I knew were going to occur during the printing stage. If there are mistakes or significant omissions, please do write to tell me.

Copyright material in Appendices 3 and 4 is reproduced by permission of the Comptroller of Her Majesty's Stationery Office, with the exception of the application form for legal advice and assistance, reproduced by permission of the Law Society of Northern Ireland, and the report of *Campbell* v *Armstrong and others*, reprinted by permission of the Editor of the Northern Ireland Law Reports.

BRICE DICKSON
University of Ulster
Jordanstown
September 1993

CONTENTS

Table of Cases

Table of Legislation

List of Tables

1

The History and Administration of the Legal System

1.1 The Early Legal History of Northern Ireland

The history of a legal system is inevitably linked to the political history of the territory where the legal system has operated. For that reason alone the legal history of Northern Ireland is long and complex. A true appreciation of it is essential, however, if the workings of the legal system today are to be properly understood. As well as throwing light on why things are as they are, the history helps us to identify those aspects of the system which are overdue for change. The importance of an historical approach will be made particularly apparent in Chapter 2 when we look at the sources of law. The first three sections of this opening chapter provide a brief sketch of the general legal history, while the following three sections describe the bodies and persons who have inherited the political and professional responsibility for operating the legal system in Northern Ireland.

The Brehon law system

Before the arrival of the Normans in 1169 Ireland was governed by Brehon law. This was a legal system based on traditional custom, the laws being formulated and applied by respected native jurists called Brehons. Brehon law continued to apply after 1169 in areas outside the Normans' control, and even in areas within their control it continued to govern the native Irish. The Normans themselves were subject to the English "common law" system, which at that time was already unifying the various local legal systems throughout England.

As the Normans extended their influence English law slowly became more important in Ireland. In 1171 King Henry II is said to have held a Council near Waterford, "where the laws of England were by all freely received and confirmed," but it is more likely that the English laws were only gradually accepted during the course of the following century. By 1300 English law applied in most of Ireland, and some 30 years later the policy of leaving the native Irish to be governed by Brehon law was reversed. By this time, however, the Irish were beginning to regroup, with the object of repelling the Norman invaders. Consequently, the influence of English law went into gradual decline. By 1500 English law extended only to the area around Dublin known as the Pale; the rest of Ireland had returned to Brehon law.

All this changed again with the Tudor reconquest, which culminated in the Flight of the Earls in 1607 and the Plantation of Ulster in the early years of the seventeenth century. The whole of Ireland was then under English control and Brehon law completely ceased to apply. In a famous piece of litigation known as *The Case of Tanistry* (1607), Brehon law was declared to be incompatible with and contrary to the common law of England and could not, therefore, remain any part of the law in Ireland. Since then the provisions of Brehon law have been referred to by judges in a few cases concerning ancient fishing rights, but otherwise Brehon law has played no part at all in the modern legal history of Ireland.

The common law system

The system of law which has existed throughout Ireland since the seventeenth century is called the common law system, though it is important to note that this is only one sense in which the expression "common law" can be used. We will encounter its other meanings in due course. The most fundamental feature of the common law system is the doctrine of binding precedent. According to this doctrine, which is explained more fully in 2.4, once a court has made a decision on a particular point of law, that decision is a binding authority on lower courts in subsequent cases concerned with the same legal point. Now that many more laws are being created by Parliament than was the case a century or so ago, there is not so much scope for judge-made law, with the result that the force of the doctrine of precedent is diminishing. It is still much stronger, however, than in countries such as France and Germany where a so-called "civil law" system operates. The law there is laid down almost exclusively in codes and even when judges interpret these codes their decisions are not binding for later cases.

Following the reconquest of Ireland in the sixteenth and seventeenth centuries the law in Ireland and England developed along much the same lines until the early twentieth century. The countries were administered differently, but the actual content of the law was almost identical. Some significant differences were created during the nineteenth century in an attempt to solve the intractable land problem in Ireland, and the two jurisdictions got out of step regarding family law and some other matters, but generally the laws remained very similar. Even since the partition of Ireland in 1920 the law throughout the two islands (with the exception of Scotland, which has more of a civil law system) has been based on the same fundamental common law concepts. The creation of separate Parliaments, though, which is described in the next section, has inevitably caused some divergences.

1.2 Parliaments

Just as the Parliament in England developed out of the King's Council (the "Curia Regis"), a Parliament in Ireland evolved, during the thirteenth century, out of the jurisdiction of the Justiciar, the King's official representative in Ireland. For two centuries there were Parliaments in both England and Ireland claiming the power to make laws for Ireland, and not until 1495 was it declared at a gathering at Drogheda that only legislation approved by the English Council could be passed by the Parliament in Ireland (Poynings' Law). The Irish Parliament continued to exist until 1800 and it did make some unapproved laws. Between 1782 and 1800 it even regained some of its former pre-eminence, because most of Poynings' Law was repealed by Yelverton's Law in 1781. From the Act of Union in 1800, until 1921, the only legislative body for Ireland was the Parliament of the United Kingdom sitting in London. But not all of the legislation enacted by that Parliament applied automatically throughout the kingdom: some Acts were applied to Ireland only at a later date (and sometimes in a piecemeal fashion), some were specifically enacted for Ireland and never applied in England, and some were not extended to Ireland at all.

With the partitioning of Ireland in 1920 separate legal systems were established for the North and the South. The North, of course, comprised six of the nine counties constituting the province of Ulster. Each part of the island was given its own Parliament as well as its own system of courts. In the South the old law continued to apply only when it was not inconsistent with the Constitution of the new state. For many years this resulted in few alterations, though in the past 20 years or so the Irish Constitution of 1937 has played an increasingly important role in the law's development in the Republic.

The Stormont Parliament

In Northern Ireland some scope for legal development distinct from that occurring in England was created by the transfer to a new local Parliament of the right to enact legislation "for the peace, order and good government" of the province. This had been the phrase used when Britain had earlier devolved power to Canada, Australia and South Africa. From 1932 the Parliament of Northern Ireland was located at Stormont, near Belfast. The matters which were "transferred" to it included law and order, local government, health and social services, education, planning, internal trade, industrial development and agriculture. Certain "excepted" and "reserved" matters, though, could be dealt with only by the Parliament at Westminster. Excepted matters were those which were of imperial or national concern, for which it was felt to be undesirable to enact local variations. They included the armed forces, external trade, weights and measures and copyright law. Reserved matters were those which were to be the preserve of the proposed Council of Ireland (which in fact was never created) and included postal services, the registration of deeds, major taxes (not, for example, road tax or stamp duty) and the Supreme Court of Northern Ireland.

The Northern Ireland Parliament consisted of two chambers - the House of Commons and the Senate - but there were also elections for representatives to sit for Northern Ireland constituencies at Westminster. The Monarch was represented in Northern Ireland by the Governor, residing at Hillsborough in County Down. The general policy of the Stormont Parliament was to keep in step with legislation enacted for Great Britain, although in certain areas Northern Ireland either failed to follow changes or introduced new laws of its own devising. As the years went by differences became particularly apparent in the laws relating to social services, education and housing.

Northern Ireland under direct rule

This devolution of powers in the North continued until March 1972, when the Stormont Parliament was suspended. "Direct rule" was introduced, with laws on transferred matters being made by Order in Council (see 2.3) and executive powers being exercised by the Secretary of State for Northern Ireland. Under the Northern Ireland Constitution Act 1973 the Northern Ireland Parliament was abolished and a new system of devolution was tried. In January 1974 powers to make some laws (called "Measures") were vested in a one-chamber elected Assembly, but this experiment collapsed in May 1974 and since then direct rule has applied once more, the arrangements being renewed annually under the Northern Ireland Act 1974.

In 1982 a new 78-member Northern Ireland Assembly, again with only one chamber and sitting at Stormont, was elected under the Northern Ireland Act 1982. It did not have any law-making powers - only "scrutiny, consultative and deliberative powers" - but the United Kingdom Government hoped that in due course some such powers could be transferred to it under the principle of so-called "rolling", or partial, devolution. Once again the experiment proved unsuccessful and the Assembly was dissolved in 1986. The signing of the Anglo-Irish Agreement in November 1985 led to the establishment of the Anglo-Irish Intergovernmental Conference, which convenes periodically to allow representatives from the Government of the Irish Republic to put forward their views on the governance of the province. It also created an Anglo-Irish Parliamentary Council which allows members of the British and Irish Parliaments to meet from time to time to discuss matters of mutual interest. The 1985 Agreement, however, is a treaty between two sovereign states and does not have the force of internal domestic law in either country.

Northern Ireland therefore continues to be controlled by the Parliament at Westminster, with the United Kingdom Government administering it through the Northern Ireland Office, a department headed by the Secretary of State for Northern Ireland (see 1.4). Public expenditure in Northern Ireland for 1993-94 is projected as £7,460 million, with approximately £900 million of this directed towards law and order. Northern Ireland constituencies elect 17 MPs to the Parliament at Westminster and three MEPs to the European Parliament. The Northern Ireland Committee of the Westminster Parliament has power to consider such matters affecting the province as may be referred to it, but in practice it now rarely meets. There is speculation that a Select Committee on Northern Ireland is to be established in the near future, along the lines of the Select Committee on Scotland. The various forms which Parliamentary law can take today are described in detail in 2.2 and 2.3.

During the period of direct rule the process of assimilation between the law in Northern Ireland and the law in England has, if anything, been fortified. Harmonization has also been fostered through the United Kingdom's membership both of the European Community (the Common Market) and of the Council of Europe (see 2.6).

1.3 Courts

The Four Courts

The Normans did not introduce a new system of law into England after the Battle of Hastings in 1066. William the Conqueror, in fact, declared that he did not wish to change the law at all. But in order to keep control over the whole country the Norman kings assumed responsibility for the administration of justice and created a new system of courts based at Westminster. These courts, supported by the royal power, gradually came to deal with the most important types of legal dispute, and it was from the rules devised by judges to settle disputes in these courts that there emerged a body of law which was common to the whole kingdom. To begin with there were three courts to handle three broad categories of case. Cases involving the King's interest in the maintenance of law and order were dealt with by the Court of King's Bench; taxation cases were heard in the Court of Exchequer; and disputes involving only "common" (*i.e.* private) individuals went to the Court of Common Pleas. These courts met regularly at Westminster, but twice a year the justices would tour the country, on Assizes, to dispense the King's justice and reassert his authority in each of the counties. Each case was decided by one judge, usually sitting with a jury of 12 "true and honest" men.

There were many disputes which could not be dealt with in these three courts. Petitions sent to the King to settle such cases were referred by him to his Chancellor (at that time usually an influential cleric) for justice to be done "according to the conscience of the case." From this practice there emerged another court, the Court of Chancery. The convention developed that the justice dispensed by the Court of Chancery was "equity", while the justice dispensed by the King's three other courts was "common law" (another sense in which that phrase has been used). It was not until 1875 in England (1877 in Ireland) that common law and equity could be administered in one and the same court; until then the two types of law had to be kept quite separate.

When the Normans established themselves in Ireland they naturally introduced a system of courts modelled on the English system. Accordingly the Four Courts (of King's Bench, Exchequer, Common Pleas and Chancery) were set up in Dublin, in a building which still bears that name. As in England, the judges in most of these courts went on Assizes throughout those parts of Ireland under Norman control each spring and summer. Cases were therefore ordered to be tried in Dublin, unless before (in Latin, *nisi prius*) the given date of trial the Assize judge came to the county where the litigants lived (hence the establishment of local *nisi prius* courts).

These four courts formed the heart of the legal systems in England and Ireland until late in the nineteenth century. Over time other courts were established to deal with special types of case and with appeals. To the four "superior" courts in Dublin were added five more: a Court of Admiralty (to deal with shipping cases), a Court of Bankruptcy and Insolvency, a Court of Probate (to deal with disputes concerning wills), a Court for Matrimonial Causes, and a Landed Estates Court (part of the effort to solve the land problem). Two appeal courts called the Court of Exchequer Chamber and the Court of Appeal in Chancery were added. For cases involving smaller amounts there was created a system of "civil bill" or "county courts" (see 5.4), and power to try less serious criminal cases was given to magistrates' courts. It can be seen that by the 1870s the court structure in Ireland had become exceedingly complicated and unmanageable.

The Supreme Court of Judicature

In 1877 a thorough reorganisation of the superior courts took place, again along English lines. The nine courts were amalgamated into one High Court which by 1900 came to have only two divisions - the Queen's Bench Division (which took over the work of seven of the old courts) and the Chancery Division (which took over the work of the other two - the Court of Chancery and the Landed Estates Court). The appeal courts were also amalgamated into one Court of Appeal. The new High Court and the Court of Appeal together constituted the Supreme Court of Judicature - a rather misleading title, since there could always be a second appeal from the Court of Appeal in Dublin to the real "supreme" court for the whole of the United Kingdom, the Appellate Committee of the House of Lords in London.

When the Government of Ireland Act of 1920 created separate court structures for the two parts of the island, the existing court system was closely followed in the North. A Supreme Court of Judicature of Northern Ireland was set up, comprising a High Court and a Court of Appeal. A Court of Criminal Appeal was added in 1930. The position remains much the same today, except that three important changes were made by the Judicature (NI) Act 1978: a third division of the High Court (the Family Division) was created, the Crown Court replaced the old system of Assizes, and the Court of Criminal Appeal was merged with the Court of Appeal. The Supreme Court of Judicature in Northern Ireland now comprises the Crown Court, the High Court and the Court of Appeal. A further appeal still lies on many occasions from the Court of Appeal to the House of Lords.

The complete hierarchy of courts is set out in Table 1; their organisation and the precise location of the Crown Court and of the so-called inferior courts (magistrates' courts and county courts) are displayed in Table 2. It can be seen that the province is divided into four circuits, seven county court divisions and 22 petty sessions districts. (From January 1994 there will be just 21 petty sessions districts because Newtownabbey district is to be merged with Belfast district). Each of the four circuits has an administrator based in the headquarters of the Northern Ireland Court Service (see 1.5, under Lord Chancellor). The county courts for Londonderry and Belfast are called Recorder's courts but their powers do not differ from those of other county courts.

The jurisdiction of the ordinary courts is more fully described in Chapters 4 and 5, while Chapters 6 and 7 examine the jurisdiction of some other specialised courts and certain tribunals. It should be mentioned that names are often given unofficially to courts whenever they are sitting to hear particular matters. Examples would be the commercial court, the companies court, the bankruptcy court, the bail court and the motions court. The motions court hears applications for interim court orders prior to the main trial of an action. The High Court also contains what is termed a Divisional Court, which is a sort of appeal court within the Queen's Bench Division and which mainly hears applications for *habeas corpus* (see 4.4) or for judicial review (see 7.1); in England this Divisional Court plays a much more important part in the legal system since it also deals with appeals on pure points of law in criminal cases first heard in the magistrates' courts or the Crown Court. England also has Divisional Courts within the Family and Chancery Divisions of the High Court.

1.4 The Government Role

The overall shape of the legal system in Northern Ireland has been determined by Parliament, whether at Westminster or at Stormont, but the duty of supervising the administration of justice on a day-to-day basis falls in particular on three members of the British Government: the Lord Chancellor, the Secretary of State for Northern Ireland, and the Attorney-General. The actual operation of the system is the professional

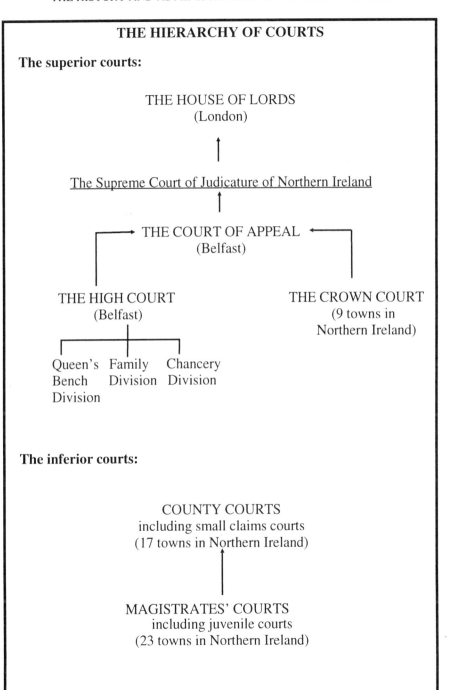

THE HIERARCHY OF COURTS

The superior courts:

THE HOUSE OF LORDS
(London)

↑

The Supreme Court of Judicature of Northern Ireland

↑

THE COURT OF APPEAL
(Belfast)

THE HIGH COURT
(Belfast)

THE CROWN COURT
(9 towns in
Northern Ireland)

Queen's Family Chancery
Bench Division Division
Division

The inferior courts:

COUNTY COURTS
including small claims courts
(17 towns in Northern Ireland)

↑

MAGISTRATES' COURTS
including juvenile courts
(23 towns in Northern Ireland)

Table 1

ORGANISATION AND LOCATION OF COURTS IN NORTHERN IRELAND

Town/city	County Court Division	Petty Sessions District	Courts
Northern Circuit			
Londonderry	Londonderry	Londonderry	Crown,Recorder's, Magistrates'
Limavady		Limavady	County, Magistrates'
Magherafelt		Magherafelt	County, Magistrates'
Coleraine	Antrim	North Antrim	County, Magistrates'
Ballymena		Ballymena	Crown, County, Magistrates'
Antrim		Antrim	Magistrates'
Larne		Larne	Magistrates'
Southern Circuit			
Armagh	Armagh and South Down	Armagh	Crown, County, Magistrates'
Banbridge		Banbridge	County, Magistrates'
Newry		Newry and Mourne	County, Magistrates'
Kilkeel		Newry and Mourne	Magistrates'
Omagh	Fermanagh and Tyrone	Omagh	Crown, County, Magistrates'
Strabane		Strabane	County, Magistrates'
Enniskillen		Fermanagh	Crown, County, Magistrates'
Cookstown		East Tyrone	County, Magistrates'
Clogher		East Tyrone	Magistrates'
Eastern Circuit			
Craigavon	Craigavon	Craigavon	Crown, County, Magistrates'
Lisburn		Lisburn	County, Magistrates'
Downpatrick	Ards	Down	Crown, County, Magistrates'
Newtownards		Ards / Castlereagh	Crown, County, Magistrates'
Bangor		North Down	Magistrates'
Belfast Circuit			
Belfast	Belfast	Belfast	Crown, Recorder's, Magistrates'
Newtownabbey		Newtownabbey	Magistrates'

Table 2

responsibility of officials such as the Director of Public Prosecutions, ,judges, magistrates and the police. A few words will be said in the next section about each of these officials, while the role of practising lawyers in the system will be described in 3.2. In this section we concentrate on the part played by government in the administration of the legal system.

Central and local government

As already explained in 1.2, Northern Ireland is now governed directly from London, the relevant government department being the Northern Ireland Office with the Secretary of State at its head and two Ministers and two Under-Secretaries as assistants to the Secretary of State. The Northern Ireland Office has some divisions based in London and others in Belfast, so that most of the staff in the former belong to the United Kingdom civil service while those working in Belfast are usually seconded from the Northern Ireland civil service. The chief of the Northern Ireland civil service advises the Secretary of State on matters which were formerly the preserve of Parliament at Stormont and co-ordinates the work of the six Northern Ireland departments. These departments are the Department of Agriculture, the Department of Economic Development, the Department of Education, the Department of the Environment, the Department of Finance and Personnel and the Department of Health and Social Services. Each of these obviously has a wide variety of matters to administer and each will encounter legal problems on very many points. Like any individual or organisation, they cannot defy the law, even though they may often be instrumental in having the law changed.

The present system of local government in Northern Ireland dates from 1973. There are 26 local authorities: two city councils (Belfast and Derry), 12 borough councils and 12 district councils. From 1993 these have been subdivided into 578 wards, distributed among 101 district electoral areas. Between five and seven councillors are elected under a single transferable vote system to represent each district electoral area. City and borough councils may call the chairperson of their council the Mayor (in Belfast, the Lord Mayor) and may designate up to one quarter of their councillors as "aldermen"; they may also confer the freedom of the city or borough on distinguished persons. Otherwise the powers and functions of all 26 authorities are the same. These are by no means as extensive as those given to local authorities in Great Britain: education and housing, for instance, are no part of their concern. But they still have responsibilities for, amongst other things, environmental health, noise, nuisances, consumer protection, litter prevention, the enforcement of building regulations and the licensing of street-trading. Like central government departments, local authorities are not above the law; their decisions can often be challenged in a court or tribunal. This has been made clear in several recent cases arising out of some councillors' opposition to Sinn Fein or to the Anglo-Irish Agreement of 1985 (see 1.2).

The Privy Council

The Privy Council of the United Kingdom should be mentioned at this stage because, as will be further explained in 2.3, it is technically this body which today makes most of the important laws for Northern Ireland. These are called Orders in Council, which are simply one type of secondary legislation authorised by statute (in this case the Northern Ireland Act 1974). There used to be a separate Privy Council for Northern Ireland, but this no longer meets and no further appointments can be made to it: its functions have been transferred to the Secretary of State for Northern Ireland.

The Privy Council consists of advisers to the Queen. Appointment to it is a recognised reward for public and political service or for attaining high political office. The total membership exceeds 400, all of them entitled to the prefix "the Right Honourable" and appointed for life, but the active section at any particular time mostly comprises the current Cabinet Ministers. Meetings are organised by the Lord President of the Council, who is sometimes (but not always) also the Minister in charge of organising Government business in the House of Commons as Leader of the House. Orders in Council are made when the Queen formally approves the draft Orders presented to her by the Government Ministers who happen to be closely involved with the matter in hand; they are signed by the Clerk of the Privy Council.

One part of the Privy Council is actually a court - its Judicial Committee. This was set up in 1833 with the task of acting as the last court of appeal for cases originating throughout the British Empire, whether civil or criminal. Vestiges of this role remain, as the Judicial Committee still hears appeals from places such as the Bahamas, the Channel Islands, the Falkland Islands, Gibraltar, Hong Kong, Jamaica, Malaysia, New Zealand and Singapore. In addition the court deals with appeals from certain professional disciplinary bodies within the United Kingdom, such as the General Medical Council and the equivalents for dentists, opticians and veterinary surgeons. This would be the only situation in which legal cases originating in Northern Ireland could find their way to the Privy Council, but the decisions taken by it on appeals from foreign jurisdictions can be of such persuasive influence that, although they do not bind judges in subsequent cases in Northern Ireland, they effectively alter the content of our common law (see 2.4).

The judges who sit in the Judicial Committee are Privy Councillors who are present or former senior judges in the United Kingdom or the Commonwealth. In most cases they are the same judges as those who sit as Law Lords in appeals to the House of Lords (see the next section). Five judges usually sit in each case, not wearing robes and using a room at 1, Downing Street in London. Their decisions take the form of "advice to Her Majesty", though dissenting opinions have been allowed since 1966.

From time to time an *ad hoc* committee of Privy Councillors is set up to consider specific matters. This is the way, for instance, in which the matters leading up to the invasion of the Falkland Islands by Argentina in 1982 were investigated. Under the Northern Ireland Constitution Act 1973 the Secretary of State for Northern Ireland retains the power to ask the Judicial Committee of the Privy Council to decide whether provisions in an Act of the Stormont Parliament, in a Measure of the 1974 Northern Ireland Assembly, or in a "relevant subordinate instrument" are void because they discriminate on religious or political grounds. This power, however, has never been exercised.

The Lord Chancellor

The Lord Chancellor occupies a unique position in the United Kingdom: he (or she, for there have been one or two female Chancellors in the distant past) is not only a Minister in the government, with a seat in the Cabinet, but also the Speaker of the House of Lords when it is acting in its legislative capacity as the second chamber of Parliament, and the senior judge when the House of Lords is acting in its judicial capacity (though these days he does not participate in many cases). Nowadays the Lord Chancellor is a distinguished lawyer appointed by the Prime Minister of the day. Often he is a former Attorney-General. An Under-Secretary of State answers questions in the House of Commons about the reponsibilities of the Lord Chancellor. With a salary of £114,082 per annum the Lord Chancellor is the highest paid member of the government or of the judiciary. The present incumbent is a Scottish judge, Lord Mackay of Clashfern.

The Lord Chancellor exercises his executive functions in Northern Ireland through the Northern Ireland Court Service, which corresponds to the Lord Chancellor's Department in London. The civil servants in this office help to arrange the business of the courts, service the judges and magistrates, and advise the Lord Chancellor on legal policy issues. It is the Lord Chancellor who is in practice responsible for the organisation of the courts, the appointment of many judges and court officials, and the general efficiency of the legal system, including the legal aid schemes (see 3.3). The Courts Service in England and Wales is to become the Courts Service Agency in April 1995; a similar shift to agency status is likely to occur in Northern Ireland at around the same time.

The Secretary of State for Northern Ireland

One of the main responsibilities of the Secretary of State, who is a member of the United Kingdom Cabinet, is the actual content of the law in Northern Ireland. It is he who must consider introducing into Parliament measures of law reform (see also 8.9) or updating social and welfare policies for the province. In addition he is generally in charge of the penal system and the treatment of offenders, a function performed in England by the Home Secretary. In this capacity he has power to refer the convictions of some criminals to the Court of Appeal for reconsideration (see 4.8), to release prisoners on licence or grant them special remission, and to grant pardons. He also has special functions under the province's emergency laws (see 4.9). In July 1993 the Secretary of State for Northern Ireland was Sir Patrick Mayhew. He is the tenth person to have held the office since 1972 and like other Cabinet Ministers he earns £63,047.

The Attorney-General

The Attorney-General is the chief law officer of the government, with responsibility for advising government departments and representing the government's interests in important legal disputes. Like the Lord Chancellor he is a political appointee (though not a member of the Cabinet) and he answers questions on legal matters in Parliament. By tradition he is meant to be non-political when giving legal advice or when acting in his capacity as head of the barristers' profession (the Bar). Before the abolition of the Stormont Parliament there was a separate Attorney-General for Northern Ireland; now the English Attorney-General acts for Northern Ireland as well, though a senior and junior barrister are appointed to be the Attorney-General's counsel in most cases requiring his involvement in Northern Ireland. Such counsel would, for example, act for the government in cases brought against it under the European Convention on Human Rights (see 2.6); service as the Attorney-General's senior counsel in Northern Ireland is frequently regarded as a passport to eventual appointment as a High Court judge. At the time of writing the Attorney-General is Sir Nicholas Lyell.

The Attorney-General has power to exercise some important discretions in selected matters involving the criminal law: his consent is required for the commencement of a wide range of prosecutions (though in most cases the consent can also be provided by the Director of Public Prosecutions: see 1.5) and he can decide that criminal proceedings which are already in progress should be terminated, by entering what is called a *nolle prosequi*. Under the emergency laws in Northern Ireland he can "de-schedule" certain offences (see 4.9). In matters concerned with the civil law (disputes between private individuals) his approval is needed for actions taken by private citizens to protect the public interest (relator actions), and exceptionally he can initiate proceedings himself. Sometimes he or his representative is asked to attend court as *amicus curiae*, that is, as a general legal adviser on points in issue in a case.

The Attorney-General's deputy is called the Solicitor-General, though he too is a barrister and a political appointee; currently he is Sir Derek Spencer. The Attorney-General appoints a Crown Solicitor for Northern Ireland, whose services are then available to any Northern Ireland executive authority or any United Kingdom government department (see 1.5). The role of ordinary barristers and solicitors in Northern Ireland is explained in 3.2.

1.5 Legal Officials

The Director of Public Prosecutions

Prior to 1972 the majority of prosecutions in Northern Ireland were conducted by police officers, but prosecutions on behalf of government departments, as well as all prosecutions for indictable (that is, serious) offences were the responsibility of Crown Solicitors and Crown Counsel. Following the recommendations of both the Hunt Report on the Royal Ulster Constabulary (1969) and the MacDermott Working Party on Public Prosecutions (1971), the role of the police in serious prosecutions was diminished and the involvement of Crown Solicitors was abolished. To take over these responsibilities the Office of the Director of Public

Prosecutions (DPP) was created. The relevant legislation is the Prosecution of Offences (NI) Order 1972, as amended. Somewhat similar arrangements now exist in England by virtue of the Prosecution of Offences Act 1985, which created the Crown Prosecution Service (CPS). However, while the CPS's activities are documented in a published Annual Report, the DPP's Office in Northern Ireland does not issue such a document.

The DPP is appointed by the Attorney-General, who may also remove him from office on the grounds of inability or misbehaviour. He must be a barrister or a solicitor who has practised in Northern Ireland for not less than 10 years. He is assisted in his work by professional and other staff working in his office in the Royal Courts of Justice in Belfast and in offices in three other towns. The present holder of the position (and only the second incumbent since 1972) is Mr A Fraser.

The chief function of the DPP in Northern Ireland is to bring prosecutions for indictable criminal offences, as well as for such less serious criminal offences as he considers should be dealt with by him. To date he has considered it right to control the prosecution of all offences arising out of incidents of a political nature as well as the prosecution of offences allegedly committed by police officers. The RUC continue to have responsibility for prosecuting minor cases. The procedures by which the DPP's Office becomes involved in conducting prosecutions are explained in more detail in 4.4.

The DPP's Office will represent the Crown in all criminal cases in the Crown Court, the Court of Appeal and the House of Lords. For these purposes it retains the services on a more or less permanent basis of three senior and three junior Crown counsel and it will function as the solicitors for these barristers. The DPP's Office also engages barristers to conduct most prosecutions on behalf of government departments in magistrates' courts when requested in writing to do so and it will act for the Crown in appeals to a county court by defendants who have been convicted in a magistrates' court. If a proposed prosecution is a private one, or one to be brought by the police, the consent of the DPP (or of the Attorney-General) is very often required before the proceedings can officially be begun and the Director can step in to take over private prosecutions if this is in the public interest. Decisions of the DPP are rarely, if ever, capable of being judicially reviewed (see 7.1).

In addition to actually conducting prosecutions the DPP can require the police to investigate incidents which appear to him to involve an offence, or to make further investigations into matters already referred to him. If someone knows of evidence relating to an alleged crime he or she is at liberty to make it known directly to the DPP's Office rather than to the police. Whenever a defendant is applying for bail (see 4.4) the DPP's Office can make representations in such cases as the Director thinks fit, which goes some way to ensuring that uniform standards on this issue are applied throughout Northern Ireland. Finally, if it appears to a coroner after an inquest (see 6.3) that a criminal offence may have been committed, the coroner must submit a written report on the case for consideration by the DPP.

The Crown Solicitor

The Crown Solicitor for Northern Ireland is appointed by the Attorney-General under section 35 of the Northern Ireland Constitution Act 1973. His or her function is to provide legal assistance to government departments and some other public bodies in Northern Ireland. Most of the work of the Crown Solicitor's Office is to do wih civil rather than criminal matters, the latter being handled instead by the Office of the Director of Public Prosecutions (see above). Usually the work involves litigation (*i.e.* court cases) because the Office represents government departments when they are sued by members of the public (*e.g.* for not properly maintaining footpaths). In addition specific tasks are assigned to the Crown Solicitor by statute: for instance, when no next of kin, or when buried treasure is found, it is the Crown Solicitor who claims the property on behalf of the state.

The Official Solicitor

The Official Solicitor represents the interests of litigants in cases where they would not otherwise be adequately protected, such as those involving children or persons who are in custody for contempt. He or she must conduct such investigations and render such assistance as may be authorised by the Rules of the Supreme Court or required by any direction of a court for the purpose of assisting the court in the due administration of justice. The present Official Solicitor (a part-time function) is Mr C. Redpath.

Judges

Information about the present judiciary in Northern Ireland is presented in Table 3. Details of the main types of case heard by the judges in each of the courts are supplied in Chapters 4 and 5. Apart from deciding cases, the judges in Northern Ireland are also involved in making Rules of Court to govern the practice and procedure for dealing with cases in each of the various courts. There are, for instance, a Supreme Court Rules Committee, a Matrimonial Causes Rules Committee and a County Court Rules Committee. These Rules are a form of secondary legislation (explained in 2.3) and they are amended and updated at irregular intervals.

Like barristers and solicitors, judges enjoy what is called "immunity from suit" when they are performing in court; this means that you cannot sue a judge for compensation even if he or she has obviously taken a wrong decision which has caused you loss.

House of Lords

The most senior judges in the United Kingdom are the Lords of Appeal in Ordinary, who hear appeals in the House of Lords whenever that body is sitting in its judicial capacity. They are appointed, as are all full-time senior judges, by the Queen, but by convention she acts on the advice of the Prime Minister, who in turn consults the Lord Chancellor. They must already have held high judicial office for two years or be barristers of 15 years' standing. At present Lords of Appeal must retire at the age of 75, but when the Judicial Pensions and Retirement Act 1993 comes into force (probably in 1994) they will have the option of retiring at the age of 70. There can be 11 Lords of Appeal at any one time, each currently earning £103,790. The best-known today are probably Lord Bridge and Lord Templeman. Usually a couple of incumbents are Scottish lawyers, and the former Lord Chief Justice of Northern Ireland, Lord Lowry, was appointed in August 1988.

Lords of Appeal - also called Law Lords - are assisted from time to time by the current and former Lord Chancellors, by other senior judges who have been appointed life peers and by retired Lords of Appeal. As an Appellate Committee the House of Lords usually sits as a bench of five judges, and never with a jury. Very important cases are sometimes heard by seven judges; an example is *Pepper (Inspector of Taxes)* v *Hart* (1992), when the Lords decided that in interpreting an Act of Parliament judges could legitimately refer to what was said by government Ministers during Parliamentary debates. Decisions on whether to grant permission for a case to be given a full hearing before the Appellate Committee are usually taken by only three Lords of Appeal (sitting as the Appeal Committee).

Many legal disputes which occur in Northern Ireland may in theory proceed as far as the House of Lords. In practice, of course, very few do

THE JUDICIARY IN NORTHERN IRELAND

Office	Number in office[1]	Qualifications for office	Retire-ment age	How addressed	Salary
Justices of the Peace	970 approx.	No formal qualifications	In office for life	"Your Worship"	Expenses only
Resident Magistrates (Deputies)	15 17	7 years' practice as solicitor or barrister	70	"Your Worship"	£54,035
District Judges (Deputies)	4 10	7 years' practice as solicitor	72	"Mr/Ms/Mrs Registrar"	£54,035
County Court Judges (Deputies)	14 41	10 years' practice as solicitor or barrister[2]	72	"Your Honour"	£78,377
High Court Masters	7	Generally, 10 years' practice as solicitor or barrister	72	"Master"	£54,035
High Court Judges	7 + Lord Chief Justice	10 years' practice as barrister	75	"My Lord" or "Your Lordship"	£90,147 (LCJ - £103,790)
Court of Appeal Judges	3 + Lord Chief Justice	15 years' practice as barrister or service as HC judge	75	"My Lord" or "Your Lordship"	£99,510
House of Lords Judges	11 + Lord Chancellor	15 years' practice as barrister or 2 years in high judicial office	75	"My Lord" or "Your Lordship"	£103,790 (LC - £114,082)

1 The only females amongst the judiciary in Northern Ireland, apart from JPs, are 3 deputy RMs, 3 deputy district judges, 3 deputy county court judges and 1 Master.

2 Deputy county court judges can be appointed from among solicitors of 10 years' standing or from the ranks of RMs; after 3 years they are eligible for appointment as full county court judges.

Table 3

- perhaps two or three a year. For minor civil cases (see Chapter 5) the final court to which a case can be taken in Northern Ireland is the province's own Court of Appeal. In some instances it is possible to take a case beyond the House of Lords into Europe, but the courts there are not really hearing "appeals" as such (see 2.6).

The Supreme Court

The judges of the Court of Appeal and the High Court are appointed by the Queen on the advice of the Lord Chancellor. In England the Prime Minister has a say in who should be appointed to the Court of Appeal, but not in Northern Ireland. These same judges, together with county court judges (see below), also sit in Northern Ireland's Crown Court (see 4.8). Since the Court of Appeal, the High Court and the Crown Court together make up the Supreme Court of Judicature of Northern Ireland, these judges are sometimes referred to as Supreme Court judges. Since 1921 there have been 33 Supreme Court judges; their names and periods of service can be found in Table 4.

Only barristers who have practised for at least 10 years are eligible for appointment (in England solicitors also qualify). They must retire when they reach the age of 75 (though the Judicial Pensions and Retirement Act 1993 will allow them to retire at 70 if they so wish); they can be removed from office before then if both Houses of Parliament so recommend, but this has not occurred in modern times.

The most important judge in Northern Ireland is the Lord Chief Justice of Northern Ireland. The office replaced that of the Lord Chancellor of Ireland in 1921. To date there have been six holders of the post: Sir Denis Henry (1921-25), Sir William Moore (1925-38), Sir James Andrews (1938-51), Lord MacDermott (1951-71), Lord Lowry (1971-88) and, from August 1988, Sir Brian Hutton. His salary is the same as that of a Law Lord, £103,790. The Lord Chief Justice is President of the Court of Appeal, the High Court and the Crown Court; in this capacity he assigns work to the judges of the various courts and has a number of other administrative responsibilities. In England the Lord Chief Justice, Lord Taylor, acts as President of the Criminal Division of the Court of Appeal, while the President of the Civil Division is the Master of the Rolls. This latter post is the one from which Lord Denning retired after 20 years' service in 1982; the present office-bearer is Sir Thomas Bingham.

The Court of Appeal of Northern Ireland consists of the Lord Chief Justice and three other judges called Lords Justices of Appeal. At present these are Higgins LJ, Kelly LJ and MacDermott LJ and there have been

11 other Lords Justices since 1921. The current salary of a Lord Justice of appeal is £99,510. In criminal cases, moreover, all judges of the High Court are eligible to sit as judges of the Court of Appeal. The Lord Chief Justice can also ask a Lord Justice of Appeal to sit in the High Court, or a High Court judge to sit even in civil cases in the Court of Appeal. (For the distinction between criminal and civil cases, see 2.1 and 5.1.)

A case in the Court of Appeal will usually be heard by three judges, always sitting in Belfast, but some matters may be dealt with by a two-judge bench and some (incidental matters) by one judge sitting alone. A jury is never involved.

The High Court of Justice consists of the Lord Chief Justice and seven other judges (a seventh position was created early in 1993). These judges are officially called puisne (pronounced "puny") judges and are referred to as "Mr Justice . . ." The seven currently in post are Campbell J, Carswell J, Kerr J, McCollum J, Nicholson J, Pringle J and Shiel J. Their salary is £90,147. There have been five other men (apart from the Lords Chief Justices and the Lords Justices) who have served as High Court judges in Northern Ireland since 1921. They may sit in any of the Divisions of the High Court, but some are seen as particularly expert in one or other Division, for example Campbell J in the Chancery Division. Except for hearings in the Divisional Court (see the end of 1.3) a High Court case will involve only one judge, always sitting in Belfast. Juries (since 1962 they have consisted of just seven persons, not 12 as in England) are now used quite rarely; they are to be found mainly in libel cases. To ease the burden on High Court judges, the Lord Chancellor may from time to time request a county court judge to sit as a judge of the High Court.

The inferior courts

County court judges, of whom there are now 14, with no fewer than 41 deputies, sit throughout Northern Ireland. Again, at least 10 years' practice as a barrister is required before a person can be considered for appointment, though deputy county court judges, who may after three years be made full county court judges, can be appointed from the ranks of resident magistrates (see below) or from solicitors of 10 years' standing. The retirement age is 72 and the salary is £78,377. County court judges are referred to as "His Honour Judge . . ." The judges who sit for Belfast and Londonderry are called "Recorders".

NORTHERN IRELAND'S SUPREME COURT JUDGES 1921 - 93

Name	Division	Period		Division	Period
Sir James Andrews	LJ	1921 - 37	LCJ	1937 - 51	
Sir Anthony Babington	LJ	1937 - 49			
Richard Best	LJ	1925 - 39			
Arthur Black	Ch	1943 - 49	LJ	1949 - 64	
Thomas Brown	QB	1922 - 44			
Sir Anthony Campbell	Ch	1988 -			
Sir Robert Carswell	QB	1984 -			
Sir Lancelot Curran	Ch	1949 - 56	LJ	1956 - 75	
Sir Maurice Gibson	Ch	1968 - 75	LJ	1975 - 87	
Sir Denis Henry	LCJ	1921 - 25			
Sir Eoin Higgins	QB/Fam	1984 - 93	LJ	1993 -	
Sir Brian Hutton	QB	1979 - 88	LCJ	1988 -	
Sir Edward Jones	QB	1968 - 73	LJ	1973 - 84	
Sir Basil Kelly	QB	1973 - 84	LJ	1984 -	
Sir Brian Kerr	QB	1993 -			
William Lowry	QB	1947 - 49			
Lord Lowry	Ch/QB	1964 - 71	LCJ	1971 - 88	
Lord MacDermott	QB	1944 - 47	LCJ	1951 - 71	
Sir John MacDermott	QB/Fam	1973 - 87	LJ	1987 -	
Sir Liam McCollum	QB	1987 -			
Sir Ambrose McGonigal	QB	1968 - 75	LJ	1975 - 79	
Sir Herbert McVeigh	Ch	1956 - 64	LJ	1964 - 73	
Robert Megaw	Ch	1932 - 43			
Sir William Moore	LJ	1921 - 25	LCJ	1925 - 38	
Edward Murphy	LJ	1939 - 45			
Sir Donald Murray	QB/Ch	1975 - 89	LJ	1989 - 93	
Sir Michael Nicholson	QB	1986 -			
Turlough O'Donnell	QB	1971 - 79	LJ	1979 - 90	
Samuel Porter	LJ	1946 - 56			
Sir John Pringle	QB/Fam	1993 -			
Charles Shiel	QB	1949 - 68			
Sir John Shiel	QB	1989 -			
Daniel Wilson	Ch	1921 - 32			

Abbreviations: LJ - Lord Justice; Ch - Chancery Division; QB - Queen's Bench Division; LCJ - Lord Chief Justice; Fam - Family Division

Note: Knighthoods have been automatically conferred on Supreme Court Judges only since 1988

Table 4

There are also four district judges, who assist the county court judges and exercise an important jurisdiction in the so-called "small claims courts" (see 5.3). They were formerly known as circuit registrars.

Magistrates' courts are not staffed by judges at all but by resident magistrates, lay panellists or (occasionally) justices of the peace. All of these offices are described below.

Statutory officers

After consultations with the Lord Chief Justice of Northern Ireland the Lord Chancellor appoints certain "statutory officers". These include the Official Solicitor (see above) and eight Masters. The Masters (and their deputies) are former legal practitioners of 10 years' standing whose job it is to deal with a variety of procedural and relatively minor substantive issues before a dispute reaches a High Court judge. In effect they exercise the jurisdiction of a judge sitting in chambers, except in respect of certain specified matters. An appeal against their decisions usually lies to such a judge. The Masters currently in post deal separately with matters relating to Queen's Bench and Appeals, Chancery, the High Court, Bankruptcy, Probate and Matrimonial, Care and Protection (for mental patients), Taxation (*i.e.* assessment of costs), and Enforcement of Judgments. There are Supreme Court Offices corresponding with each of the Master's roles, that for Queen's Bench and Appeals being called the Crown Office. A Master earns £54,035 per annum, the same as a resident magistrate.

The main administrators in county court divisions are called chief clerks (formerly Clerks of the Crown and Peace), while those in magistrates' courts are called clerks of petty sessions.

Resident magistrates

One of the major differences between the legal systems of Northern Ireland and England is that in Northern Ireland the responsibility for trying less serious criminal offences lies with full-time, legally qualified magistrates called "resident magistrates" (RMs). In England much of this work is still done by part-time justices who have no formal legal qualifications, though they undergo periodic training after they are appointed. The explanation for this difference is to be found in history: at the end of the eighteenth century there were parts of Ireland where there were not enough "proper" persons to act as ordinary part-time justices, so it was found necessary to appoint full-time magistrates (not necessarily lawyers) who were required to reside in these areas to assist the justices. This worked so well that during the nineteenth century the practice of appointing resident magistrates was extended throughout the whole of the island. Until 1935 the part-time justices could also sit with the RMs in magistrates' courts in Northern Ireland, but in that year this power was taken away, so that only resident magistrates can now sit in these courts, which deal mainly with minor criminal offences. The lay justices, who are called Justices of the Peace, do however retain an important role in the legal system (see below).

Today only barristers and solicitors of seven years' standing are eligible for appointment as RMs. They are appointed by the Queen on the recommendation of the Lord Chancellor. There are currently 15 in office, with 17 deputies. They must retire when they reach the age of 70 and their salary is £54,035. In court they are addressed as "Your Worship".

In addition to trying comparatively minor criminal offences, resident magistrates conduct committal proceedings in the more serious criminal cases (see 4.7). They also deal with some private (or civil) law disputes and are responsible for a number of matters which are more administrative in nature than judicial, such as the renewal of licences for public houses (see 5.2). They are immune from being sued for causing loss to litigants unless they act entirely beyond their powers (*i.e.* "without jurisdiction"): see *McC* v *Mullan* (1984), a Northern Ireland case which reached the House of Lords.

Justices of the Peace

The people who act as lay magistrates in Northern Ireland are called Justices of the Peace (JPs). The office is a very ancient one, first established in Ireland (as in England) in the fourteenth century. In England and Wales JPs still act as full-scale magistrates, but as noted above their powers have been severely limited in Northern Ireland since 1935.

Persons become JPs through appointment under the Queen's Commission of the Peace, which is issued for each county court division by the Lord Chancellor. They remain in office for life. The Lord Chancellor selects persons on the basis of recommendations made to him by local advisory committees in each county court division. The composition of these committees is secret, but the chairman is usually the Lord Lieutenant of the county (a representative of the Queen). Nominations can be submitted by any person or group and should be forwarded through the Assistant Secretary of Commissions in the Northern Ireland Court Service. Those appointed will invariably be respected people who, over the years, have gained the trust and the admiration of the local community. In Northern Ireland today there are approximately 970 JPs, of whom maybe 10 per cent are women. They receive no payment for their services, only out-of-pocket expenses.

Most of the powers which JPs have at the moment may be exercised only within the county for which they have been appointed. Their main task is the signing of summonses, warrants and various official forms (such as forms relating to state pensions). Summonses are documents which direct people to appear in court on a certain day in order to answer a particular allegation (see 4.2 and the sample document in Appendix 4). Warrants are documents authorising the police to arrest someone who is suspected of having committed a crime or to search premises where, for instance, stolen goods are thought to be hidden; or they may take the form of written authorisation for extending a person's detention or committing a person for trial or to prison on remand.

JPs have the power to conduct committal proceedings (see 4.7) and, provided the accused person consents, they can try summarily some minor criminal offences, such as vagrancy or poaching. Two justices must be appointed to every Board of Visitors for prisons in Northern Ireland (see below). They retain as well the somewhat controversial power to "bind over" persons to keep the peace or be of good behaviour. This power, which derives from the common law and the Justices of the Peace Act 1361, enables JPs (and RMs) to require people to forfeit a sum of money or serve a period of imprisonment if they break a promise to keep the peace or be of good behaviour during the stipulated period, which must not exceed two years. Strangely, such persons do not first have to be convicted of a criminal offence.

Other officials

There are several other officials whom you may encounter if you have a brush with the law. The army, which includes the Royal Irish Regiment and the Military Police (the "red caps"), continues to assist the RUC in maintaining law and order in Northern Ireland and has been granted special powers to that end (see 4.9). Traffic wardens have all the powers of police officers as regards the control of road traffic. Some organisations, such as the Ministry of Defence and port authorities, are empowered to set up their own police services for specific purposes.

Process servers and bailiffs are private individuals or firms who are engaged by both public and private bodies to deliver official documents or to enforce court orders. If you are forming a company you will have dealings with the office of the Registrar of Companies, and if you attempt to do your own conveyancing when moving house you will need to make use of the Land Registry, the Statutory Charges Register or the Registry of Deeds. The Registrar General, with his headquarters in Belfast and officers in every district council area, has responsibility for recording all births, deaths and marriages.

1.6 The Police, Probation and Prison Services

The police service

The police service in Northern Ireland is the Royal Ulster Constabulary. It was formed in 1922 to replace the Royal Irish Constabulary, which policed the island until partition. Following civil disturbances in 1968-69, an Advisory Committee was set up under the chairmanship of Lord Hunt to examine the recruitment, organisation, structure and composition of the RUC and to recommend as necessary whatever changes were required to provide for the efficient enforcement of law and order. Most of Lord Hunt's recommendations were subsequently implemented through the Police Act (NI) 1970.

The force, however, still has to work in exceptionally dangerous conditions and its members are armed. Between 1969 and 1992, 189 police officers and a further 98 reservists were killed in terrorist incidents. Attacks on police patrols and police stations are still common, and they are not always carried out by republican paramilitaries. During 1986, following the signing of the Anglo-Irish Agreement in November 1985, there were well over 500 incidents of serious intimidation of RUC officers, and 121 police families had to be moved from their homes. For further details of the level of terrorist crime, see Table 9 in 4.2.

The RUC is currently organised on the basis of three regions (North, South and Belfast), 12 divisions and 37 sub-divisions. In addition there is a traffic division, with headquarters in Belfast and four regional sub-divisions. There are approximately 170 police stations throughout the province. The maximum permitted size of the service is 8,500 officers, with a further 5,000 in the Reserve (3,200 of them full-time). Approximately 10 per cent of the force are detectives and 3 per cent are in the Traffic Branch. The Special Branch, dealing with undercover anti-terrorist work, numbers more than 650 officers. Understandably the force finds it difficult to recruit Roman Catholics; at the moment less than

8 per cent are of that religion. At the head of the force is the Chief Constable (Sir Hugh Annesley until mid-1994), with two Deputy Chief Constables, two Senior Assistant Chief Constables and nine Assistant Chief Constables. The total expenditure on the RUC in 1991-92 was £523 million.

Police activities

As in other legal systems, the primary role of the RUC is to prevent and detect crime. Despite the troubles, the crime rate in Northern Ireland is comparatively low (see 4.2) and the detection rate is quite high when compared with that of the other 51 UK police forces - in 1992 it was 34.4 per cent. The police have been assisted in their work during the past 24 years by the British army, though the avowed policy now is that the police have an independent responsibility in all areas and that the soldiers are merely there to give support when needed. The interrogation practices of the force were investigated in 1977 by the European Court of Human Rights (*Ireland* v *UK*, and see 2.6) and in 1978 by a Committee of Inquiry headed by an English county court judge, Judge Bennett. Various recommendations for making the practices more acceptable were put forward and have since largely been implemented. Further inquiries have been undertaken into alleged shoot-to-kill incidents which occurred in 1982; these were the subject of the controversial Stalker-Sampson report in 1987, which led to investigations of breach of discipline but not to any criminal prosecutions.

The RUC is accountable to the Police Authority for Northern Ireland, and complaints against its officers must be considered by the Independent Commission for Police Complaints; the role of both these bodies and of visitors to police stations is described in more detail in 8.7. Her Majesty's Inspectorate of Constabulary for England and Wales acts as an advisory body to the Northern Ireland Office and the Police Authority regarding such matters as recruitment and equipment for the RUC; they also carry out *ad hoc* inspections of the force. The police officers' representative bodies in the province are the Superintendents' Association of Northern Ireland and, for lesser ranks, the Police Federation for Northern Ireland.

As part of its programme in community affairs the RUC runs a five-a-side football competition and "Blue Lamp Discos" for young people. Its contact with school pupils is maintained through the Police Educational Programme (PEP), which now runs in 60 per cent of all schools in Northern Ireland, as well as through rambles, an inter-school quiz and sixth-form seminars. More than 100,000 young people have participated in the Ramble Scheme since 1974. The police also try to deal with the problems of juveniles in a sympathetic manner through a Juvenile Liaison Scheme (see 6.1). The system for consulting with members of local communities is as yet somewhat underdeveloped: every district council has a Community and Police Liaison Committee or a security committee (or both), but although police officers sit on these there is not as much contact with community groups in some areas as there should be. The neighbourhood policing scheme, on the other hand, is considered by the RUC to be most satisfactory, as are the support schemes set up to provide assistance to the victims of burglary.

In England the powers of prosecution which were formerly vested in the police forces were transferred to the Crown Prosecution Service by the Prosecution of Offences Act 1985. The RUC still possesses such powers in minor cases but the Office of the Director of Public Prosecutions (explained at the start of 1.5) will deal with whichever of these offences it considers appropriate. The police's continuing monopoly over the investigation of crimes, however, is a limiting factor on the DPP's complete autonomy. In 1982 the practice emerged of using "supergrasses", or "converted terrorists", from some of whom evidence was obtained in exchange for immunity from prosecution ("turning Queen's evidence"); in these cases the evidence was collected by the police but the immunity was granted by the DPP. A total of 223 defendants had been tried on the word of a supergrass by the end of 1986; 53 convictions remained outstanding after appeals had been heard, but in all of these cases there was evidence to corroborate the testimony of the supergrass.

If the police decide not to prosecute someone for an alleged offence, any person with a sufficient interest *(locus standi)* in the matter can initiate a private prosecution instead. But private prosecutions are time-consuming and expensive (no legal aid is available), and the Attorney-General can always apply for them to be terminated if he does not feel that they are in the public interest (see 4.5). It is believed that only one private prosecution has ever reached the trial stage in Northern Ireland, and no conviction was obtained. As an alternative course of action, if an interested person feels aggrieved at the police's failure to investigate a crime or prosecute a suspect, an application can be made to the High Court for the "prerogative" order of *mandamus* which, if granted, will compel the police to carry out their duty (see 7.1). It is not possible to sue the police if you are the victim of a crime which the police negligently failed to forestall.

It is to the Chief Constable of the RUC that applications for firearm certificates must be made; an appeal against a refusal lies to the Secretary of State for Northern Ireland. At the end of 1992 there were 87,456 firearm certificates on issue, covering a total of 129,250 lawfully held weapons.

The probation service

The probation service in Northern Ireland is now administered by the Probation Board. This was set up in 1982 with up to 18 members, appointed by the Secretary of State and drawn from a wide spectrum of the community. The Board is serviced by a small secretariat based at its headquarters in Belfast. In July 1993 its Chairperson was Mr Sean Curran and the Chief Probation Officer was Mrs Briege Gadd. The Board has adopted a corporate plan for 1993-97; this emphasises the need to reform offenders *within the community*. There are 34 probation offices throughout the province, all of which are listed in the telephone directory. In 1991-92 the cost of running the probation service was approximately £8.5 million.

The chief aim of the Probation Board is to prevent reoffending. In supporting the work of Northern Ireland's 120 or so maingrade probation officers it seeks to reduce the number of custodial sentences imposed by the courts. Probation officers, operating under the Probation Act (NI) 1950, write social enquiry reports (SERs) on offenders found guilty in a court. These reports are compulsory for offenders who are under 17 years of age; for older offenders they are provided only if the court so requests and if the offender consents. The reports attempt to give an objective assessment of the offender to the judge or magistrate, set out the courses of action available to the court, and make recommendations as to which would be most appropriate in the particular case. In 1992 just over 55 per cent of all SERs were written for adult offenders in magistrates' courts, 15 per cent concerned juvenile offenders, and the remainder dealt with defendants in the Crown Court or appeal courts. The Probation Board acknowledges that usage of SERs in magistrates' courts varies noticeably between court locations and that there are wide variations in sentencing practice.

Probation officers now have a Manual which covers in one volume those aspects of law and procedure affecting their work in the courts, the community and prisons. They also adhere to minimum standards of practice issued by the Board with regard to the supervision of probation orders and community service orders. A court can place an offender on probation for a period between six months and three years. In 1992 there were 1,134 new orders made; 50 per cent of these were for one year and 35 per cent were for two years. The order is not intended as a punishment but rather as an offer of rehabilitation. To that end the probation officer assigned to the case will befriend, give guidance to, and supervise the offender. This kind of supervision within the community is not only better for the offender, it is also vastly cheaper than containment in prison. The recidivism rate for those placed on probation (that is, the proportion of offenders who reoffend) is also quite low; at the moment it is running at about 33 per cent.

Probation officers also help to run the community service order scheme, whereby offenders aged 17 or over can be ordered to perform a set number of hours of community service (see 6.1). This is proving increasingly successful as a means of reintegrating offenders as law-abiding members of society. Various local initiatives have been developed to provide opportunities for community service: Northern Ireland, despite all its problems, may in some respects be better than elsewhere in this respect because of its comparatively low crime rate and its still identifiable small communities.

The probation service provides welfare services for prisoners, prisoners' families and people recently released from prison. In this capacity the officers certainly act not so much as legal officials but as specialised social workers. Whenever life sentence prisoners are taking part in the "working out" scheme during the months before their release on licence, probation officers help to counsel them.

Rehabilitation services

In some of its work the Probation Board is obviously supplemented by various voluntary bodies. Indeed the Board has a statutory responsibility to fund some of these voluntary projects. The Extern Organisation and the Northern Ireland Association for the Care and Resettlement of Offenders (NIACRO) are prominent groups in the voluntary sector which find that the services they provide overlap with those of the Probation Board. The Save the Children Fund offers training courses for professionals who work with young people in trouble with the police. The Probation Board also helps to fund child-minding and family centre facilities at Belfast, Maze and Magilligan prisons; it supports as well the Dismas House project (a hostel for ex-prisoners), the Belfast Rape Crisis Centre and the growing number of victim support schemes throughout the province.

It is worth noting that under the Rehabilitation of Offenders (NI) Order 1978 an individual's sentence (whether or not it involved imprisonment) may in certain circumstances become "spent", which means that from then on that person must for most purposes be treated as someone who has not been convicted of, or even charged with, the offence in question. Such a rehabilitated person can even sue for libel or slander if someone later refers to the fact that he or she has been convicted of the offence, and the failure to disclose a spent conviction is not in law a proper ground for prejudicing a person as regards employment (except in relation to work with people under 18 years of age) . The period which must elapse before a sentence becomes spent depends on the type and severity of the original sentence. For a prison sentence of up to six months, for instance, the rehabilitation period is seven years, while for sentences of between six and 30 months the period is 10 years. Prison sentences of more than 30 months are excluded altogether from the scheme. If a person is placed on probation the rehabilitation period runs simultaneously with the probation period, or for one year after the conviction, whichever is longer.

The prison service

This service, though operating within a separate jurisdiction, is run along similar lines to its equivalent in England and Wales. Social and political factors, however, have led to some divergences.

There are at the moment six prison establishments in Northern Ireland: Belfast Prison (Crumlin Road), Maze Prison, formerly Long Kesh (near Lisburn), Magilligan Prison (near Londonderry), the male and female prisons at Maghaberry (near Lisburn) and the Young Offenders' Centre for males at Hydebank Wood on the outskirts of South Belfast. The total strength of the prison service in June 1993 was 3,180, plus a further 355 civilians employed as administrators, teachers, nurses etc. Only about 7 per cent of the service is Roman Catholic and just 5 per cent women. The officers are trained at the Prison Services College in Millisle, Co. Down. The service is run by the Northern Ireland Office, one of the departments of the United Kingdom Government; it issues an annual report on the administration of the prison service by virtue of its obligation under section 5 of the Prison Act (NI) 1953. In 1991-92 the total cost of running the prison service in Northern Ireland was approximately £132 million. This means that the cost per person sent to prison that year was more than £27,000.

The prison population

Unlike the position in many other countries, the prison population in Northern Ireland is now declining. It reached a peak of almost 3,000 in 1978 but since 1989 the average daily population has been about 1,800. In 1991 the average daily population of *sentenced* prisoners was 1,446, the remainder being prisoners on remand. About 470 prisoners are held in Maze Prison, and about 500 (including more than 300 on remand) in Belfast. The number of *receptions* into prison in 1991 was 4,828, almost unchanged from the level 10 years previously; clearly a large number of short custodial sentences are still being imposed for minor offences. For instance in 1991-92 about 1,500 people were sent to prison for non-payment of fines. This represents 55 per cent of all prisoners *sentenced* during that year but on any one day only three per cent of the prison population was made up of these short-term prisoners. Conversely, in 1991-92 only 1 per cent of *sentenced* prisoners were sent to prison for life or "at the Secretary of State's pleasure" but on any one day some 23 per cent of the prison population fell into that category.

At the end of March 1992 there were 1,462 sentenced prisoners in Northern Ireland's jails. Amongst these were 24 females, 47 fine defaulters, 283 serving up to two years, 551 serving between two and 10 years, 246 serving more than 10 years and 335 serving life or an indeterminate sentence. The majority of prisoners were in jail because they had been convicted of crimes involving personal violence; 137 had committed sexual offences, 363 had committed burglary, robbery or theft and 40 had committed a motoring offence.

The prison régime

The normal prison régime, although maligned in some quarters, actually compares quite favourably with that in other parts of the United Kingdom, Ireland and Western Europe. It is regulated partly by unpublished circulars issued to prison governors by the Northern Ireland Office and partly by the Prison Rules (NI) 1982. The Rules require that prisoners should engage in useful work. Some are employed in servicing the prisons themselves, while others work in prison industries making items such as shoes, clothing and metalwork. As regards education, over half of Northern Ireland's prisoners enrol for courses, ranging from the most basic to Open University level. The most popular subject is art. In 1991 seven prisoners obtained degrees from the Open University, including three who were awarded First Class Honours.

The Young Offenders' Centre at Hydebank Wood, which opened in 1979, has places for 300 young men, mainly aged 17 to 21, who have been sentenced to less than three years in custody. (The few females in this category are housed at Maghaberry.) The régime is officially described as "brisk", with the inmates gaining privileges by using their time in a positive and constructive way. The Centre offers extensive education, vocational training and physical recreation facilities. Young persons aged 15 or 16 are sometimes held in the Centre when a court has certified them to be unruly or guilty of serious misconduct, even though they may not have been convicted of any crime (see 6.1). Borstal training was abolished in Northern Ireland in 1980.

There is no parole system comparable to that which operates in England. Instead prisoners can earn up to 50 per cent remission on their sentences, though for prisoners convicted of terrorist offences this is reduced to the one-third rule which applies in England. "Lifers" and "SoSPs" (persons imprisoned at the Secretary of State's pleasure for committing murder when under 18 years of age - in March 1992 there were still 17 such persons in prison) have their cases examined, after 10 and eight years respectively, by the Life Sentence Review Board, which seeks the views of the judiciary and makes recommendations to the Secretary of State. Judges sometimes recommend minimum sentences at the time of trial, but these recommendations have no binding force in law. The Secretary of State can then decide to release such a prisoner on licence. If life or indeterminate sentence prisoners are given a release date, it is usually about a year in advance so that during the pre-release period (usually served at Belfast Prison) the prisoner can take part in a scheme of work and home leaves. Even after release the prisoner remains on licence for the rest of his or her life and can be recalled to prison when the Secretary of State considers this necessary to avoid danger to the public. In 1991-92, 30 prisoners were released on licence in this fashion and a further 38 were at various stages of the pre-release scheme.

Discipline and welfare

Each prison in Northern Ireland has a Board of Visitors, which is appointed by the Secretary of State and must include at least two Justices of the Peace; there were 75 persons serving as Visitors in March 1992. The Board has to meet at least once a month, sending copies of its minutes to the Secretary of State, and the prison must be visited by one member of the Board at least once a fortnight. The Board's function is to satisfy itself on behalf of the general public as to the state of the prison premises, the administration of the prison and the treatment of the prisoners. Every Visitor has free access at all times to all parts of the prison. He or she can hear any complaint or request which a prisoner may wish to make, if necessary out of the sight and hearing of prison officers. The Boards draw the attention of the prison governors to particular matters and report regularly to the Secretary of State. For the Young Offenders' Centre there is a corresponding Visiting Committee consisting of 15 members.

Discipline in the prisons is primarily the responsibility of the governors, but the most serious punishment a governor can impose is loss of 28 days' remission. Any serious or repeated offence which a governor believes requires a more severe punishment may be referred to the Secretary of State and it is for him to decide how the case should be handled. He may ask officials in the Northern Ireland Office to deal with it or he may delegate the case to the relevant Board of Visitors (not to a governor), which will appoint between two and five of its members to deal with the case; in either event the maximum penalties which can be imposed are loss of up to 180 days' remission and/or confinement in a prison cell for up to 56 days.

At disciplinary hearings before Boards of Visitors prisoners must be allowed to present their own case and to call and cross-examine witnesses. As well they may be granted "assistance by way of representation" (see 3.3). Prison governors also have a discretion to allow legal representation in hearings where they preside. Representation should be allowed where the charge is serious or the penalty grave, where points of law are likely to arise or where a prisoner might be unable to present his or her case properly. Judicial review (see 7.1) is available in respect of disciplinary hearings in a prison, but there are no rights of appeal. In the 12 months up to the end of March 1992, 54 cases of offences against discipline were referred to the Boards of Visitors or Visiting Committee; legal representation was granted in eight cases.

In the 1980s there have been several serious incidents in Northern Ireland's prisons. A hunger strike at Maze Prison, following the long-running "blanket" and "dirty" protests, led to the deaths of 10 prisoners in 1981. The European Commission of Human Rights rejected a case taken by the protesters largely because their conditions were said to be self-inflicted, but the Commission did criticise the inflexibility of the prison authorities. Some of the demands of the prisoners, such as the right to wear their own clothes, were eventually conceded. In 1983 there was a mass escape of 38 prisoners from Maze Prison; this was investigated by Sir James Hennessy, whose report recommended better inspection and self-assessment arrangements. Periodic inspections are conducted by Her Majesty's Inspectorate of Prisons and by the International Committee of the Red Cross.

From time to time there have been protests at Magilligan and Belfast Prisons over the issue of segregating loyalist and republican prisoners, especially at visiting times. In November 1991 two remand inmates at Belfast Prison were killed by an explosive device planted in a dining hall; a subsequent report by Lord Colville endorsed the policy of segregation but suggested steps to make the prisons more safe. Since 1982 many organisations have expressed concern at the level of strip searching of women prisoners in Northern Ireland; by the end of 1988 there were indications that this practice was being significantly curtailed although a mass strip search did unexpectedly occur in March 1991. By the end of 1992 the Government had also become less inflexible as regards requests from Northern Irish prisoners serving sentences in Great Britain to be transferred back to a jail in Northern Ireland.

Voluntary groups active in the area of prisoners' welfare include the Northern Ireland Association for the Care and Resettlement of Offenders, the Extern Organisation, the Prison Fellowship of Northern Ireland and the Peace People. The Butler Trust has also funded many worthwhile projects.

2

The Branches and Sources of Northern Ireland Law

2.1 The Branches of Law

In Chapter 1 we concentrated on the history of the present-day legal system and described briefly the role of various officials in administering that system. In this chapter we will examine more closely the ways in which the legal system actually creates, applies and develops the law. Our aim here is not to investigate the nature of law or consider what exactly the law is on a certain point; we are taking for granted a conception of law as a set of socially binding rules and principles and are simply inquiring into how those rules and principles come to be fashioned. The bulk of our inquiry will concern the two main sources of law identified in Chapter 1 - Parliament and the courts - but we begin with a short explanation of the ways in which law may be divided into several branches. All of these branches consist of rules derived from each of the main sources of law.

Criminal law and civil law

The commonest way of classifying law is to distinguish between criminal and civil law. Criminal law is that part of the law which prohibits acts deemed to be contrary to public order and the interest of society as a whole. It calls these acts "offences" and prescribes a variety of punishments for any person convicted of committing them. Some offences, such as murder or rape, are extremely serious; others, such as failure to wear a seatbelt, are comparatively minor. But they are all crimes and as such are dealt with by a special set of courts applying special procedures (see Chapter 4).

Most non-lawyers tend to think that criminal law is far and away the chief branch of the law. In fact it is only one relatively small part of it. Students who study for a law degree at a university usually spend less than one-tenth of their time on criminal law. Senior judges may spend a quarter of their time on criminal cases, but judicial involvement is not a good way of measuring the law's impact. It has to be remembered that as well as controlling public order and determining how people should be punished for disrupting it, the law must make provision for regulating practically every sphere of human behaviour. It lays down rules for enabling citizens to achieve certain objectives (such as renting a house, buying a car, running a business, making a will, getting married) and it creates principles for the settlement of private disputes - disputes which do not involve breaches of public order. All the law which is not criminal law is sometimes referred to as "civil" law, though, like "common" law, that expression has a variety of meanings depending on the context.

The main feature which distinguishes crimes from civil wrongs lies not in the nature of the behaviour being questioned but in the method by which the behaviour is dealt with by the legal system. A single piece of behaviour can constitute both a crime and a civil wrong (*e.g.*, damaging someone's property or stealing something), but the criminal aspects of the incident will be dealt with by criminal courts (where the accused person - the defendant - is "prosecuted", "convicted" or "acquitted", and if convicted, "punished") and the civil aspects by civil courts (where the defendant is "sued", held "liable" or "not liable", and if liable, compelled to pay "damages"). In both criminal and civil appeals the party appealing is termed the appellant; in civil cases the opposing party can then be called the respondent. Under such legislation as the Criminal Justice (NI) Order 1980 a criminal court can at times award compensation to the victim of a crime without the need for separate civil proceedings, but this power is rarely used in practice (see 4.6). A civil court, moreover, occasionally awards "punitive" damages and it may issue a "declaration" that certain behaviour would be criminal if it were to be carried out. In such cases the distinction between criminal and civil proceedings becomes somewhat blurred.

"Contempt of court" is another area of law that causes confusion between criminal and civil law. There are in fact two types of contempt recognised by the law. One is the *crime* of contempt, which is committed when a person says, writes or does something which might obstruct the administration of justice, be that criminal justice or civil justice. Examples would be where a member of the public becomes unruly in a courtroom or where a newspaper publishes an article revealing that a person being tried for an offence has a string of previous convictions. The other type of contempt is known as *civil* contempt and it occurs whenever a person disobeys a court order, such as an order requiring him or her to reveal the source for an article he or she has written or an order requiring a person to pay compensation to someone he or she has injured. For each type of contempt a person can be fined or committed to prison; indeed for contempt "in the face of the court" (*e.g.* unruly behaviour in the courtroom) a person can be committed to prison summarily, without a hearing.

It should be noted that applications to be compensated by the state for loss suffered as a result of criminal activity are actually civil law claims and are dealt with accordingly (see 5.5). Applications for judicial review (see 7.1) are also civil law matters, even though the review applied for relates to the decision in a criminal case.

Branches of civil law

The names of the various branches of the civil law are mostly self-explanatory. They include land law, family law, contract law and company law. Each of these can in turn be subdivided and some of the subdivisions overlap with other subdivisions or with other main branches; examples are landlord and tenant law, housing law, labour law, partnership law, bankruptcy law, banking law and consumer law. Of the less obviously named branches, the law of torts is for the most part concerned with the compensation of people for injuries caused to themselves or damage caused to their property through someone's recklessness or carelessness; the law's term for such carelessness is "negligence". A subdivision of tort law is the law on libel and slander (or "defamation"). Other torts include trespass, nuisance, false imprisonment and interference with goods.

The expression "property law" is sometimes used to refer to those branches of the civil law which inform us about our rights and duties in relation to the things we own or rent or in which we have some other kind of interest. As the most important form of property is land (or "realty") - an expression which in law embraces the buildings erected on land - the term property law is often used to mean the same as land law. Strictly speaking it should also refer to the law concerning property which is not land. There are innumerable forms of such property (collectively known as "personalty"), ranging from the most tangible - such as cars and antiques - to the most intangible - such as shares in a company, premium bonds or copyright in a book. To discourage too much property becoming vested in one person, our law has devised methods for splitting up the interests which might be held in a single piece of property: someone who owns a house, for instance, might rent it to someone or give an interest in it to a building society in return for a loan (a mortgage). A specific device which both English and Irish law have developed for splitting up people's interests in property is the "trust". If a fund of money, for instance, is held on trust, the purse-strings are controlled by persons called trustees and the people who actually receive payments out of the fund are called beneficiaries of the trust. It is in the form of trusts that most charities carry on their work.

Public law and private law

Some branches of the civil law, together with the criminal law, are sometimes lumped together to form the category known as "public law" in contrast to "private law". While private law regulates the relations between individuals, public law regulates the relations between individuals and public bodies, including the state. Thus the branch of public law called constitutional law tells us about the way in which we are governed and what our civil liberties are. This is a particularly important branch of Northern Ireland law. Administrative law deals mainly with the power of government ministers and departments and the controls exercised by the courts over administrative tribunals (see 7.1). Some of the principles developed within administrative law, such as those concerned with natural justice (e.g. each side to a dispute must be given a fair hearing), are beginning to infiltrate into private law subjects such as contract and tort law. Welfare law explains the operation of the welfare state, setting out the conditions which must be satisfied before people will qualify for state benefits. International law can be part of public law or private law: it is public whenever it concerns the relations between states but private whenever it deals with the relations between individuals from different states.

Substantive law and procedural law

All the branches of law so far mentioned can be labelled "substantive" legal subjects because they concern the actual substance or content of the law: they reveal to us our rights, our duties and our privileges. "Procedural" or "adjectival" legal subjects, on the other hand, regulate the methods by which the substance of the law is applied. The law on criminal procedure determines how crimes are to be prosecuted, how the rights of an accused person are to be protected and how punishments are to be enforced. The law on civil procedure similarly lays down the steps which must be taken whenever a civil dispute develops into a civil legal action. Chapters 4 and 5 of this book are mostly concerned with criminal and civil procedure. The law of evidence contains a mass of detailed rules to specify the sort of testimony and documents which can be used in either a civil or a criminal court to support an argument.

All of these procedural subjects are important because if the rules of procedure are not properly complied with it can happen that substantive legal rights are lost. For example, it is a general rule of civil procedure that a legal action claiming compensation for personal injuries must be brought within three years of the injuries coming to light; if the action is not brought within this limitation period, the right to claim compensation is lost (or "time-barred").

2.2 Primary Legislation

All the branches of law described in the previous section have at least one feature in common: the rules which they contain are derived not only from legislation, which is law created by Parliament, but also from judicial precedent, which is law laid down by judges. Practically every legal issue is governed partly by statute law and partly by judge-made law. Two other sources of law are custom and the opinions of deceased eminent scholars, but in practice these are resorted to very infrequently; both legislation and judge-made law take priority over them. On the rare occasions when the law as laid down by Parliament is in conflict with the law as laid down by judges, it is parliamentary law which must prevail. If parliamentary law is itself at odds with earlier parliamentary law, the later in time must prevail.

Legislation consists not just of Acts of Parliament - which are called "statutes" - but also of the myriad number of orders, rules, regulations and schemes which are made under the authority of an Act of Parliament. This latter body of laws is called secondary, subordinate or delegated legislation, but to all intents and purposes it is just as binding on the general public as the primary legislation enshrined in statutes. Secondary legislation is considered in more detail in the next section.

There is actually a third type of legislation which ought to be mentioned in passing: legislation created under the Royal Prerogative. This takes the form of Prerogative Orders in Council, whereby the Queen simply assents to proposals put before her by senior Ministers who have been appointed Privy Councillors (see 1.4). The matters regulated by the Royal Prerogative in this way are limited to particular fields such as the civil service, the armed forces and coinage. When in 1984 the Prime Minister wished to ban trade unions at Government Communications Headquarters at Cheltenham (GCHQ), she issued a ruling under a power conferred on her by a Prerogative Order in Council, namely the Civil Service Order 1982.

Prerogative Orders with a legislative character are inserted as an Appendix in the annual volumes of United Kingdom statutory instruments (explained in the next section) but are quite different from Parliamentary Orders in Council, which are made under the authority of an Act of Parliament. Prerogative Orders are not themselves statutory instruments, whereas Parliamentary Orders are. In a sense the Prerogative Orders are subordinate legislation (because Parliament can qualify the power to make them) but not secondary legislation (because Parliament's authority is not required for their creation). They invariably apply throughout the United Kingdom, not just to one part of it (England and Wales, Scotland or Northern Ireland).

The primacy of statute law

In the United Kingdom, unlike some countries such as the Republic of Ireland or the United States of America, it is not possible for the courts to refuse to apply primary legislation on the grounds that it is invalid or in some way unconstitutional. Nor can the courts attempt to alter the wording of such laws. Parliament at Westminster is supreme; whatever it enacts cannot be queried. Only a later Parliament can undo the things which a previous Parliament has done. Constitutional lawyers call this "the doctrine of parliamentary sovereignty". The only qualification which needs to be added to this, as regards the United Kingdom as a whole, is that membership of the Common Market means that whenever United Kingdom domestic law, whether parliamentary or judge-made, runs counter to the law emanating from the European Community, it is the latter which must be given priority even by British judges. We return to this European Community dimension at the end of this chapter (see 2.6).

As regards Northern Ireland, however, it has to be remembered that the Government of Ireland Act 1920 effectively provided the province with something which the rest of the kingdom still does not possess - a written constitution. The legislative powers of the Stormont Parliament were deliberately restricted by the Act: excepted and reserved matters could be dealt with only by the Parliament at Westminster (see 1.2). If the Belfast Parliament trespassed into these areas, courts in Northern Ireland were entitled to declare the legislation (whether primary or secondary) to be unauthorised. As regards primary Stormont legislation, this almost happened in a case called *R (Lynn)* v *Gallager* (1937). The Milk and Milk Products Act (NI) 1934 required all sellers of milk in

Northern Ireland to have a licence from the Ministry of Agriculture. Mr Gallagher was refused a licence because his dairy farm was situated outside Northern Ireland, even though he sold milk within the province. Upon his conviction for the crime of selling milk without a licence Mr Gallagher, on appeal, tried to argue that the 1934 Act was beyond the power of the Stormont Parliament to make because, by section 4(1) of the Government of Ireland Act 1920, that Parliament could not make laws in respect of trade. The Court of Appeal of Northern Ireland and the House of Lords held that the 1934 Act was not one in respect of trade but one in respect of the peace, order and good government of Northern Ireland and so was valid.

Different types of statutes

Statutes are made by being first drafted and then enacted. The precise methods of drafting and enactment differ according to the type of statute in question. For the moment we can identify three types. In the first place there are public general Acts, which are statutes affecting the whole public and with which we are principally concerned here; they are by far the commonest type of primary enactment, with about 60 now being created by the Westminster Parliament each year (in 1991 there were 69, in 1992 there were 61). Secondly, there are local Acts, which are statutes concerned only with a particular locality. Thirdly, there are private Acts, which are directed purely towards specific individuals or companies. (In 1992 there were 21 local and private Acts.) Between 1921 and 1972, during which time Northern Ireland possessed its own Parliament, Acts of all three types were passed, examples of the second and third types being respectively the Londonderry Corporation Act (NI) 1970 and the Allied Irish Banks Act (NI) 1971. One of the private Acts passed at Westminster in 1992 was the Ulster Bank Act, which allows for the company structure of that bank to be re-organised.

Private Acts should not be confused with Private Members' Bills, which are proposals for laws introduced and piloted through Parliament by an MP who does well in a ballot at the start of the Parliamentary session. Only two or three of these Bills eventually get passed into law, most of them being opposed by the government, but famous examples of those which did are the Abortion Act 1967, introduced by David Steel MP, and the Obscene Publications Act 1959, introduced by Roy Jenkins MP. In 1991 two Private Members' Bills led to the Badgers Act 1991 (protecting badger setts) and the Smoke Detectors Act 1991 (requiring all new buildings to be fitted with smoke detectors). It is rare for a Private

Members' Bill to extend directly to Northern Ireland, although some of them later lead to equivalent legislation for the province in the shape of an Order in Council (see 2.3). Only two Private Members' Bills have been successfully piloted through the House of Commons by Northern Ireland MPs: Gerry Fitt MP introduced what became the Chronically Sick and Disabled Persons (NI) Act 1978 and Martin Smyth MP introduced the Disabled Persons (NI) Act 1989. Both Acts largely reflect earlier legislation already in place for England and Wales. A member of the House of Lords can also introduce a Peer's Bill; this is how Lord Dunleath was able to proceed with the Education (NI) Act 1978.

Since the imposition of direct rule (see 1.2), the United Kingdom Parliament continues to enact the three types of statute for Northern Ireland, though it rarely resorts to the second and third type. Even the first type is seldom used specifically for the province: such Acts are normally applied to the whole of the United Kingdom (*e.g.* the Consumer Credit Act 1974). The main way in which legislation confined to Northern Ireland is now enacted is by adopting the Parliamentary Order in Council procedure under the Northern Ireland Act 1974. This is an example of secondary legislation and is therefore described more fully in the following section.

Whenever the Westminster Parliament wishes to enact a law concerning an "excepted" matter (see 1.2), it must embody it in a public general Act, for example the Northern Ireland (Emergency Provisions) Act 1991. If the subject of the proposed law is a "transferred" matter then such an Act will be employed only if the government wishes to ensure a full parliamentary debate, for example the Fair Employment (NI) Act 1989. (For legislation dealing with "reserved" matters, see the paragraphs dealing with Orders in Council in 2.3.) Acts confined in operation to the province will usually have the words "Northern Ireland" or "Ulster" either as key words in the title or within brackets before the word "Act". Statutes of the Stormont Parliament 1921-1972 are distinguished from English statutes with similar titles by adding the phrase "Northern Ireland" *after* the word "Act", as in the Legal Aid and Advice Act (NI) 1965.

Some statutes are passed merely to *consolidate* previous statutes, that is, not to change the law but simply to bring into one place the various enactments relating to a particular matter. Examples are the Income and Corporation Taxes Act 1988 and the Social Security Contributions and Benefits (NI) Act 1992. Occasionally statutes are passed in order to *codify* existing statute and judge-made law on a topic. These statutes represent a fresh start on the topic and usually change the existing law. An example is the Theft Act (NI) 1969.

The drafting and enacting of statutes

Acts of the United Kingdom Parliament are officially made by "The Queen in Parliament". This means that they must be approved by the House of Commons, the House of Lords and the Monarch. Since 1911, however, the power of the House of Lords to curb the legislative zeal of the House of Commons has been severely restricted. The Monarch, moreover, no longer refuses to assent to an Act of Parliament presented to her. As the House of Commons is usually dominated by Members of Parliament belonging to the political party which has formed the government, it is in practice the government which decides what legislation should be passed. The government's intentions are made clear in the Queen's Speech at the beginning of each Parliamentary session.

The great majority of public general Acts start life as proposals put to the Cabinet, either by a Cabinet committee or by a particular government department through its representative on the Cabinet. Sometimes the proposals will have been preceded by a government White Paper on the topic. From the Cabinet the proposals are sent in the form of departmental instructions to the Office of Parliamentary Counsel, whose staff have the task of actually drafting the legislation. A similar office existed in Northern Ireland when there was a Parliament at Stormont; it still exists in the form of the Office of Legislative Counsel, which now confines its attention to drafting Orders in Council issued under the Northern Ireland Act 1974 and helping with the drafting of Northern Ireland statutes to be enacted at Westminster.

Legislative drafting is a specialised skill. The draftsman has to translate the department's policy instructions into unambiguous legal language, being careful not to distort the government's intentions or leave any gaps. The Act must also be tied in with whatever legislation already exists on the topic. During the legislation's passage through Parliament the draftsman must always be at hand to advise Ministers and prepare any necessary amendments.

Passage through Parliament, or the enactment of the legislation, is usually a long and complicated process. The standard procedure is for a Bill to be introduced into the House of Commons, where it is dealt with in five stages: the first reading stage (a formality), the second reading stage, the committee stage, the report stage and the third reading stage. It is at the committee and report stages that detailed amendments to the

Bill are mostly considered. It is then sent to the House of Lords, where similar stages must be gone through, and if any amendments are suggested these must return to the House of Commons to be considered further. In most cases, mainly because of the government's majority in the House as a whole and in committees, the final form of the law differs little from that put forward at the initial stages. The Bill is then accorded the Royal Assent and immediately becomes an Act. The House of Lords can delay a Bill only by a year: thereafter the House of Commons can enact the Bill notwithstanding the opposition of the Lords. The most recent example of this happening is the War Crimes Act 1991.

The granting of Royal Assent, however, does not automatically bring the Act into force. This will be so only if the Act contains no other indication as to when or how it is to be brought into force. Often an Act says that it is to come into force only when a "commencement order" has been made (often by a government Minister). The Equal Pay Act (NI) 1970 was not brought into force until 1976. The Employment of Children Act 1973 and the Easter Act 1928 (which provided for a fixed date for Easter) are examples of Acts where the mechanism for bringing them into force has still not been activated! There is a constitutional convention to the effect that legislation should not be retrospective in operation, but occasionally this is ignored, as when the government needs to validate some actions which would otherwise be illegal. An example is the Northern Ireland Act 1972, which declared that as from 1920 the law was different from that laid down by the judges in *R. (Hume)* v *Londonderry Justices* (1972).

The enactment of legislation usually takes months, though urgent Bills can be dealt with in a day or two. The Northern Ireland Act 1972 obtained its second reading in the Commons and the Royal Assent within the space of four-and-a-half hours. In 1974, following the Birmingham pub bombings, the Prevention of Terrorism Act was passed in great haste too.

The form of statutes

Today statutes are set out in a traditional format, an example of which is given in Appendix 3. The Act reproduced there, the Fatal Accidents Act (NI) 1959, is an unusually short Act and has since been repealed and replaced by the Fatal Accidents (NI) Order 1977, but it displays most of the standard features. We can note nine of these:

(1) *The chapter number* (18). This is the number given to the Act at the time of its publication; its purpose is simply to make identification of the Act easier.

(2) *The long title*. This provides a brief summary of the Act's purposes and effects; it expands upon the Act's short title, which is simply the Fatal Accidents Act (NI) 1959 (see (8) below).

(3) *The date* (15th December 1959). This is the date on which the Act was finally made, that is, the date on which the Royal Assent was given. As there is no other provision in this Act specifying when it is to come into force, the Act can be presumed to be in force as from the date given after the long title.

(4) *The enacting words* ("Be it enacted . . ."). This is a standard formula placed at the beginning of all Northern Ireland statutes simply to indicate which Parliament made the statute. The enacting words for United Kingdom statutes differ accordingly.

(5) *Sections*. Each Act is divided into sections, which are numbered 1, 2, 3, etc. Sections are in turn divided into subsections, which are numbered (1), (2), (3), etc. Subsections can then be split into paragraphs: (a), (b), (c) etc. The next subdivision, not used in the Fatal Accidents Act (NI) 1959, is called a subparagraph: (i), (ii), (iii), etc. Reference is made to a subparagraph by writing as follows: s.1(3)(b)(ii) (pronounced as "section one, three, b, two"). While a statute is passing through Parliament it is called a Bill, not an Act, and its provisions are divided into clauses, not sections, but further subdivisions are still called subsections and paragraphs.

(6) *Marginal notes*. The words in the margins beside each section summarise the effect of the section for ease of reference; strictly speaking they do not constitute part of the law. Whenever other statutes are mentioned in sections a reference is placed in the margin to enable the reader to find them more easily when looking for them in a library.

(7) *Definition section*. Most statutes contain a section near the end defining more precisely some of the expressions used earlier. The Fatal Accidents Act (NI) 1959 makes do with defining some words in section 2(2); note that an exact definition of "benefit" is provided, whereas only partial explanations of "insurance money" and "pension" are given. This leaves it open to a judge to say that those terms embrace other funds as well.

(8) *The short title etc. section*. Every statute ends with a section giving the short title of the Act; when a statute is passed dealing with a topic

for which legislation already exists, the Acts can be referred to together, as section 3(1) of the Fatal Accidents Act (NI) 1959 illustrates. The final section also contains a provision concerning the operation in time of the Act: see section 3(4) of the 1959 Act. In United Kingdom statutes the final or penultimate section will normally say whether the statute is to apply in Scotland and in Northern Ireland as well as in England and Wales; some statutes apply in only a part or parts of the United Kingdom, for example the Marriage (Wales) Act 1986 applies only in Wales while the Congenital Disabilities (Civil Liability) Act 1976 applies throughout the United Kingdom except Scotland.

(9) *Schedules.* Many Acts contain one or more Schedules setting out in tabular form the statutory provisions repealed by the Act. Sometimes a Schedule will also set out the amendments provided for by the Act, but if there are not too many of these they may be catered for in the body of the Act itself, as in section 1(4) of the Fatal Accidents Act (NI) 1959. Occasionally the Schedules contain more substantive provisions, such as guidelines for the application of a particular standard mentioned in the Act. Schedules are not self-enacting: somewhere in the Act there must be a provision stating that the Schedules are to have the force of law: see section 3(3) of the 1959 Act.

An important formal feature of statutes which is not illustrated by the Fatal Accidents Act (NI) 1959 is the division of longer Acts or Schedules into Parts. This is simply a method of ensuring that all the provisions concerned with a particular matter are bunched together in the same place within a statute. To help the reader to find a particular provision some pieces of very long legislation are now published with an index.

The problems of looking for statute law

Even if you can recognise and read a statute when you find one, this will not be much help to you unless you know how to look for it in the first place. The trouble is that most Acts of Parliament are designed to operate prospectively, this is, for the future and not the past. They remain in force even after the Parliament which made them has been dissolved. When new legislation is enacted, insufficient attention is sometimes paid to the statutes which are already in force. It can thus be very difficult to understand the current legal position on a certain matter if there are several statutes purporting to deal with it, some dating back a long time.

In Northern Ireland the problems are accentuated by the fact that - as noted in Chapter 1 - since the fourteenth century there have been many Parliaments claiming the power to legislate for the area which is now Northern Ireland. As a result the Northern Ireland "statute book" - the collection of the statutory provisions currently in force in the province - is very large indeed. The collection comprises the work of six separate legislatures:

(1)   the Parliament in Ireland, from 1310 to 1800,
(2)   the Parliament of England, from 1226 to 1707,
(3)   the Parliament of Great Britain, from 1707 to 1800,
(4)   the Parliament of the United Kingdom, from 1800 to the present,
(5)   the Parliament of Northern Ireland, from 1921 to 1972, and
(6)   the Northern Ireland Assembly, 1974, the enactments of which are not called Acts but Measures.

Many of the statutes of these Parliaments remain in force, or partly in force, even though they are of virtually no significance in practice: about 50 statutes of the Parliament in Ireland still apply, as do about 70 statutes of the Parliaments of England and Great Britain. In more recent times statutes have included provisions to repeal earlier statutes which are being superseded and indeed sometimes whole Acts are passed purely to rid the statute book of redundant laws - for example, the Repeal of Unnecessary Laws Act (NI) 1954 and the Statute Law Revision (NI) Act 1980. It can still be difficult, though, to determine precisely the current statutory position on a particular topic. The difficulty is compounded when one realises that some statutes passed by Parliament at Westminster have not made it clear whether they are meant to apply in Northern Ireland as well as in the rest of Britain, though the rule is that if the Act is silent on the matter it is presumed to apply throughout the United Kingdom. In 1991 there were 38 United Kingdom statutes (out of 69 passed altogether) which applied wholly or partly in Northern Ireland.

Were it simply a matter of knowing which statutes have been repealed and which are still in force, the problem would be fairly manageable. But we have to remember that statutes can be amended as well as totally repealed. When this occurs (an example is provided by section 1(4) of the Fatal Accidents Act (NI) 1959, reproduced in Appendix 3) the statute is not re-enacted in its new form: you have to read it in its original form and then read what the amending statute provides. Amendments can be introduced by Acts which have very little in common with the original statute, sometimes by a Law Reform (Miscellaneous Provisions) Act or an Administration of Justice Act. They can even be introduced by secondary legislation, described in the next section.

To make the search for the statute law easier, Her Majesty's Stationery Office publishes various auxiliary volumes. The statutes themselves are published and sold singly at the time they are enacted as well as collectively in bound or loose-leaf volumes at the end of each calendar year. These annual volumes have continued to be produced since 1972 even though they now contain not primary legislation but the Orders in Council made under the Northern Ireland Act 1974. Each pre-1972 volume contains tables showing the United Kingdom and Northern Ireland Acts repealed or amended by Northern Ireland Acts during that year, as well as tables showing the Northern Ireland Acts affected by United Kingdom Acts passed during the year and the full list of United Kingdom Acts passed that year which are applicable in Northern Ireland. The annual index to the statutes also lists the amendments made to Acts by secondary legislation.

Every three years or so (the latest is up to the end of 1990) an index is published to all the statutory provisions currently in force in Northern Ireland, arranged under distinct subject-headings; at roughly the same interval another table is published of all the statute law which affects, or has affected, Northern Ireland, this time arranged in chronological order and with amendments and repeals noted (the latest volume is up to the end of 1989). Both these lists amount to weighty tomes (in fact the Index to the Statutes is in two volumes), but they are indispensable because they also include references to statutes passed for the whole of the United Kingdom. They permit you to tell at a glance what primary legislation exists on any matter and whether primary legislation which once existed has been amended or repealed. The position can be so complicated, however, that mistakes and omissions are not uncommon.

The *Statutes Revised*, Northern Ireland is a 16-volume collection of the public general Acts of the Parliaments of Ireland, England, Great Britain, the United Kingdom and Northern Ireland which have affected Northern Ireland down to 1950, whether or not they deal with matters which were finally placed within the legislative competence of the Parliament of Northern Ireland. The texts are reprinted as amended, with the amending and repealing schedules therefore excluded. During 1982 the Statutory Publications Office of the Department of Finance and Personnel produced in loose-leaf form a nine-volume second edition of the *Statutes Revised*, which sets out in chronological order the text, also amended, of all the statutes affecting Northern Ireland between 1921 and 1981. Unfortunately this excludes the relevant United Kingdom statutes enacted since 1920, but a four volume series (A-D) appended to the edition reprints the amended texts of all pre-1920 legislation, from whatever parliamentary source, still in force in Northern Ireland. Cumulative supplements to *Statutes Revised* are now published annually to show what changes have occurred during the past year.

All United Kingdom statutes, as well as being published singly and in annual collections, are indexed by the two-volume *Index to the Statutes* published every two years. Two private publishing companies also produce versions of these statutes with comments and annotations: these are the series known as *Halsbury's Statutes* and *Current Law Statutes*. The latter now include an index to each statute as well as, for consolidating statutes, a Table of Derivations showing where provisions were previously to be found in legislation and a Table of Destinations showing where old provisions now appear in the new statute. The last volume for each year also now includes the full text of the Private Acts passed during that period and an alphabetical list of *all* the statutes passed since 1700 (including those repealed: there are about 17,500 of these). *Statutes in Force* provides the service for England and Wales which *Statutes Revised* provides for Northern Ireland; it comprises scores of loose-leaf volumes.

Computer-based information retrieval

The advent of computerised information retrieval systems is greatly facilitating the search for primary (as well as secondary) legislation. By keying in the appropriate question, one can discover within seconds the relevant legislation on a particular point. The full text of the up-to-date version of this legislation can be displayed on a screen and printed out if desired. Moves are afoot to include Northern Ireland legislation on databases used in these systems, but at the time of writing the transfer has not yet been achieved. Only legislation passed at Westminster is today accessible. The use of computers is also affecting searches for judge-made law (see 2.4).

2.3 Secondary Legislation

All pieces of secondary legislation are ultimately the offspring of a parent (or "enabling") Act of Parliament. They are used to lay down the law in more detail than is normally contained in primary legislation, or where it would be too time-consuming to invoke the full Parliamentary process just to make a fairly minor alteration in some existing legislative scheme. The parent Act will give power to a rule-making authority to issue detailed laws on a particular matter. The rule-making authority is usually a government department but it can also be, for instance, the Privy Council (which makes Orders in Council), a local authority (which makes bye-laws), or a committee of judges and lawyers (which makes Rules of Court). The exact title of the particular secondary legislation will depend on the wording of the parent Act: it may provide for Orders in Council, orders, rules, regulations, directions, schemes or bye-laws. Nothing turns on the difference in title - all of these varieties are equally binding as laws of the land, though some Orders in Council do have special features explained below.

"Non-legislation"

There are various semi-official documents which the lay person often believes have the force of law but which in fact do not. Even though they are sometimes issued pursuant to a power conferred by statute, they can only influence the judges' views on what the law should be. Such publications include the Highway Code, the Codes of Practice on Closed Shops and Picketing (issued for Great Britain by the Department of Employment), the Code of Practice on Fair Employment (issued by the Fair Employment Commision: see 8.2), the codes of practice agreed to by various trade associations, the standing orders issued to the prison service by the Northern Ireland Office and the Codes of Practice issued under the Police and Criminal Evidence (NI) Order 1989 (see 4.3). The Immigration Rules 1990, issued pursuant to the Immigration Act 1971, are another very important example. The Inland Revenue frequently issues policy statements which are treated by the courts as having this semi-legislative status: the statements declare that the Inland Revenue will make extra-statutory concessions, that is, not charge tax on certain specified payments. Statements of practice published by insurance companies, and circulars put out by the Home Office and other government departments on a wide range of legal matters are also in this category. Judges, Masters and registrars announce what are called "Practice Directions" in order to provide for better organisation of proceedings within the courts.

Just because a matter is catered for in some such semi-official document (which may not even be available to the general public) rather than in a piece of secondary legislation does not mean that it is of little legal significance - it more usually means that strict legal standards are deemed inappropriate for the matter. Consequently, issues as diverse as the level of permissible noise from ice-cream vans and the strip-searching of persons in police custody are dealt with by this kind of document.

Types of secondary legislation

Although all pieces of secondary legislation have the same legal status, they nevertheless differ in form. Quite apart from the variations in their titles, alluded to above, it is helpful to distinguish between three different types of secondary legislation affecting Northern Ireland. The first two are special because they are made in England; only the third type is made within Northern Ireland itself. Because of this difference in the origins of secondary legislation it can often be quite difficult, as in the case of primary legislation, to determine exactly which law is applicable in the province. However, the difficulty is not as acute as in the case of primary legislation because secondary legislation did not become common until the nineteenth century. We shall look at the three types of secondary legislation separately.

Statutory instruments

In England and Wales most of the secondary legislation is published in the form of consecutively numbered "statutory instruments". Some of these, being made under the authority of an enabling Act which extends beyond England and Wales, are applicable in Northern Ireland. Thus, for example, the Consumer Credit (Quotation) Regulations 1980 apply in Northern Ireland because the enabling Act was a statute in force throughout the United Kingdom, namely the Consumer Credit Act 1974; but the Packaging and Labelling of Dangerous Substances Regulations 1978 do not apply in Northern Ireland because in this case the enabling Act (the Consumer Protection Act 1961) does not apply outside England, Wales and Scotland.

Many statutory instruments are commencement orders for primary legislation, some of which will apply to Northern Ireland. In 1992 there were 100 commencement orders (all of them reproduced in the last volume of *Current Law Statutes* for that year).

Furthermore, some Westminster statutes have an effect only within Northern Ireland, so obviously the legislative powers delegated by such Acts can themselves be effective only within Northern Ireland. Their title will contain the words "Northern Ireland" before the word "Rule", "Regulation", "Order", etc. An example is the Emergency Provisions

(Compensation) (NI) Rules 1991, made under the authority of section 63 of the Northern Ireland (Emergency Provisions) Act 1991 (see 5.5).

In 1991, 458 statutory instruments were made affecting Northern Ireland as well as other parts of the United Kingdom (out of 2,905 made altogether; in 1992 the number was 3,351); eight others, excluding the Orders in Council described next, were made affecting only Northern Ireland (*e.g.* the Northern Ireland Act 1974 (Interim Period Extension) Order 1991 - the provision which extended the direct rule arrangements for Northern Ireland for a further 12 months). Quite a few of the former category are instruments made to comply with the United Kingdom's obligations as a member of the Common Market; section 2(2) of the European Communities Act 1972 is one of the most important enabling provisions in our law.

Orders in Council

Orders in Council are in fact just one species of the more general category of statutory instruments described above. They are often viewed as the most important type of secondary legislation because they are formally made by the Queen on the advice of her Privy Councillors (*i.e.* senior government Ministers of the day; see 1.4). But in fact they carry no more weight than any other type of delegated legislation and in appropriate cases can be impugned by Parliament or by the courts to just the same extent (see below).

There are a number of Acts providing for the making of Orders in Council which might apply in Northern Ireland as well as in other parts of the United Kingdom, for example the Administration of Justice Act 1985. However, the reason for listing Orders in Council here as a separate type of secondary legislation is that there is one enabling Act, the Northern Ireland Act 1974, which in effect substitutes legislation in the form of Orders in Council for the legislation which, had it not been abolished, the Parliament at Stormont would have enacted. More precisely, Orders in Council under the 1974 Act are used to make laws for Northern Ireland on subjects which, being "transferred matters" under the Northern Ireland Constitution Act 1973, would have been legislated for by the Northern Ireland Assembly if it had survived the first few months of 1974. "Reserved" matters under the Northern Ireland Constitution Act 1973 are also dealt with by Orders in Council. Only "excepted" matters need to be legislated for by an Act of Parliament at Westminster. "Law and order" is a reserved matter but "terrorism" is an excepted matter, which is why there is a Northern Ireland (Emergency Provisions)

Act rather than an Order. It is to be noted that the categories of "transferred", "reserved" and "excepted" matters are not the same under the Northern Ireland Constitution Act 1973 as they were under the Government of Ireland Act 1920 (see 1.2).

Orders in Council made under the Northern Ireland Act 1974 are published and numbered as United Kingdom statutory instruments, a separate number being given to them for publication in annual collections of Northern Ireland Orders in Council. These collections continue the series known as Acts of the Northern Ireland Parliament, so many people would view these Orders as having, to all intents and purposes, the status of primary legislation. This is not strictly the case, because unlike primary legislation they can be challenged by the courts (see below). During the last five years there has been an average of 22 of these Orders in Council each year. An example is provided in Appendix 3 (the Occupiers' Liability (NI) Order 1987). As we shall see below, it is not unusual for Orders made under the 1974 Act to sub-delegate law-making powers to other authorities, even though the general rule for secondary legislation is that further delegation of powers is not possible. These Orders can also amend or repeal primary legislation, which again is contrary to the normal rule for secondary laws.

It should be noted that not every item of legislation given the title "Order" will in fact be an Order in Council. However, it is rare for a statutory instrument applying only in Northern Ireland to be called an Order unless it is an Order in Council made under the Northern Ireland Act 1974; an example is the District Electoral Areas (NI) Order 1993. The word "Order" is also used for some more ordinary pieces of legislation which fall within the third type described below. These are not statutory instruments at all. Examples would be the Statutory Sick Pay (Rate of Payment) Order (NI) 1991, made under the Social Security (NI) Order 1982 (which *was* an Order in Council) and the commencement orders for primary legislation mentioned earlier. See also the example of a statutory rule reproduced in Appendix 3, namely the Planning Applications (Exemption from Publication) Order (NI) 1991.

Statutory rules

Statutory rules are made by rule-making authorities in Northern Ireland under a power conferred by an Act of the United Kingdom Parliament, by an Act of the Stormont Parliament or by an Order in Council made under the Northern Ireland Act 1974. They are really the Northern Ireland equivalents of the statutory instruments made for the rest of the United Kingdom (see above). Sometimes they differ from the corresponding statutory instruments in title alone, the actual content remaining virtually identical. The title will always contain the words "Northern Ireland" placed in brackets *after* the words "Rules", "Regulations", "Order", etc. A typical illustration of statutory rules would be the Students Awards Regulations (NI) 1991, which were made by the Department of Education for Northern Ireland under the Education and Libraries (NI) Order 1986 and which are almost identical to the Education (Mandatory Awards) Regulations 1992, made under the Education Acts 1962 and 1973.

As in the case of Orders, not all laws with the title "Rules" will in fact be what they seem. They may not be statutory rules at all but statutory instruments, for example the Emergency Provisions (Compensation) (NI) Rules 1991 cited above. They are recognisable from the position of the words "Northern Ireland" *before* the word "Rules". To repeat, however, the difference in title does not affect the legislation's status.

In 1991 there were 546 statutory rules made for Northern Ireland. They were issued by 14 different rule-making bodies, the commonest sources being the Departments of Agriculture and of the Environment, and they obviously dealt with a huge range of subjects. But some statutory rules are of a recurring variety. One such is the statutory rule known as a commencement order, which sets a date for the coming into force of provisions in other legislation, for example the Education Reform (1989 Order) (Commencement No. 4) Order (NI) 1991. Another recurring variety is the statutory rule which sets new financial limits for those originally stated in a parent Act or in a previous statutory rule, for example the Fisheries (Licence Duties) Bye-laws (NI) 1991.

Like statutes, statutory rules can also be subdivided into public, local and private rules, though here too the distinctions are not very important. The local and private rules usually concern roads or road traffic, one example being the Road Races (Circuit of Ireland Rally) Order (NI) 1986. Bye-laws made by local authorities are another example; they can be made by district councils for, generally speaking, the good rule and government of the whole or any part of the district, provided they are confirmed by a government department. They can also be made by such bodies as the Fisheries Conservancy Board for Northern Ireland (an example is given in the previous paragraph), Trustees of the Ulster Folk and Transport Museum, Northern Ireland   Railways and Harbour Authorities. In 1991, 63 of the 546 statutory rules were local.

The making of secondary legislation

Whatever type of secondary legislation is eventually made, and in whatever form, it is invariably drafted only after a period of consultation with interested parties. Except occasionally, the final drafting is performed by civil servants within the legal branches of the government department concerned, not, as is the case with primary legislation, by Parliamentary Counsel.

Orders in Council under the Northern Ireland Act 1974 are given special treatment. Proposals for new Orders are first considered by a committee of senior civil servants, the Policy Co-ordinating Committee, and then by a committee of government Ministers, the Legislative Programme Committee. Instructions for a draft Order are then sent to the Office of Legislative Counsel in Belfast. When a draft has been prepared and then approved by the two above-mentioned committees it is circulated to the public in the form of a "Proposal for a Draft Order in Council" and is accompanied by an Explanatory Document. Usually no more than six weeks are allowed for comments. The Northern Ireland Committee at the House of Commons may be consulted if the area being dealt with is a contentious one. The comments made on the proposal are considered and the draftsman then prepares a final draft for laying before Parliament.

Speaking very generally, the precise method of creating secondary legislation depends on the importance of the secondary legislation in question. Usually the most important - and Orders in Council made under the 1974 Act fall into this category - must be laid in draft form before both Houses of Parliament, and be approved by both Houses, before being presented to the Queen for her formal assent. This process puts the onus on the government to find time for Parliament to debate and affirm the legislation before it can finally be made; if no debate takes place then no further action can be taken. Secondary legislation which is urgent, and for which no time is immediately available for a parliamentary debate, can be made without first being laid before Parliament, but it must cease to have effect if each House does not approve it within a specified period, usually 28 or 40 days. No Order in Council for Northern Ireland has been made under this urgent procedure since 1987. Both of these legislative processes may be termed "affirmative" procedures because the legislation does not have effect, or ceases to have effect, unless it is affirmed.

An alternative is the "negative" procedure, whereby the legislation takes effect, or continues to have effect if already made, unless a "prayer" in either House specifically annuls it within 40 days. This procedure is usually employed for Orders in Council and statutory rules which are almost identical to English legislation already enacted and for which a separate parliamentary debate is deemed to be unnecessary. In such cases the English Act will contain a section saying that equivalent legislation can be made for Northern Ireland under the negative resolution procedure and the preamble to an Order in Council will state that the Order is being made for purposes corresponding to those of the provisions of the equivalent English Act. In 1991 and 1992, for example, 17 of the 45 Orders in Council made under the Northern Ireland Act 1974 were made by way of this negative resolution procedure: thus the Redundancy Fund (Abolition) (NI) Order 1991 reflects section 13 of the Employment Act 1990 and the Firearms (Amendment) (NI) Order 1992 reflects the Firearms (Amendment) Act 1992. When this negative resolution procedure is used the draft Order is not preceded by a published proposal but is simply made by the Privy Council and laid before Parliament. Under all of these procedures, howevever, the legislation must be affirmed or annulled in its entirety; it cannot be amended, though it can be withdrawn and re-laid later in a revised form.

Less important secondary legislation may be required to be laid before Parliament but is not subject to the affirmative or negative procedures. Such legislation cannot be debated, but ministerial questions can be asked about it, and because it must be laid it cannot usually come into force before the date of laying. If it is essential that the statutory instrument comes into force before being laid, the Speaker of the House of Commons and the Lord Chancellor (who is Speaker of the House of Lords) must be notified. The least important secondary legislation need not be laid before Parliament at all, though again questions can be asked about it if an MP happens to have his or her attention drawn to it. The statutory instruments which are afforded this most cursory treatment are mostly local or private in nature. An unfortunate consequence of direct rule in Northern Ireland is that the secondary legislation which in the days of Stormont was subject to the negative resolution procedure is no longer required to be laid before Parliament at all. This is due to the fact that the replacement of Stormont Acts by Westminster Orders in Council required the whole of the legislative machinery for Northern Ireland to be, as it were, "taken down a gear": delegated legislation which was previously subject to the negative procedure at Stormont is now subject to no parliamentary scrutiny whatsoever.

It should be noted, finally, that the making of secondary legislation is not the same as the bringing of it into force. Secondary legislation which is required to be laid before Parliament - even if already made (and not just in draft form) - cannot come into force before it is laid, except very rarely. As well, even if the legislation does not need to be laid, or is laid in draft form and made later, it may still itself provide (and usually does) that it is not to come into force until a certain period has elapsed after it has been made.

Controls on secondary legislation

Parliamentary controls over secondary legislation

Secondary legislation is controlled by two bodies: Parliament itself and the courts. Parliament's control comes into play not only at the stage when the parent Act is being enacted - for its delegating provisions can then be debated and amended - but also at the stage when, as is often required, the secondary legislation itself is laid before Parliament to undergo either the affirmative or negative procedure. The time allowed for debates on such procedures on the floor of the House of Commons is usually just 90 minutes. In addition (or more usually instead) they can be discussed for two-and-a-half hours by a Standing (or Merits) Committee of the House of Commons and the debate there will obviously be influential on the way MPs vote on resolutions in the House. By constitutional convention the House of Lords does not vote down secondary legislation proposed by the government.

All United Kingdom statutory instruments - except Orders in Council made under the Northern Ireland Act 1974 - can also be scrutinised from a technical rather than a merit point of view by a Joint Select (or Scrutiny) Committee of the House of Commons and the House of Lords. The Committee consults the rule-making authority concerned if it thinks that the instrument is technically defective, and the attention of the whole House of Commons can then be drawn to the matter.

The specific task of inspecting Northern Ireland secondary legislation to see if it is technically defective is performed by an official called the Examiner for Statutory Rules, currently Mr P L Oakey. The Examiner looks at all the secondary legislation which is required to be laid before Parliament but which is not subject to the affirmative or negative procedures. This means that he examines about half of all the statutory rules which are ultimately made. About 50 sets of rules per year are not required to be laid before Parliament at all. The Examiner issues a report every few months (the 34th report was published in June 1993). In it he draws the attention of the Clerk of the Northern Ireland Assembly (a post which was retained even after the Assemblies of 1974 and 1982-86 were dissolved and which is still occupied by Mr John Kennedy) to those statutory rules with which the Examiner is dissatisfied on one or more grounds.

These grounds include the existence of an unjustifiable delay in publishing or laying the rule, doubts as to whether the rule is *intra vires* (*i.e.* within the powers conferred by the parent Act), and the fact that the parent Act has tried to prevent the courts from challenging the rule. In practice the Examiner also complains if there is a gap of less than the conventional 21 days between the laying of a statutory rule and its coming into force. He ensures as well that the Commons Select Committee on European Legislation scrutinises those Northern Ireland statutory rules which give effect to an EC obligation. At the end of the day the Examiner finds fault with only a tiny minority of the rules examined. Whenever he has complained that a rule may not be *intra vires*, the appropriate rule-making authority has either lobbied to have the parent Act extended or has itself repealed the offending provision in the rule.

The Assembly which operated in Northern Ireland from 1982 to 1986 (see 1.2) was consulted about proposals for Orders in Council emanating from government departments. On a few occasions the views expressed by Assembly Members led to changes being made in the final form of the legislation.

Judicial control over secondary legislation

Control by the courts over secondary legislation is sometimes described as judicial review, another form of which is described in 7.1. It takes the form of a decision that a piece of secondary legislation of whatever nature is *ultra vires* (*i.e.* beyond the powers conferred by the parent Act). Whether such is the case or not can often be a very controversial legal issue, as is illustrated by the conflicting speeches of the Law Lords in the Northern Ireland case of *McEldowney* v *Forde* (1971). The issue arose there indirectly and not in judicial review proceedings properly so called, but the difficulty of the point was nonetheless great. The question was whether the Minister of Home Affairs for Northern Ireland was acting *ultra vires* the Civil Authorities (Special Powers) Act (NI) 1922 when he added "republican clubs and any like organisation howsoever described" to the list of associations which were unlawful under that Act. The decision turned on whether this action was "for the preservation of the peace and maintenance of order" and by a majority of three to two the Law Lords held that it was.

The scope of the powers conferred by a parent Act was also in issue (again indirectly) in *R. (Hume)* v *Londonderry Justices* (1972). There the High Court decided that the granting of power to an army officer to order an assembly of persons to disperse was beyond the power of the Stormont Parliament (and its delegates) because the Government of Ireland Act 1920 said that the Parliament of Northern Ireland was not to have power to make laws "in respect of the army". In *Dunkley* v *Evans* (1981), on the other hand, an English court held that the West Coast Herring (Prohibition of Fishing) Order 1978, which was made under the Sea Fish (Conservation) Act 1967 and prohibited herring fishing within a defined area, was not totally invalid just because the defined area included an area of the sea adjacent to the coast of Northern Ireland which was expressly excluded from the scope of the 1967 Act; the Order was invalid only as regards that particular area of sea.

These are all instances of secondary legislation being challenged for substantive violation of the parent Act. Procedural violations, such as not consulting the right people before making the statutory rule or including a provision which prevents the courts from pronouncing on the rule's validity (so-called *ouster clauses*), are also grounds for judicial review, but again the exact attitude of the courts to these problems is somewhat unpredictable. In *R* v *Secretary of State for Health* (1992) a court invalidated the Oral Snuff (Safety) Regulations 1989 because the principal manufacturer of the product in question had not been properly consulted in advance. In all cases where secondary legislation is held to be *ultra vires* it ceases to have any force in law and can be disobeyed with impunity. In recent years there have been several well publicised cases of ministerial statutory instruments being successfully challenged in the English courts (*e.g.* the cases involving opticians' fees and board and lodging allowances for claimants of supplementary benefit).

The form of secondary legislation

Pieces of secondary legislation are more numerous and often more lengthy than pieces of primary legislation. The Insolvency Rules (NI) 1991, for example, run for 948 pages (596 of which are taken up by prescribed forms). Appendix 3 reproduces a typical example of a short Order in Council made under the Northern Ireland Act 1974. It is the Occupiers' Liability (NI) Order 1987, which supplements the Occupiers' Liability Act (NI) 1957 and alters the judge-made law on whether an occupier of premises owes a duty of care to people who trespass on those premises. The following features of a typical Order in Council may be noted:

(1) *Its number.* Each Order in Council made under the Northern Ireland Act 1974 is given both a United Kingdom statutory instrument number (here it is 1280) and a Northern Ireland Order in Council number (here it is 15).

(2) *Dates.* The date on which an Order in Council is made is the date on which the Queen assents to her Privy Councillors' recommendations (here, 21st July 1987). The date on which the Order comes into force is provided for in the body of the Order (see article 1); sometimes it does not come into force until a further statutory commencement order is made naming an appointed day.

(3) *The enacting words.* ("Now, therefore, Her Majesty..."). This is another example of a standard formula; the preliminary phrase beginning "Whereas a draft..." is called the preamble.

(4) *Articles.* Each Order is divided into articles (not sections), with the further subdivisions being referred to as paragraphs and subparagraphs. The numbering and lettering systems are the same as for statutes, for example article 3(1)(a).

(5) *The first articles.* These are devoted to defining the title of the Order, its commencement date, and how it is to be interpreted (see also 2.5). In statutes, by contrast, these matters are usually dealt with by sections at the end.

(6) *Explanatory note.* This is provided at the very end of all secondary legislation in order to give a brief indication of the effects of the legislation. It is comparable to the long title of a statute, but, unlike the long title, it forms no part of the actual enactment and should not be used as an aid to interpretation of the legislation. As secondary legislation can be worded in an obscure way, it is often helpful to begin by reading the explanatory note to get an idea of the purpose of the legislation.

Appendix 3 also reproduces a short, but fairly normal, statutory rule: the Planning Applications (Exemption from Publication) Order (NI) 1991. There are no special features of this which require highlighting. We can see that its number in the collection of statutory rules for 1991 is 473, and the attached explanatory note is very helpful in placing the rule in context. Note that even though it is a statutory rule it is actually entitled an "Order" (because the Planning (NI) Order 1991 says that the Department of the Environment may do certain things "by order" and hence its provisions should be called articles; if it were entitled "Rules" or "Regulations", the provisions would be referred to as rule 4, regulation 5, etc).

The problems of looking for secondary legislation

As with statutes, secondary legislation is published singly as well as collectively in annual bound volumes. Many of these are summarised in the multi-volume *Halsbury's Statutory Instruments*, which are regularly updated. Orders in Council made under the Northern Ireland Act 1974 are published in the series which used to contain the Acts of the Stormont Parliament. Each annual volume, as well as reprinting the Orders themselves, includes tables showing the United Kingdom and Northern Ireland Acts (and previous Orders in Council) which have been repealed, amended or otherwise affected by Orders in Council made during the year. Further tables indicate the United Kingdom Acts passed during the year which apply in Northern Ireland and the effects of these Acts on previous Irish Acts, Northern Irish Acts and Orders in Council. The consequences for earlier Acts and Orders of the statutory instruments and statutory rules made during the year are also tabulated.

The last volume for each year of the statutory rules for Northern Ireland contains a list of that year's United Kingdom statutory instruments which affect the province (other than Orders in Council made under the 1974 Act) and there is an index categorising the rules on the basis of the authorities which made them. Further tables supply lists of the changes made by the year's statutory rules not just to earlier Acts and Orders (information which is also given in the annual volume of Orders in Council, see above) but also to earlier statutory rules. A large index to all the statutory rules in force, arranged under subject headings, is published every three years - the last one published, in 1991, goes up to the end of 1988 - but this does not give details of the amendments which later statutory rules may have made to earlier ones: the fully amended text can be gleaned only from reading all of the relevant rules together.

2.4 Judge-Made Law

The courts are almost as important a source of new law as Parliament. The law which they create is sometimes referred to as case law or common law, as opposed to Parliament's statute law; this is yet another sense in which the expression common law can be used. Generally speaking, new law is created by the courts in two types of situation: where existing statute law has nothing at all to say about the point in issue, and where that which statute law does have to say is unclear. In the latter situation the role of the courts is to interpret the existing legislation; the techniques they adopt in doing so are examined more closely in the following section. For the moment we shall concentrate on situations where the courts make law untrammelled by any existing pronouncement on the matter by Parliament.

Decisions by judges on novel points of law enter the corpus of case law by being reported in one or more of a series of law reports. Only a very small fraction of judicial decisions are reported in this way, and not all of those which do get reported are significant, for they may simply confirm a point which was already fairly well settled. Reported decisions, however, are important because they are available thereafter for lawyers and judges to refer to in future cases in order to back up an argument; what has been decided in the past is a good guide for what should be decided in the present (or, as it is sometimes put, "like cases should be decided alike"). The convention once was that the decisions by courts never really created new law at all - the judges were simply "finding" the law in earlier cases and were "declaring" what it was; today, though, there are few lawyers who still adhere to this somewhat fictional view of the judicial function. Whether we like it or not, judges do make law.

With the advent of computer-based information retrieval systems (of which the best known for legal information is LEXIS), the importance of *unreported* cases has grown. Transcripts of these were previously kept in court libraries, which were not very accessible. Lawyers will some-times search through unreported cases to see whether they do after all contain a ruling which can be taken as authoritative on a particular point. Reported Northern Ireland cases *are* now included in the databases of information retrieval systems. However, the House of Lords has expressed some scepticism about the utility of citing computer-searched unreported cases.

Law reports

In Northern Ireland there are two main series of law reports: the Northern Ireland Law Reports and the Northern Ireland Judgments Bulletin. Both are published under the auspices of the Incorporated Council of Law Reporting for Northern Ireland. The former is the senior series because it was begun in 1925, but all the reports, before they are published, are checked by the judges to make sure that an accurate account has been given of what was said in the case. The Northern Ireland Law Reports appear in four parts per year and contain cases determined in the superior courts in Northern Ireland and on appeal therefrom to the House of Lords. The Judgments Bulletin, sometimes called the Bluebook from the colour of its cover, has been published since 1970, appearing now almost on a monthly basis and simply reproducing the judges' speeches in a case without an editor's summaries of the facts and decisions or details of the barristers' arguments (which are occasionally given in the Northern Ireland Law Reports). Most cases reported in the Judgments Bulletin are later reported in the Law Reports too. An index to all Northern Ireland cases reported since 1921 has been published and a supplement has brought it up to date to 1975. The Bar Library (see 3.2) has produced more recent updates.

Appendix 3 reproduces a reported case from the Northern Ireland Law Reports: *Campbell* v *Armstrong and Others* (1981). The summary at the start of the case, written by the editor of the series, is called the headnote. There then follows a list of the previously reported cases (and their references) mentioned by the judge in this case, some of which are Northern Ireland cases and some English. If you read the report you will see a typical example of how a judge goes about deciding a dispute on the basis of existing case law and statute law. The case also illustrates the process of statutory interpretation, which is discussed in the next section.

In England there are several series of law reports. The "official" ones are the Law Reports (divided into four series for Appeal Cases - that is, decisions in the House of Lords and Privy Council - Queen's Bench cases, Chancery cases and Family cases, these last three also containing Court of Appeal decisions in each category) and the Weekly Law Reports. The most commonly used "unofficial" (*i.e.*, privately published) series is called the All England Law Reports. The quality newspapers in England publish short reports of important decisions; the most respected of these series is that issued in *The Times*. All law reports are referred to by well established abbreviations, for example All ER stands for the All England Law Reports. In a typical year there would be no more than 100 new cases reported in Northern Ireland. In England there would be as many as 2,500.

In both Northern Ireland and England the decisions of inferior courts (magistrates' courts and county courts) are virtually never reported, because if a truly novel legal point arises in such courts the case will almost inevitably be appealed to a higher court, where the decision will be reported. In practice, of course, by no means every novel point is appealed, often because the litigants cannot afford the time or money involved. This means that many important points never get the full legal airing they deserve and hence, to the general public's amazement, the law on many commonplace problems can be hazy.

For some areas of the law special series of law reports have been devised to help publicise lower courts' decisions as well as the decisions of higher courts which would not otherwise qualify for inclusion in one of the major series. In Northern Ireland we have special series of this sort for decisions of the Lands Tribunal, industrial tribunals and social security appeal tribunals (see Chapter 7). Decisions of courts and tribunals which might not otherwise get reported but which may nevertheless be of some legal interest are noted in the Bulletin of Northern Ireland Law, a publication of the Servicing the Legal System programme of the Queen's University of Belfast, which attempts to list all developments of legal interest to Northern Ireland on almost a month-by-month basis.

The rules of the doctrine of precedent

In the vast majority of court cases the dispute is really about the facts of the case - what was done, by whom, and when - rather than about the law which is applicable to those facts. Do not expect to visit a courtroom and see the lawyers and judges poring over law books. But when law reports do need to be referred to then the doctrine of "precedent" comes into play. This doctrine (already mentioned in 1.1), which is sometimes referred to by the Latin phrase *stare decisis* (meaning "stand by things that have been decided"), states that a lower court is *obliged* to follow a higher court's earlier decision in a similar case unless the previous decision can be "distinguished". A higher court can overrule a lower court's decision, but this just means that the higher court is changing the law from that time onwards, not that the losing party in the earlier decision (which may have been taken years previously) can now have that decision reversed.

As the highest court in the Northern Ireland legal system is the House of Lords, the decisions of that court are obviously binding on all the other courts in Northern Ireland. Strictly speaking this is only true of the House's decisions in cases originating in Northern Ireland, but in practice all of its decisions are treated with the greatest respect. It has even been accepted that an English or Scottish House of Lords decision must be followed in preference to a conflicting decision of the Northern Ireland

Court of Appeal. Decisions of the Judicial Committee of the Privy Council (see 1.4) are not absolutely binding on courts in either Northern Ireland or England, but their authority is nevertheless persuasive. Within the province itself decisions of the Court of Appeal are binding on the High Court and Crown Court, and their decisions in turn are binding on the county courts. Magistrates' courts, at the very bottom of the hierarchy, are bound by all other courts.

Decisions of courts at equivalent levels

The rules are less clear when a court on one level is confronted with an earlier decision of another court on the same level. For many years the House of Lords adhered to the practice of holding itself bound by its own previous decisions however much it had come to disagree with them. But by 1966 it was apparent that this practice was leading to the law becoming fossilised while the courts waited for Parliament to enact reforming legislation; it also encouraged judicial resort to spurious distinctions and tenuous refinements in order to escape injustices. In that year, accordingly, the Law Lords issued a Practice Direction stating that in future, while they would normally treat former decisions of the House as binding, they would depart from them whenever it appeared right to do so. In the years since, this new power has been sparingly exercised: there are perhaps ten *clear* instances of its use but on more than one occasion the House has refused to overrule an earlier decision even though it thought that it was wrong.

In England there has been considerable controversy over whether the Court of Appeal in that jurisdiction should be bound by its own previous decisions. The great advocate for its not being bound was Lord Denning, who as Master of the Rolls was in charge of the Court of Appeal's Civil Division from 1962 to 1982. But as often as Lord Denning refused to follow former cases, even one in which he himself had participated, the House of Lords, on appeal, said that he was incorrect to do so. On this stricter view the Court of Appeal can refuse to follow its own earlier decisions in only three situations: (1) where there are in fact two such decisions which conflict, (2) where the earlier Court of Appeal decision is inconsistent with a subsequent House of Lords decision, and (3) where the earlier decision was announced without proper consideration having been given to earlier cases or statutes pointing the other way (in legal language, *per incuriam*). There is also a practice whereby a Court of Appeal consisting of three judges is not bound by decisions taken by a Court of Appeal consisting of only two judges, but, conversely, a court consisting of more than three judges is not considered to have more binding authority. In appeals in criminal cases the Court of Appeal tends to adopt a more flexible attitude to its own previous decisions in cases where the appellant's loss of liberty would be too high a price to pay for case law uniformity. There is also flexibility in cases where the previous decision is an old one which has not since been cited.

As it operates in a different jurisdiction the Court of Appeal in Northern Ireland is, strictly speaking, not bound by decisions of the English Court of Appeal. But it still accords these decisions the greatest respect and will follow them unless there are very strong reasons for not doing so. As regards its own earlier decisions, the Court of Appeal in Northern Ireland adopts the same practice as the Court of Appeal in England. In situations where there is no possibility of a further appeal to the House of Lords - as for nearly all civil cases begun in the province's magistrates' courts or county courts (see Chapter 5) - the Court of Appeal here may disregard its earlier decision if it considers that it is plainly wrong or too vague and that to follow it would be unjust or unfair. There has to be this flexibility, for otherwise the law would stagnate. In the days before the reorganisation of the courts in the 1870s (see 1.3), it was possible for all judges of the Irish Court of Appeal to sit together as a full Court of Appeal in order to review its previous decisions, and the House of Lords would sometimes ask all the High Court judges to advise it on a certain point, but both these practices have long since been abandoned.

In England and Northern Ireland the High Court will abide by its own previous decisions unless persuaded that these are wrong. Each of these High Courts will also be deferential to earlier decisions of its counterpart, especially if in other respects the law on the matter in question is the same in both countries. One can say the same about the attitude of today's Court of Appeal and High Court in Northern Ireland to decisions of the Court of Appeal and High Court in Ireland taken before partition of the island in 1920: they are not technically binding but will be followed unless patently wrong.

In England, the Divisional Courts (see 1.3) adopt the same attitude to their own previous decisions as does the Court of Appeal. Because the Divisional Court in Northern Ireland rarely sits, it is not possible to state what practice it favours.

The *ratio decidendi* of a case

Of course, whether an earlier decision is wrong or not is largely a matter of opinion, which underlines the fact that the doctrine of precedent is not always as limiting a constraint on the inventiveness of judges as might at first be imagined. It must be stressed, moreover, that the doctrine of precedent obliges lower courts to follow higher courts only if the earlier decisions are exactly in point. This makes it essential to deduce from every reported case the precise principle for which it may later be cited as an authority. This nub of the case is called, in Latin, the *ratio decidendi* or simply the *ratio*, that is to say the legal principle on which the case was decided. Whatever is said by the judges which is not directly on the main point is called *obiter dictum*, literally "something said by the way". Only the *ratio* of a case is binding on later judges. The later judge can avoid applying it only if the facts of the case being dealt with can be significantly *distinguished* from those of the earlier case; lawyers may expend much time and expertise in attempting to find a valid distinction from an earlier case in order to avoid the rigours of the doctrine of binding precedent.

2.5 Statutory Interpretation

However elaborately it is phrased, no rule embodied in primary or secondary legislation can hope to cater for all the circumstances which may arise for consideration. It can be taken for granted that administrators and judges will need to interpret the legislation in order to decide whether or not it applies to a given fact situation. For instance, if Parliament were to pass a law making glue-sniffing a criminal offence and included in the Act a list of the substances which were to be treated as glue for the purpose of this offence, a court of law might still have to decide what exactly amounted to "sniffing". The people who draft legislation obviously try to reduce the uncertainties as much as possible, but the need for judicial interpretation is ultimately inescapable; human foresight and the English language cannot avoid it. Indeed the task of statutory interpretation is one which occupies a great deal of the time of our judges; certainly the majority of reported cases involve a point of interpretation at some juncture. An example from the Northern Ireland Law Reports is the case of *Morton v The Air Ministry* (1946), where Black J. had to decide whether the words "local or other public authority", contained in an Act of the Stormont Parliament, referred to government departments; he held that they did not. Another illustration is provided by *Campbell v Armstrong and Others*, the sample case reproduced in Appendix 3.

The doctrine of binding precedent applies to the topic of statutory interpretation as much as to any other in the law. This means that if the

Northern Ireland Court of Appeal were to pronounce on whether inhaling the vapours of glue through one's mouth qualifies as sniffing glue, then all the lower courts in Northern Ireland would have to construe the same Act in the same way. Very often a pertinent English decision exists on the point of interpretation and if the English legislation is identical to the Northern Ireland legislation then the English court's decision will virtually always be followed in this jurisdiction. (There is legislation concerning glue-sniffing in Scotland: the Solvent Abuse (Scotland) Act 1983 talks of "misusing a volatile substance by deliberately inhaling, other than for medical purposes, that substance's vapour". In the rest of the United Kingdom it is the supply of glue which can sometimes be a criminal offence, not the sniffing of it: see the Intoxicating Substances (Supply) Act 1985).

Every piece of legislation within one jurisdiction is unique and the interpretation placed on it by judges will rarely be relevant to the interpretation of other legislation even if the very same words are in issue. But there are certain approaches to the whole process of interpretation which judges tend to apply to all sorts of statutes. They range from what really amount to general philosophies concerning judicial activity to what are in practice quite specific presumptions. Over the centuries the law has fluctuated in its adherence to these various approaches, some of which conflict. Controversy still rages today, so one cannot be dogmatic in asserting that a statutory provision must be interpreted with such and such an attitude in mind. All the approaches, it is readily admitted, have exceptions. With these qualifications in mind, we can briefly attempt to state the prevailing views on statutory interpretation in Northern Ireland today.

The rules of interpretation

In the first place the court should try to ascertain the intention of Parliament when it drafted the particular provision. Until very recently the judges were obstructed in their efforts to do this by the rule that reports of proceedings in Parliament (*i.e. Hansard*) could not be looked at to see what the MPs and peers who voted for the provision thought it meant. In England Lord Denning more than once deviated from this practice but he was roundly criticised by the House of Lords for doing so. In *Pepper (Inspector of Taxes)* v *Hart* (1992) the House of Lords (by a majority of six Law Lords to one, the Lord Chancellor dissenting) finally accepted that the rule should be relaxed so as to allow reference to clear statements made by a Minister or other promoter of the legislation and to other parliamentary material which was necessary to understand these statements and their effects.

The intention of Parliament can also be deduced from the long title of the Act, the unambiguous effects of other provisions in the Act, the omissions from the Act, the state of the pre-existing law, official reports preceding the enactment of the legislation, the practical consequences of preferring one interpretation over another, and the conventional maxims of interpretation which it must be assumed the draftsman was aware of when the Act was written (see below). The most important indication of Parliament's intention, though, is the ordinary meaning of the words themselves; if one of the interpretations being contended for is at variance with that ordinary meaning, it is likely that the ordinary meaning will be preferred. To that extent a purely literal approach to interpretation is shunned. A purposive approach - oné which asks the question "What was Parliament really getting at?" - is nowadays adopted.

Left at that, one might conclude, to return to our hypothetical example, that inhaling glue vapours through the mouth is tantamount to "sniffing" it. Literally, sniffing is a process carried out only through the nose; colloquially, however, glue-sniffing is used to describe a variety of types of solvent abuse and the intention of Parliament would probably be frustrated if inhaling through the mouth was held not to be covered by the Act. But it is at this point that countervailing principles, presumptions and maxims concerning statutory interpretation must be brought into play. One of these is that a statute which creates a criminal offence must be interpreted as narrowly as possible so as to preserve a person's freedom of action. Another is that the express mention of one of a class of things by implication excludes other items of the same class, so that if the Act in one place refers to sniffing as meaning sniffing through the nose, then inhaling through the mouth should be taken as not covered by the same word. In some instances these principles and presumptions are so well embedded in our law that they cease to be merely arguments to be taken into account by the judge and become instead obligations requiring the judge to decide the case in a certain way; an example is the principle that one cannot take advantage of one's own illegal act in order to claim a right under a statute - for instance a murderess cannot claim a widow's pension if the person she killed was her husband *(ex turpi causa non oritur actio* - a claim cannot be based on an immoral foundation).

Some questions of interpretation recur so frequently that Parliament has provided set solutions. These are to be found in the Interpretation Act (NI) 1954 and the Interpretation Act 1978. The former covers the interpretation of Acts of the Northern Ireland Parliament as well as Orders in Council made under the Northern Ireland Act 1974 (see article 2 of the sample Order in Council reproduced in Appendix 3). The latter covers Westminster legislation applying in Northern Ireland. They deal with such problems as the meaning of "month", whether "man" includes "woman" and whether the singular includes the plural. The Law Commission (see 8.9) is still seeking to persuade the government to adopt more systematic measures for the avoidance of problems in statutory interpretation.

2.6 European and International Sources

There are many agencies in the world which promote the conclusion of international agreements. When the government of the United Kingdom signs these agreements, which may be called treaties, conventions or covenants, it does so on behalf of the people of Northern Ireland as well as those of Great Britain. But merely signing the treaty does not render it a part of United Kingdom national law, nor, usually, does it oblige the United Kingdom to comply with the treaty's provisions *vis -à-vis* other states. For the treaty to be made a part of our national law it must be "ratified". This is achieved by incorporating the treaty into national law by Act of Parliament; sometimes the treaty will be appended to the Act in a Schedule, at other times its provisions will be reworded but with more or less the same effect; it is Parliament's prerogative to depart from the terms of the treaty to whatever extent it wishes. For the treaty to be made a part of the international law binding the United Kingdom it is usually enough if it has been ratified by the government. This is normally taken to have occurred after it has been signed and laid before Parliament for 21 days (the so-called "Ponsonby" rule). However, recent controversy over whether the Maastricht Treaty could be ratified by the government alone, even with the disapproval of Parliament, indicates that the exact constitutional position is somewhat obscure.

Examples of domestic statutes incorporating treaties into our national law are the Recognition of Divorces and Legal Separations Act 1971, the Carriage of Passengers by Road Act 1974 and the State Immunity Act 1978. These implemented Conventions which were concluded, respectively, in 1968, 1973 and 1972, each by a different international agency. Occasionally, because of differences between the pre-existing law in Northern Ireland and that in England, separate legislation is required for the province when treaties are incorporated into Northern Ireland law, for example the Adoption (Hague Convention) Act (NI) 1969. A good example of a treaty which is binding upon the United Kingdom in international law but not as yet in domestic law is the European Convention on Human Rights and Fundamental Freedoms, discussed below. Another such treaty is the Anglo-Irish Agreement, signed in November 1985 and since ratified by both the British and Irish Parliaments.

The only context in which the sources of Northern Ireland law are to be found outside the United Kingdom altogether - that is, without the government's participation in its creation at all - is that of public international law, the area of law which concerns relations between states. This has some of its sources in international custom and in the decisions of international tribunals such as the International Court of Justice at The Hague in the Netherlands. It is sometimes said that EC law is another such context, but strictly speaking this is not so: as will be explained below, EC law has effect in Northern Ireland only because a United Kingdom statute says so.

European Community law

When, on 1st January 1973, the United Kingdom joined the European Economic Community (the Common Market) as well as the European Coal and Steel Community and the European Atomic Energy Community, the treaties establishing these Communities (including the Treaty of Rome 1957) were incorporated into United Kingdom law by virtue of the European Communities Act 1972. According to the most commonly accepted interpretation of this Act the rules of the common law of the three United Kingdom legal systems (England and Wales, Scotland and Northern Ireland), as well as existing and future United Kingdom legislation, have effect subject to European Community law. In 1973 European Community law thereby became a new source of law in Northern Ireland; judges in Northern Ireland must interpret "domestic" Northern Irish law in a way which complies with the provisions of EC law.

European Community law falls into three categories: (1) the provisions of the various treaties setting up the Communities, which can be said to constitute the primary law of the EC; (2) the Regulations, Directives and Decisions of the Community institutions, that is, the Council of Ministers and the Commission, whose measures can be called the secondary law of the EC; and (3) the rulings and decisions of the Court of Justice of the European Community, the case law of the European Community. At present the European Parliament does not have any law-making powers.

Some of the legislative acts in the second category (namely, Regulations and most Decisions) are "directly applicable" in member states of the EC, which means that they have the force of law without the need of any further national legislation. Sometimes they are said to be "self-executing". Regulations are binding in their entirety on all member states, while Decisions are binding only on those states, corporations or individuals to whom they are addressed. Because Regulations are of a more abstract nature than Decisions their administrative details often require to be implemented by specific domestic legislation (see 2.3); they nevertheless become operative when the Regulation says so in order that European Community law shall be uniform throughout the EC at any one time, so that if the British Parliament has not passed any implementing legislation it is still possible for people in the United Kingdom to rely directly upon the Regulation in any legal dispute. Decisions, on the other hand, are always binding on addressees without the need for any further implementation.

Directives, despite their name, are not directly applicable: they are binding only as to the result to be achieved by them and each member state is free to decide upon the means for giving the Directives legal and administrative effect. The Directive may, however, set a time limit for the implementation of its provisions. Thus, by a Directive of July 1985 the United Kingdom had to alter its law on liability for defective products by July 1988, which it did by the Consumer Protection Act 1987 and the Consumer Protection (NI) Order 1987. By 1992, moreover, there were no fewer than 13 Directives on various aspects of company law. If a Directive clearly aims to confer rights and duties on individuals, a person who suffers loss as a result of his or her government's failure to change national law within the time specified can sue the government to recover compensation for losses suffered (*Francovich* v *Italy*, 1991). As mentioned above in 2.3, the European Communities Act 1972 enables subordinate legislation to be made by the relevant Minister or government department in connection with the performance of obligations and the exercise of rights under the European treaties.

It is now clear that courts throughout the United Kingdom can refuse to apply even an Act of Parliament if the judges are of the view that the Act conflicts with EC law. In the *Factortame* case (1990) the House of Lords, following a ruling by the European Court of Justice, held that provisions in the Merchant Shipping Act 1988, and regulations made thereunder, should be "disapplied".

The European Court of Justice

The European Court of Justice, which sits in Luxembourg, is staffed by 13 judges and six advocates-general, all of whom are chosen by the governments of the 12 member states of the European Community. The judges are selected from the people who are eligible for appointment to the highest judicial posts in their own countries or who are jurists of recognised competence. They are appointed for six years at a time. Britain's first judge, Lord Mackenzie Stuart, was appointed in 1972 and was reappointed twice. His successor was Sir Gordon Slynn, now a Law Lord. The current judge is Judge David Edward. The judges elect their own President, for a three-year term.

Advocates-general are similar to the court advisers used in continental legal systems but unfamiliar in common law countries. One of them is allocated to each case coming before the Court of Justice. In reporting to the judges their task is threefold: to suggest a solution to the case, to relate that solution to the existing law, and to set out the likely future developments in the law. But the advocates-general do not actually participate in the drafting of the Court's judgments nor in the discussions which lead to the Court's decisions. Although their submissions are not binding on the Court, they are reported alongside the Court's judgment (which is usually very terse and provides no detail of any dissenting opinions) and they serve as useful background material explicating the judgment. Since 1973 the Court's judgments have been published in English in the European Court Reports.

The Court of Justice has jurisdiction to hear many different types of case involving European Community law, but the most important are probably those concerned with the validity or interpretation of acts of the Community institutions. If such matters arise during the course of a case before any national court or tribunal of a member state they can be referred to the Court of Justice under article 177 of the Treaty of Rome; the opinion of that Court is then handed back to the local court so that it can be applied to the facts of the particular case. Such referrals can take several months to complete. Examples of referrals made in Northern Ireland are those made by the resident magistrate in the case of *Pigs Marketing Board (Northern Ireland)* v *Redmond* (1978) and by the President of Industrial Tribunals in *Johnston* v *Chief Constable of the RUC* (1986). Courts and tribunals "of last instance", that is, those against whose decisions there is no further appeal, are *obliged* to refer such matters to the Court of Justice unless the correct interpretation is quite clear; the Northern Ireland Court of Appeal is a court of last instance in several matters and so is affected by this obligation.

The judgments of the European Court of Justice are binding on the national courts and authorities of the 12 European Community countries. In response to the decision in the *Johnston* case in 1986, for example, concerning the claim that sex discrimination could be justified on the basis of national security, the United Kingdom Government passed the Sex Discrimination (Amendment) Order 1988. However, if the national authorities continue to default, the most that the Court can do is to make an unenforceable declaratory judgment against the government in question; it cannot hold national law to be void. In the vast majority of cases, of course, the national authorities do eventually comply with the Court's judgments.

The Court of Justice, in line with the practice followed in the civil law countries which constitute the majority of EC member states, adopts what to British and Irish lawyers seems an unashamedly creative attitude when faced with problems of statutory interpretation. However, judges in the United Kingdom are beginning to imitate their European counterparts when EC legislation requires to be interpreted. Through time this is bound to lead to a more "purposive" approach to the interpretation of national legislation as well (see 2.5). British draftsmen may take a leaf out of the European book and begin to draft legislation in more general terms. The Court of Justice is also much less committed than British courts to the notion of binding precedent in case law (it can refuse to follow its own previous decisions) and this too may gradually persuade British judges to slacken a little their adherence to that notion.

The Court of First Instance

In 1989 a second court was established at Luxembourg to help take the burden off the Court of Justice. Called the Court of First Instance it hears disputes between the staff of the European Community and their employers, disputes over the rules on commercial competition and cases arising from the Coal and Steel Treaty. Appeals lie to the Court of Justice on points of law or serious breaches of procedure. The Court comprises 12 members, each appointed for renewable six-year terms, but there are no separate advocates-general to assist these judges. Usually cases are dealt with by chambers of three or five judges. The British judge is currently Mr Christopher Bellamy.

The European Convention on Human Rights

The European Court of Justice should not be confused with the European Court of Human Rights, which sits in Strasbourg in France. The Court of Human Rights has the job of interpreting the European Convention for the Protection of Human Rights and Fundamental Freedoms, which was drawn up by the Council of Europe in 1950. The Council of Europe is an international organisation formed in 1949 and now comprising 28 European states; it is distinct from the European Community, being more active on social and cultural fronts than in economics or politics. The United Kingdom was amongst the first to ratify the Convention on Human Rights in 1951, but although the Convention entered into force in 1953 our government has not yet taken legislative action to incorporate it into domestic law; it is not therefore part of our national law, but it is binding on the United Kingdom internationally. However, courts in the United Kingdom do occasionally look to the Convention as an aid to the interpretation of ambiguous domestic statutes or to the establishment of the modern common law position on issues concerning human rights.

The states which are parties to the Convention may be proceeded against for an alleged violation of the Convention by other such states or, if they admit this right (as they all now do), by their own individual citizens. During 1992 there were 1,861 individual applications registered under the Convention. Complaints are first considered by the European Commission of Human Rights, which decides whether they are "admissible" within the terms of the Convention. They will not be admissible, for example, if all avenues for redress in the national courts have not yet been exhausted or if more than six months have elapsed since the date of the final decision in the national courts. If they are admissible, the Commission will carry out an inquiry and seek to bring about a friendly settlement. If no such settlement is possible, the Commission will issue a report on whether there has been a breach of the Convention. It will also decide whether to refer the case to the Court of Human Rights, a course of action which the defendant state can insist upon too but not, as yet, the individual applicant. If no referral has occurred within three months of the Commission's report being issued, the Committee of Ministers of the Council of Europe can look at the case. This Committee is a political rather than a legal body and can reach a decision only if two-thirds of its members agree.

There are as many Commissioners and judges eligible to sit in the European Commission and Court of Human Rights as there are member states of the Council of Europe; each government nominates one Commissioner and one judge. The Commissioners are full-time officials but the judges are part-timers. A minimum of seven Commissioners or judges sit in any one case, the decision being by majority vote. At the moment the British Commissioner is Mr Nicholas Bratza and the British judge is Sir John Freeland. Decisions of the European Court of Human Rights are binding on all the states involved in the case, though in practice states wait some time before altering their national law to bring it into line with the pronouncement of the Court. On occasions the Court may also order a national government to pay compensation to an aggrieved party.

The Convention's effect on Northern Ireland's law

The European Court of Human Rights has held against the United Kingdom more frequently than against any other state (in more than 30 cases altogether) and in 1991 and 1992 more applications were registered against the United Kingdom than against any other state with the exception of France (202 and 222 for the UK as opposed to 400 and 353 for France). As a result of decisions by the Court of Human Rights the Government has had to change the United Kingdom's law on (amongst other things) contempt of court, the closed shop, immigration law, telephone tapping, prisoners' rights and corporal punishment in schools.

Many of the cases brought against the United Kingdom Government have originated in Northern Ireland. The Court has issued judgments in five of these and at least 20 Northern Irish cases have been dealt with by the Commission. Several further cases are pending, although the rate of application may slow down if it becomes clearer that the Commission and Court are unwilling to interpret the Convention in a way which may make the job of the security forces in Northern Ireland more difficult. Following a partially substantiated complaint by the Irish Government in the 1970s, the instructions to security forces in Northern Ireland with regard to interrogation techniques had to be altered (*Ireland* v *UK*), and following a complaint by an individual the law on homosexual offences in Northern Ireland was reformed (the *Dudgeon* case). However, a challenge to the legality of the use of plastic bullets in Northern Ireland failed before the European Commission (*Stewart* v *UK*, 1985). In November 1988 the Court held in the *Brogan* case that detention for more than four days and six hours under the Prevention of Terrorism (Temporary Provisions) Act 1984 was a breach of Article 5 of the Convention, which requires detainees to be brought promptly before a judge. The government then officially "derogated" from the Convention in this respect; in a subsequent challenge to this derogation (*Brannigan and McBride* v *UK*, 1993) the Court held that it was valid under Article 15 of the Convention, which allows states to derogate if there is "a public emergency threatening the life of the nation" and if the steps taken are not more than "strictly required by the exigencies of the situation".

In the Republic of Ireland the Government was obliged to introduce a civil legal aid scheme after a woman successfully complained before the European Court of Human Rights that Article 6 of the Convention, giving her the right of access to courts, was being breached because of the prohibitive costs involved in seeking a decree of judicial separation from her husband (the *Airey* case). In the *Open Door Counselling* case (1992) the Republic's ban on the provision of abortion information was ruled unlawful. However a challenge to the Republic's broadcasting ban, which prevents Sinn Féin representatives from speaking on the air waves, has been held valid *(Purcell* v *Ireland*, 1991).

The Standing Advisory Commission on Human Rights in Northern Ireland (see 8.6) has recommended that a Bill of Rights based on the European Convention should be enacted for Northern Ireland and the Committee on the Administration of Justice (see 3.1) has published proposed drafts of a Bill which draw heavily on the Convention while going substantially beyond it in several important respects. In 1978 the members of a Select Committee of the House of Lords could not agree on whether a Bill of Rights was desirable for the United Kingdom as a whole but were unanimous that, if there were to be a Bill, it should be based on the European Convention. It rejected the proposal that the European Community should, as a body, become a party to the Convention. Numerous attempts to have the European Convention incorporated directly into British law have failed in the House of Commons but there is a growing campaign to achieve this and it is now supported by both the Labour and Liberal Democrat Parties as well as by pressure groups such as Charter 88.

3

Legal Services

3.1 Seeking Legal Help

Identifying a legal problem

When non-lawyers think of law they usually connect it in their minds with bodies such as the police, the courts and judges. Chapters 1 and 2 may have reinforced this impression, but at this point it is necessary to make it clear that the legal system consists of a great deal more than just police work and court cases. In fact only a very small fraction of legal matters ever involve such steps.

Legal problems arise at very many points in our lives but in the overwhelming majority of instances they are easily solved and no further difficulty ensues. They may arise because you want to achieve some objective but you do not know what is the "legal" way of going about it: what forms must be filled in, whose permission must be sought, what fees must be paid, etc. Typical instances are when you want to make a will, buy a house, borrow money or set up a business. Alternatively, problems may arise during some quite ordinary everyday activity: something goes wrong and you suddenly find yourself having a dispute with another party. For example, you may buy some article in the shops only to discover when you take it home that it does not work properly; you may be in regular receipt of income support but you find that it is not meeting your needs; you may be sacked from your job; you may have an accident while driving your car; or you may be unable to produce a television licence when the Post Office detector van calls at your house. The other party in such disputes may be an individual, a firm or a branch of government.

Before you are able to seek legal help with any of these problems you must be aware that the problem facing you is indeed a legal one. The existence of a legal problem is by no means always as obvious as may be imagined. You may be in breach of legal regulations but not know this; you may be legally entitled to some benefit or award but, again, be ignorant of this right; you may be perfectly aware that you are in dispute with someone, but neither of you may think of it as a legal dispute - you may simply consider it to be an administrative or an organisational wrangle.

But once you begin to think that the law may have something to say about your predicament, you should act quickly. First of all you should tell a friend or a relative about it. As often as not, just talking over the problem with someone can help you to see another way out of it. Your attention may be drawn to some aspect of the situation which enables you to clear things up. But if this is not so and you feel the need for further advice or assistance, there are many bodies who may be able to help. Before you consult them you should try to gather together all relevant documents relating to your case. If you have already written letters about it, it will help if you have kept copies of these, or at any rate a summary of what was said in those documents or during telephone conversations. A list giving the precise dates of the various stages in the dispute up to this time can also be most useful.

Advice agencies

There are basically two types of bodies which can give you advice on legal matters. We can call them "private" and "public" agencies. The private agencies consist of organisations to which you may belong that either run an advisory service to allow you to cope yourself with particular kinds of problems or are prepared to treat your problem as in effect their own problem and to act on it accordingly.

Examples of these private agencies are trade unions, employers' and traders' associations, some clubs, tenants' groups, claimants' groups and insurance companies. If you are a member of a trade union, for instance, you will often find your union more than willing to take up a grievance relating to your employment in an attempt to remedy it on your behalf. Insurance companies too will often offer to act for you, as in disputes concerning road accidents. If you are a doctor, the Medical Defence Union may pay your legal costs when you are sued for medical negligence. Obviously the schemes which each of these private organisations operates will differ widely in the degree of assistance they provide; some will expect personal and financial commitments from you, others will not. But the mere fact that someone else is interested enough to help you find a way out of your predicament can be a great comfort!

The public agencies are those which exist for the benefit of all people in the community, whether or not they have joined a scheme. Some are general agencies: they will advise you on practically every problem you bring to them, even if it is just telling you where you can go for more specialised help. Others deal only with particular types of problems. All of them should be ready to help not just on the legal aspects of your problem but also on its other dimensions - its personal, social and financial features. They will also provide their services free of charge, though needless to say they welcome donations so that they can develop their work. For the most part they are staffed by volunteers who may or may not have professional expertise in the field; if they do not, they should certainly be able to advise you on where to contact the professionals. We shall examine a few of these public agencies in more detail.

Citizens' Advice Bureaux

Probably the best known agencies accessible to the general public are the Citizens' Advice Bureaux (CABx). Begun in 1964, there are currently 28 Bureaux in Northern Ireland, plus seven "extension" offices; the addresses can be found in the telephone directory. Their opening hours vary.

When you visit a CAB you will be interviewed in private by one of the advisers. A written record of your case will be made so that if some other adviser has to take over the case at a later stage he or she will know at a glance what has already happened. In most cases it does not take more than half-an-hour for the adviser to listen to your story and let you know what action is recommended. Sometimes the advice will be that you yourself should take certain steps; at other times the adviser will be happy to write letters or make contacts on your behalf. It is wonderful what effect an approach by a semi-official person such as an adviser can have on the other party to a dispute: it shows your sincerity and it may be just enough to persuade the other side to see things your way.

If your case is a complex one or involves a lot of money the adviser will probably want you to contact a solicitor. Every CAB in Northern Ireland has a "referral list" which gives the names of practising solicitors in the area who have agreed to receive cases passed on to them by the Bureau; the adviser should be able to tell you a little about some of these solicitors so that you can decide more easily which of them you think would handle your case best. Some of the CABx actually have solicitors present acting as advisers: they will be there on a rota basis, ready to be consulted about any case which requires their expertise. If it transpires that the case is one which should be dealt with by a solicitor acting in his or her office rather than as an adviser, it is possible for the solicitor in the Bureau to take over your case in a professional capacity. This is only allowed, however, if the solicitor has been previously granted a "waiver" by the professional body for solicitors, the Law Society of Northern Ireland (see 3.2); without this waiver it would be a breach of the rules against touting and advertising which are imposed on all solicitors.

All the CABx in Northern Ireland belong to the Northern Ireland Association of Citizens' Advice Bureaux, which provides the local Bureaux with up-to-date information about changes in the law. It also provides training facilities for the advisers. In 1992-93 the grant from the Department of Education for the work of the Northern Ireland Association was just over £250,000; a further £104,000 was made available by the Making Belfast Work initiative. The money was largely used for the salaries of 17 staff in the regional office. NIACAB has a Board with a representative from each Bureau; its chairperson is Mr Will Glendinning and the Regional Director is Mr Derek Alcorn. The National Association of Citizens' Advice Bureaux, based in London, publishes many pamphlets dealing with various aspects of the law likely to be encountered by advisers. Although the details of law and procedure are often different in Northern Ireland, most of these pamphlets are very useful here. Your local bureau should be able to tell you if any parts of the pamphlets do not apply.

During the year ending 31st March 1993, CABx throughout the province handled a total of 151,107 new enquiries, with the five Belfast offices receiving nearly one-third of these. By far the largest category of enquiry was social security, which accounted for 35 per cent. A further 22 per cent concerned consumer, trade or business matters, 11 per cent related to housing and land issues and a further 11 per cent to employment. More than 220 volunteers undertook approximately 1400 hours of work per week in order to deal with this flood of enquiries. The year also saw a 70 per cent increase in the number of cases (708) where CABx workers represented members of the public in tribunals. Indeed nearly one-quarter of all persons taking cases to the social security tribunals now receive help from CABx and the Northern Ireland Association has appointed a Tribunal Rights Worker to help train CABx staff in the skills involved in work of this nature.

The service provided by CABx is obviously a vital one. The Royal Commission on Legal Services, which reported as long ago as 1979, recommended that the network of CABx throughout the United Kingdom should be expanded and it thought that salaried lawyers should be seconded where necessary to act as supplementary internal advisers. The Government supported this recommendation in 1983, but since then it has not proved so willing to provide the required money for an expansion of CAB services on the scale required. Consequently local CABx depend for most of their funding on district councils or on charitable donations.

Other advice centres

A second important type of generalist advice agency are the local advice centres. Like the CABx, these exist to give advice on all sorts of matters, not just those involving legal issues. As their name implies, the centres are the result of local initiatives and are often funded, in part at least, by the local district council. Not all are open daily, since their staff are often volunteer advisers or community workers who have many other responsibilities to fulfil. A few of the advisers are qualified lawyers, but most are not. The Law Society does not grant a waiver (see above) to solicitors who do voluntary work in an advice centre, so they are not allowed to take over any of the cases privately.

At the moment there are approximately 70 local advice centres in Northern Ireland though they may not always call themselves this. During their busiest periods they may handle a total of 2,000 inquiries a month. You can expect the same sort of personal attention and confidentiality as you would find in a Citizens' Advice Bureau, though unfortunately the centres do not enjoy the relatively comprehensive back-up services which are provided to the CABx. They receive some information kits and training from the Belfast Law Centre (see below) but not always on a very systematic basis.

Various other advice agencies exist in Northern Ireland, most of them designed to deal with problems which are peculiar to a particular locality or kind of person. There are many community and tenant organisations, and other bodies such as Alcoholics Anonymous, Belfast Housing Aid, Gamblers Anonymous, Gingerbread (for one-parent families), Relate, the Samaritans, Shelter and Women's Aid. There is a Consumer Advice Centre in Belfast which deals with the wide range of consumer affairs. For further details of these agencies, apply to the addresses given in Appendix 2, or consult either *The Northern Ireland Index: A Guide To Voluntary Action* (published by the Northern Ireland Council for Voluntary Action) or the latest *Legal Aid Solicitors List*, published annually by the Law Society of Northern Ireland. Both publications should be available in local libraries.

The Belfast Law Centre

One of the disadvantages of the advice agencies so far described is that they are limited in what they can do. They can give advice and write letters; on occasion they will represent a claimant at a tribunal, or at any rate help the claimant to present his or her case there, but they cannot otherwise do the work of practising lawyers. Their big advantage is that they do not charge for their services. To meet the need for an agency which not only does not charge but can operate almost as a firm of private solicitors, offices called Law Centres have been established throughout the United Kingdom. The first one to be set up in Britain was in North Kensington in London in 1970. Today there are about 60 throughout the United Kingdom and one in Dublin. The Belfast Community Law Centre began work in 1977. It changed its name to the Belfast Law Centre in 1980.

The Centre in Belfast reaches out to a larger geographical area than any other Law Centre in the United Kingdom and fewer than 10 per cent serve comparable populations. As well as its premises in Belfast it maintains a Northern Area office in Ballymena, a Southern Area office in Lurgan and a Western Area office in Derry. At the end of March 1992 it employed 10 permanent staff in Belfast and six outside Belfast. Three of the Belfast workers, including the Director of the Centre (Mr John O'Neill), are qualified solicitors. They have been granted "waivers" by the Law Society, which in effect permit the Centre to act as a firm of solicitors provided that it does not engage in the major areas of work in which private practitioners operate, such as buying and selling houses or dealing with wills, matrimonial disputes and most criminal work. As a result, the bulk of the Law Centre's cases concern social security, housing, debt and employment problems; immigration law is a growing specialism.

The latest annual report of the Law Centre shows that in 1991-92 a total of 3,450 queries were made to it, a rise of 18 per cent over the previous year. Approximately 10 per cent of these were "retained" by the Centre for further attention; the remainder were either dealt with immediately (83 per cent) or passed on to solicitors or other advisory bodies (7 per cent). By far the largest proportion of queries relate to social security (61 per cent in 1991-92). It is difficult to be completely objective, but about 70 per cent of all retained cases are eventually settled to the total or partial satisfaction of the Law Centre's staff.

Generally speaking, the Law Centre deals with cases only if they have been referred to it by another advice agency, such as a Citizens' Advice

Bureau. About 50 such agencies are member organisations of the Law Centre, but cases can be referred from other sources as well. In 1991-92 nine per cent of the referrals were from social security offices. The member organisations elect the management committee of the Law Centre and must be independent advice groups: no government agency, statutory body or group with a vested interest may be a member. However the Centre's "closed door" principle has not prevented the proportion of queries originating from unapproved referrals rising to about one-half of the total number of queries made. The Centre does not advertise its existence widely, and is not in the telephone directory, but still it is kept very busy.

The sort of case which the Law Centre will be most happy to deal with is a test case on some new point; if it can obtain a favourable ruling from a court or a tribunal, this will help all the other people who may be encountering the same problem. Its recent forays in this respect include one case on a private landlord's duty to keep rented premises in good repair and another on the government's duty to make single payment awards under the social security system to particular claimants rather than in the form of a credit slip redeemable at a shop. In 1992 the Centre successfully challenged in the European Court of Justice the validity of the residence rules in the family credit regulations for Northern Ireland; seven further cases in 1991-92 involved applications for judicial review of the decisions of welfare agents such as the social fund inspectors (see 7.1 and 7.2).

In concentrating on test cases the Law Centre comes close to advancing group interests, much in the way that in the United States "class actions" can be brought on behalf of a large number of people. This is a welcome development, for the legal system of Northern Ireland is otherwise a highly individualised one, that is, each problem has to be dealt with as it affects a particular person. The review body on civil justice (see 5.1) recommended in 1989 that the Lord Chancellor should institute a study by a law reform agency (see 8.9) of the arguments for and against extending the availability of representative or class actions; four years later, unfortunately, no further progress on this can be reported.

Educational role

Since 1985 an especially important part of the Law Centre's work has been the provision of training and information to other groups giving advice, mainly in the area of welfare rights. Four staff are employed full-time on this work. As well as providing basic training for new advice workers the Centre runs specialist courses on topics such as debt, access to housing, disability and the Child Support (NI) Order 1991. In each of the four Health and Social Services Board areas the Law Centre organises a Regional Support Group for all advice workers in the locality and in 1991-92 it ran 16 information days on a variety of topics in Ballymena, Belfast, Derry and Lurgan. In all more than 260 advice-giving agencies and community groups are assisted in this fashion. The Law Centre, along with the Northern Ireland Association of CABx, has also been instrumental in establishing an Advice Services Working Party, which aims to develop advice services throughout Northern Ireland by, for instance, encouraging liaison between agencies in the voluntary and statutory sectors. In 1992, with a view to improving the quality of advice-giving in the province, it published a booklet entitled "Standards and Guidelines for Advice Agencies". The Law Centre itself supplements this guidance by distributing a variety of informational material on welfare matters and through its quarterly magazine *Frontline*.

The Belfast Law Centre has always set great store by its educative and preventive role in society. It seeks to avoid potential problems becoming real ones as well as to make people more aware of their rights and duties. In 1991, for example, it launched a publicity campaign to make people aware of their entitlement to backdated claims for supplementary benefit in certain circumstances; as a result no fewer than 21,630 people applied to have their entitlement re-examined. In some parts of England this active role has brought Law Centres into conflict with local and central government. In 1979 the Royal Commission on Legal Services suggested that Law Centres should transform themselves into Citizens' Law Centres in line with the model proposed in that Report. The Law Centres Federation (the umbrella organisation for existing law centres in the United Kingdom) disagreed with this suggestion. To date the government has not forced through a radically new system, but it has been reluctant to continue to fund some centres and one or two have had to close. The effect of reforms to the legal aid schemes has been to make even greater demands on Law Centres. It is to be hoped that adequate funding will be provided to cope with this. At present the Belfast Law Centre runs on a budget of approximately £300,000 per annum, most of it granted by the Northern Ireland Office and the Department of Health and Social Services.

Pressure groups

The distinction between an advice agency and a pressure group is not always a clear-cut one. In some respects it could be said that the Consumer Advice Centre, for example, is as much one as the other, for it combines its advisory work with some degree of campaigning about consumers' rights. Of the organisations which are primarily pressure groups the most prominent in Northern Ireland on legal matters is now the Committee on the Administration of Justice (the CAJ). The Northern Ireland Association of Socialist Lawyers, prominent during the early 1980s, is now dormant. The CAJ comprises committed volunteers prepared to investigate alleged injustices and to work for improvements in the legal system. Its various sub-groups carry out research, publish booklets and make submissions to the government. As a rule they do not hold themselves out as offering legal advice to individuals, but in a few instances they have helped people to present their cases more persuasively to the authorities.

Some groups with headquarters in England have also taken an interest in the Northern Ireland legal system - and not just in the emergency laws which have been introduced to deal with the troubles. Worthy of mention are British Irish Rights Watch, the Child Poverty Action Group, the Howard League for Penal Reform, JUSTICE, the Legal Action Group, and Liberty (formerly the National Council for Civil Liberties). Each of these groups has individual members in Northern Ireland. If you wish to join or be put in touch with local members, write to the offices in England at the addresses listed in Appendix 2.

Legal Information Forum

In February 1993 a new association was formed with the aim of improving access to legal information for everyone in Northern Ireland. Known as the Legal Information Forum, and chaired by the librarian at the Bar Library in Belfast, the association is the first outcome of a report entitled "Extending Access to Legal Information: A Northern Ireland Case Study", which was commissioned by the Northern Ireland Library and Information Plan in 1992. The Forum intends to train non-specialist librarians and information workers in the provision of legal information and will be publishing a Northern Ireland Legal Information Directory.

3.2 The Legal Professions

Consulting a solicitor

Should your case be one which you want to take to a solicitor - perhaps after having been advised to do so by an advice agency - you will need to know how to deal with a solicitor and what the implications may be. Finding a solicitor should present no problem. You or your family may have dealt with one in the past and you may want to use the same person again; a friend or somebody at an advice agency may recommend someone to you; as a last resort you can cast your eye down the list of solicitors in the Yellow Pages of the telephone directory and choose one whose office is close to where you live. It is best to call in person or by telephone in order to arrange an appointment. Bear in mind that some solicitors do not handle certain types of case, so you may have to shop around a little.

You should not be apprehensive about consulting a solicitor; he or she should be able to let you know quickly what your legal position is on the matter and what you should do next. But always prepare yourself well before arriving at the solicitor's office: rehearse your story with a friend beforehand and bring along all the relevant documents. If you are worried about the costs involved, you can ask if the solicitor will see you under the fixed-fee interview scheme, which provides you with a 30-minute interview for £5.00 (see 3.3). If the solicitor is unwilling to see you under that scheme, you can certainly ask when you make your appointment how much the initial interview will cost. The cost may be covered by the legal advice and assistance scheme described in the next section. At each interview you can ask how much the proposed next step in the case is likely to cost and whether you will be eligible for legal aid, advice or assistance. You may even contact more than one solicitor and compare their estimated charges before you decide which to engage.

The work of a solicitor

Solicitors became a distinct self-governing profession in Ireland with the creation of the Law Society of Ireland in 1830. In 1922 a Royal Charter was granted to solicitors in Northern Ireland to permit the setting up of the Incorporated Law Society of Northern Ireland. Under a statute passed in 1938 (superseded by an Order in Council in 1976, itself amended in 1989) the Law Society obtained the power to issue regulations governing the education, the accounts and the professional conduct of solicitors. The current Accounts and Practice Regulations were issued, with the approval of the Lord Chief Justice, in 1985 and 1987 respectively. All solicitors must register with the Law Society every year (though they need not necessarily become members) and an annual practising certificate will be granted only if the Law Society is sure, amongst other things, that the solicitor is properly insured against loss wrongfully caused to clients.

Today, solicitors' offices are found throughout the province; more than 400 are listed in the telephone directory. They vary in size from the small one-person office to the large firm which may have several partners and employ several "assistant" solicitors - these are fully qualified solicitors who do not have a stake in the ownership of the firm. The firm will also employ secretarial staff and perhaps one or two apprentices; unlike English firms, solicitors in Northern Ireland do not employ assistants called legal executives. The size of the firm should not affect the quality of the service provided, nor should it greatly influence the charges. Remember that solicitors are at bottom professional business people, who need to pay overheads and make a profit. In a sense they are handicapped in this activity because the Law Society does not permit them to advertise or attract business through, for example, price-cutting or sharing offices with non-solicitors. The rules on these matters have recently been relaxed a little, and may soon be more so.

The daily work of a solicitor can be very varied. Most of it is office work, though solicitors do have what is called "the right of audience" in magistrates' courts and county courts (and in some Crown Court matters), which means that they can speak on behalf of their clients in those courts. Traditionally that is the role of barristers, who still, as we shall see, retain the exclusive right of audience in the higher courts. The largest single category of solicitors' work is conveyancing (the legal transfer of land and buildings), which occupies about one-third of their time and represents an even greater proportion of their income; the other important categories are matrimonial work, succession work (*i.e.* dealing with the consequences of a death), criminal work and compensation claims. If the firm is large enough it will probably have a litigation department to deal with those cases which may involve court actions; the vast majority of such actions are eventually "settled" (*i.e.* compromised) out of court and it is an essential part of a solicitor's function to try to arrange such a settlement.

The time and cost involved in actually bringing matters to court are such that it is a step to be taken only as a very last resort; even during the course of a court hearing the two sides to a dispute may agree to settle it, which then leads to a judgment by consent (see 5.1). In order to reduce the pressure on courts, and to keep down costs, the Law Society also offers a conciliation and mediation service for parties involved in commercial disputes. Initiated in January 1993, the Alternative Dispute Resolution Scheme requires a fee to be paid to the Law Society and to the mediator; these are shared between the parties and are likely to be considerably less than the fees due after a court hearing.

Though varied, much of a solicitor's work is fairly routine. If it does not involve a dispute with another party, it is called non-contentious work, the charges for which are calculated on a different basis from that used for contentious work (see 3.4). All solicitors can now also function as Commissioners for Oaths, and 14 act as notaries public. The former are required as witnesses for certain official documents, though they cannot witness documents prepared by themselves or by their opponents in a case. Notaries public are lawyers who can witness documents for use abroad. As regards two matters solicitors have a virtual monopoly: the drawing up of a conveyance on the sale of land and the taking out of probate or letters of administration when someone dies. It is a criminal offence, with some minor exceptions, for anyone who is not a solicitor to undertake either of these tasks if payment is demanded for the work. In England the first of these monopolies was removed when the Administration of Justice Act 1985 provided for the licensing of non-solicitor conveyancers, but as yet this freedom of trade has not been extended to Northern Ireland. Solicitors can however now engage in work traditionally left to other professionals. Thus, since its formation in 1988 the Law Society's Financial Advice Service has made it the largest mortgage broker in Northern Ireland, with practically every firm of solicitors able to channel advice on where to obtain the best loan.

Information relevant to the solicitors' profession in Northern Ireland is included in the Law Society's monthly magazine called *The Writ*. As well as the regional associations of solicitors which exist throughout Northern Ireland (the Belfast Solicitors' Association is 50 years old), there are associations for solicitors interested in particular kinds of legal work, such as the Family Law Association and the Criminal Bar Association.

Complaints against solicitors

If you wish to complain about a solicitor you should first of all discuss the matter thoroughly with the solicitor involved. You should realise that, because technically they are officers of the Supreme Court, the primary duty of solicitors is not to their clients but to the courts. They certainly must act for you to the best of their ability but this does not allow them to conceal evidence or to ignore established procedures. However, if you are not satisfied with your solicitor's explanation in relation to your complaint you can write to the Law Society about the matter. All complaints are dealt with by the Secretary of the Law Society and the more serious cases are considered by the Professional Conduct Committee, on which two non-lawyers are entitled to sit. This Committee may either reprimand the solicitor or refer the case to the Disciplinary Tribunal. The latter is independent of the Law Society and it too contains lay representatives; it has the power, amongst other things, to strike a solicitor off the Solicitors' Roll, to impose a fine of up to £3,000 and to order the solicitor to remit all or part of the legal fees for the work in question. An appeal against a decision of the Disciplinary Tribunal can be taken by any person affected by it to a judge of the High Court and in some instances there can be a direct appeal from the Professional Conduct Committee to the Lord Chief Justice.

The Law Society's Professional Conduct Committee will consider complaints alleging negligence only if the behaviour would amount to professional misconduct or to inadequate professional services. Other cases of negligence must be processed in the ordinary way through the civil courts (see 5.4 and 5.6) or dealt with under the Solicitors' Complaints Arbitration Scheme. This was set up in 1988 under the auspices of the Chartered Institution of Arbitrators, though by mid-1993 it had not been used even once. The client and the solicitor can each pay £46 to allow an independent arbitrator to examine all the documents in the case and come to a decision (there is no hearing as such). The loser may be ordered to refund the other party's fee for the arbitration and cannot take the matter further (*e.g.* to a court).

The Lay Observer

Since 1977 Northern Ireland has had an official called the Lay Observer, a non-lawyer whose job it is to report on the nature of complaints made to the Law Society about the conduct of solicitors and the manner in which the complaints are dealt with by the Society. The reports are officially made to the Lord Chief Justice, the Department of Finance and Personnel and the Council of the Law Society, but they are printed and can be purchased through Her Majesty's Stationery Office. The current Lay Observer is Mr John Stanley and in his report for 1991-92 he reveals that there were 308 complaints against solicitors. Of these, 84 related to conveyancing (presumably mostly of homes), 72 to personal injury claims and 32 to the administration of a deceased person's estate. The most frequent complaint was of delay or inaction (138 cases), followed by 86 cases of alleged unethical behaviour and 27 of disputed accounts. The Lay Observers have repeatedly expressed satisfaction with the manner in which complaints are handled by the Law Society, though only a random sample of 25 per cent of the cases are closely examined in any one year. Whatever the outcome of a complaint, the Lay Observer has no power to punish a solicitor or to compensate a complaining client.

In order partly to alleviate public anxiety at the lack of scrutiny of solicitors' and other legal services the government has declared its intention to appoint a Legal Services Ombudsman for Northern Ireland, a post already in existence for both England and Wales and Scotland thanks to the Courts and Legal Services Act 1990. Such an Ombudsman, as befits his or her title (see 8.1), would have much greater investigative powers than those of the present Lay Observer.

The work of a barrister

In a small proportion of the cases handled by solicitors it will be necessary for the services of a barrister to be used. Barristers, or "counsel" as they are sometimes called, are experts in advocacy and have the sole right of audience in the higher courts. They began to organise themselves in Ireland as a professional body (the Bar) as long ago as the thirteenth century and in 1541 their headquarters became the King's Inns in Dublin. Following partition, judges and practising barristers in Northern Ireland formed their own Inn of Court of Northern Ireland in 1926. The governing bodies of the profession are the Inn of Court's "benchers", who include the 11 Supreme Court judges, and (more importantly) the Executive Council of the Inn of Court, which now has a Chief Executive (Mr Brendan Garland). The Bar Council, elected by practising barristers, oversees standards within the profession and in effect acts as the profession's "trade union"; its current chairperson is Mr Patrick Coghlin QC.

In contrast with solicitors, who mostly work in firms, barristers are self-employed and are not permitted to form partnerships. In England they share premises known as chambers and are referred to as having tenancies in those chambers. In Northern Ireland (as in Scotland and the Republic of Ireland) the tradition is for all barristers to work out of a Bar Library, which is situated in Belfast in the Royal Courts of Justice, Chichester Street. That is usually where solicitors will contact them.

There is therefore no need for barristers' clerks, who in England effectively act as business managers in each of the chambers and take a commission on the fees earned. In Northern Ireland the fees are negotiated directly between barrister and solicitor. As it is technically the solicitor who engages the barrister, even though the client may have asked for a particular barrister to be used, the barrister cannot sue the client for fees if they are not paid; by legal custom the barrister cannot sue the solicitor either. A barrister who is offered a "brief" by a solicitor must undertake to work on the case unless he or she does not have the time, or a proper fee is not offered, or he or she is in some way personally involved in the case; this is known as the "cab-rank principle". There is little specialisation at the Bar in Northern Ireland, so it is rare for a barrister to avoid work on the ground that it is not within his or her usual sphere of practice (therefore requiring too much time to perform properly).

Experienced barristers may apply to the Lord Chief Justice to "take silk", that is, to become a Queen's Counsel (QC). After appointment as a QC a barrister will not generally appear in court without a "junior", as all other barristers are called, and will charge higher fees. The distinction between these senior and junior barristers is sometimes reflected in talk of the Inner and Outer Bars. Most judicial appointments are open only to practising barristers of a certain number of years' standing (see 1.5), so needless to say most of the judges are former QCs. The first ever female QC was appointed in 1989. In June 1993 there were 36 QCs and 294 junior barristers registered as members of the Bar Library in Northern Ireland. There are in addition a few practising barristers who do not belong to the Bar Library and many more non-practising barristers whose membership of the Bar Librray has lapsed.

A solicitor will need to consult a barrister whenever an expert's opinion is required as to the chances of successfully arguing a particular point in court. The client cannot approach the barrister directly: he or she must be briefed by a solicitor, a rule which is intended to filter out the less difficult cases so that barristers can concentrate on the more important ones. A written opinion by the barrister will often satisfy the client's needs, and even if the case does eventually come to court the client will probably meet the barrister there for the first time: only in a few cases is it deemed necessary for there to be a "conference" with the barrister and solicitor prior to the day of the trial. For cases being heard in the High Court (see 5.6) it is the barrister who drafts the pleadings. Once a barrister is involved in a case he or she will advise the client whether or not to accept an offer of settlement. Otherwise that advice can be given by a solicitor, though sometimes counsel is briefed purely to advise on settlement negotiations.

The work of barristers, it can be seen, is somewhat different from that of solicitors. That the legal systems of England and Northern Ireland should retain this division of labour at all is an anomaly of history. Many other countries whose legal systems are based on the English "common law" system - among them the United States of America and Canada - have long since abandoned the distinction, though it remains in the Republic of Ireland. The main argument for fusing the two professions is that it would reduce costs, but at the moment there are so many vested interests at stake that fusion is an extremely far-off ideal. A tiny step towards fusion was taken by the European Communities (Services of Lawyers) Order 1978 which, under strict conditions, allows lawyers qualified in other EC member states to provide services in the United Kingdom which could otherwise be provided only by barristers or solicitors. This cross-border legal activity has been facilitated by the creation of the Single European Market in 1993. Further steps towards fusion have yet to result from the United Kingdom Government's green paper on the legal professions, published in 1989.

Complaints against barristers

Complaints should be directed to the Complaints Committee of the Bar's Executive Council, which may conduct a hearing on the matter. No lay persons sit on this Committee, however, and it does not have power to suspend or disbar a barrister; this can be done only by the benchers, who deal with the serious cases of misconduct. Again, if a client wishes to allege that a barrister has been negligent, he or she will need to begin a civil action. Barristers and solicitors are immune from being sued in respect of their performance as advocates in court (just as judges are immune in respect of their performance as adjudicators), but they can be sued in connection with pre-trial work.

Legal education

There is practically no instruction given in law to school-children in Northern Ireland. The province's Schools Examinations and Assessment Council does not have a syllabus in law at either GCSE or "A" Level. Any examinable courses which are followed will therefore usually be organised from England and will deal with English law. In October 1993 the Northern Ireland Curriculum Council launched its *Law in Schools* materials with a view to exposing secondary school children to some elementary legal principles. There is a School of Law at the Queen's University of Belfast and a Department of Public Administration and Legal Studies at the University of Ulster. Both institutions offer a variety of undergraduate and postgraduate degree, certificate and diploma courses, some taken through study at evening classes. Other colleges of further education provide lower-level instruction in law.

The way to become a solicitor or barrister in Northern Ireland is to complete successfully the vocational course organised by the Institute of Professional Legal Studies at Queen's University. A person can apply for this course if he or she has a law degree (of at least second class honours for intending barristers) or, having another kind of degree, has completed a Certificate in Academic Legal Studies at Queen's University (two years full-time or three years part-time). All applicants, however, must also sit an admissions test specifically designed to assess their aptitude for practising law and some candidates will be interviewed. In 1993 there were 90 places on the Institute's course, of which approximately 20 were for prospective barristers and the remainder for trainee solicitors. Department of Education bursaries were available for all but 20 of the 90 places, the rest being fee-paying. Every year there are many more applicants than there are places.

For intending solicitors the Institute course is now a component part of a two-year "apprenticeship". The first four months are spent in a solicitor's office, the student having found a so-called "master" before gaining admission to the Institute. The next year consists of lectures and vocational exercises at the Institute, at the end of which the student sits examinations for a Certificate in Professional Legal Studies. The service in a solicitor's office is then continued for a further eight months. This qualifies the student for a restricted practising certificate, which means that for two years he or she cannot practise on his or her own account or in partnership, but only as an assistant solicitor in a firm or under a solicitor in a public body or government service. "Apprentice" solicitors of this variety are the equivalent of what are termed "articled clerks" in England. A further prerequisite for a full practising certificate is attendance at Continuing Legal Education seminars.

For intending barristers the Institute course runs for nine months, from October to June. They then obtain their Certificate in Professional Legal Studies and are "called to the Bar" in the following September. For a further 12 months they must serve a "pupillage", acting as "pupils" to experienced "masters" (barristers of at least eight years' standing at the

Bar). During the first three months of this year they accompany their master to court and learn how things are done in practice; during the next three months they can take cases by themselves in the motions court (see 1.3), but only after the first half of the year can they accept other types of fee-earning work. It may be some months before they actually begin to receive an income from the briefs which they have handled for solicitors.

In exceptional cases the arrangements just described for admission to the legal professions may be altered. This is particularly so for applicants who have already worked as a law clerk in a solicitor's office for seven years, for university lecturers in law and for persons who are professionally qualified in other jurisdictions.Indeed, if you qualify as a solicitor in England and Wales or the Republic of Ireland you can be admitted as a solicitor in Northern Ireland immediately; barristers can equally transfer provided that they have practised for at least three years. Lawyers who qualify in Scotland cannot transfer so easily.

The troubles in Northern Ireland have coincided with a dramatic increase in the numbers wishing to practise law: in 1965 there were 500 solicitors and about 60 barristers, but by mid-1993 there were more than 1,000 solicitors and 330 barristers. There is one barrister in Northern Ireland for every 5,500 residents; in England and Wales the ratio is 1:9,000 and in Scotland it is 1:25,000. The number of would-be students remains high today, despite the sizeable expenses which must be incurred and the low incomes received during the lengthy training periods. Unfortunately, unlike the situation in England, there is no longer an increasing workload to absorb all the fresh recruits. The problem is a constant headache for the Council of Legal Education for Northern Ireland which, as the governing body of the Institute of Professional Legal Studies, has the responsibility for deciding policies and setting standards concerning admission to the Institute.

Lawyers not in private practice

Not everyone who obtains a law degree or qualifies as a solicitor or barrister will actually want to try to practise law. Many will find employment in other positions where they can use their legal knowledge in less direct ways. Government departments (including the Northern Ireland Court Service), district councils, the Housing Executive, public companies, watchdog bodies and teaching institutions all engage such persons in various capacities. On account of the smallness of the province, however, there is obviously not the variety of opportunities that there would be in Great Britain. Few qualified solicitors who are so employed will want, or be permitted, to continue to hold a practising certificate, but barristers, being otherwise self-employed, are usually a little more free in this respect. One disincentive, perhaps, is the requirement laid down by both the Law Society and the Bar Council that their members must at all times be covered by a professional indemnity insurance policy, the premium on which can be very costly. Occasionally an employer will pay this on the employed lawyer's behalf.

The future of the professions

In 1989 the government published three green papers relating to the legal professions in England and Wales; similar proposals were made later that year for Northern Ireland and a policy paper was issued in 1991. As a result of these proposals, the main professional division is unlikely to remain that between barristers and solicitors but instead to become one between lawyers who are certified advocates and those who are not. Advocates will be allowed to contract directly with clients, while all lawyers will be permitted to practise in firms offering other business services. Lawyers will be able to issue advertisements, and it will become lawful to supply legal services on a "no win, no fee" basis. The Lay Observer in Northern Ireland is to be replaced by a Legal Services Ombudsman similar to existing commercial ombudsmen (see 8.1). On the whole the government's proposals were welcomed, except by the Bar. It remains to be seen to what extent they will be implemented.

3.3 Legal Aid, Advice and Assistance

There are three quite separate state schemes for the provision of financial assistance in legal matters, and the first of them has a variant which really constitutes a fourth scheme. By and large these schemes operate regardless of the nature of the legal problem involved, but a few special problems are not covered, such as libel and slander actions or queries about the law outside Northern Ireland. Some matters are catered for by separate specially designed schemes, like the assistance which the Equal Opportunities Commission and Fair Employment Commission are empowered to give in some cases of alleged discrimination on the grounds of gender, marital status, religion or politics (see 8.2 and 8.5). Individuals may also receive financial assistance from purely private sources; your employer or trade union may help , or a club to which you belong (*e.g.* the Automobile Association). It is also possible to take out an insurance policy against the incurring of legal expenses, though of course these will vary in the degree of protection that they provide. If you have rights to such private help but resort instead to the state schemes, the state schemes may be able to seek an indemnity (*i.e.* reimbursement) from the sources of private help; this applies mainly to insurance policies.

Probably the most attractive of the non-state schemes is the fixed-fee interview scheme, which a few solicitors still operate. Under this the client can receive half-an-hour's interview with a solicitor for a nominal flat fee (inclusive of VAT) of £5, an amount which has not changed in several years. This contrasts with the £20 or more which would normally be charged for such a period. Anyone can qualify for this assistance, though it is at the discretion of the solicitors participating in the scheme whether or not they will see a particular person under it. The names of the solicitors who may be prepared to give a fixed-fee interview are indicated in the *Legal Aid Solicitors List*, which is published annually and available from the Legal Aid Department of the Law Society of Northern Ireland, and from Citizens' Advice Bureaux, public libraries, etc. The scheme can even be used as a means of discovering whether you would be likely to qualify for help under one of the state schemes.

The three state schemes provide for legal advice and assistance, legal aid for civil court proceedings, and legal aid for criminal court proceedings. It is not possible to enjoy assistance under the first scheme at the same time as you are receiving aid under one of the other two schemes, but it can happen that aid under both the second and third schemes is given to a person who is involved in civil as well as criminal proceedings arising out of the one incident. We will now examine each of these schemes separately. They operate on the basis of the Legal Aid, Advice and Assistance (NI) Order 1981 and numerous complex regulations made thereunder or under previous legislation. New consolidated regulations have been anticipated for several years. These will probably reflect changes introduced into English law by the Legal Aid Act 1988. Radical reductions to the financial limits were announced early in 1993 and these are reflected in the figures given hereafter.

When the Law Society takes a decision on a legal aid matter it is not possible to appeal against that decision to the courts. It is possible, though, to take judicial review proceedings (see 7.1), and at times the judges give guidance on the schemes in the course of their judgments.

The legal advice and assistance scheme

When this scheme was started in Northern Ireland in 1974 it was confined to the giving of oral advice. It was extended to written advice in 1978 and was sometimes referred to as "the £25 scheme", as that was the limit on the value of the assistance which could be granted under it. In 1980 this limit was raised to £40 and in 1983 to £50; it now stands at £86.50. The scheme is popularly referred to as "the green form scheme", because of the colour of the appropriate application form. This is reproduced (in black and white!) in Appendix 4.

The decision whether to grant legal advice and assistance is made by a solicitor. When you go for your initial interview, whether this is under the fixed-fee system or not, you can ask the solicitor to calculate whether you qualify under the legal advice and assistance scheme. Solicitors can even accept applications from persons residing outside Northern Ireland, but they cannot grant assistance in any matter which has already attracted assistance unless they first obtain the permission of the Law Society.

Eligibility

The eligibility test applied by the solicitor is a purely financial one: the "merits" of your legal position are irrelevant. The stipulated financial limits are revised every year. As from April 1993 you will not qualify if you have what is termed "disposable capital" of more than £1,000. This is an absolute disqualification, regardless of how low your weekly income is. "Disposable capital" basically means the savings you have in a bank, post office, building society or premium bonds, or any "valuables" such as jewellery; the value of capital assets such as a privately owned house, household furniture or personal clothing is ignored because these items are considered to be "indisposable", and the same applies to the value of the subject matter of the actual dispute (*e.g.* a car whose ownership is being contested). Even if your disposable capital is less than £1,000 you will qualify for advice and assistance only if you are in receipt of income support or family credit, or if you have a "disposable income" of less than £147 per week. "Disposable income" basically means your take-home pay minus your regular living expenses (for rent, rates, hire-purchase payments and other necessary outgoings).

Your solicitor will help you to work out your disposable capital and disposable income. Normally the capital and weekly income of your husband or wife must be included in the calculations as well. If you have dependants - a spouse, child, or other relative - certain sums can be counted as indisposable capital (£335 for the first dependant, £200 for the second, and £100 for others). Allowances are also made in the assessment of disposable income: £25 for a spouse, £22.15 for a child aged 11 to 15, etc (these allowances were reduced in April 1993 from, respectively, £40.69 and £26.75). The solicitor will also be able to tell you whether you will be required to make a contribution to the advice and assistance granted to you and, if so, how much. You will have to contribute if your disposable income exceeds £61 per week, the size of the contribution depending on your exact income. It will vary between £7 and £86, being always approximately £55 less than your disposal weekly income. The solicitor will usually agree to the payment of these contributions by instalments, if that is necessary. In England and Wales the contributory part of the green form scheme has been abolished, so that only persons in receipt of income support, family credit, disability working allowance or less than £61 weekly disposable income are now eligible for assistance, albeit free of charge. It is likely that a similar change will be made to the Northern Ireland scheme before long.

A solicitor is entitled to give you £86.50 worth of advice and assistance under the green form scheme, which represents about two hours' work and excludes an allowance for VAT. If the work which needs to be done will be worth more than £86.50 the solicitor can apply to the Law Society for an extension on the upper value of the work he or she can do. The Law Society will grant the extension if it is satisfied that it is reasonable for the advice and assistance to be given and that the estimated amount of the costs to be incurred in giving it is fair and reasonable.

Since the introduction of the Police and Criminal Evidence (NI) Order 1989 (the PACE Order: see 4.3) a person detained in a police station is entitled to have access to a solicitor. To provide for such cases the legal advice and assistance scheme has been amended to allow solicitors who attend such detainees (often, of course, at unsocial hours and at very little notice) to receive up to £150 without needing to apply for special authority from the Law Society.

The assistance by way of representation scheme (ABWOR)

The solicitor can do all kinds of legal work under the legal advice and assistance scheme, including the preparation of applications for civil or criminal legal aid certificates (see below). He or she may write letters for you, draft documents (such as a will), negotiate with someone, take statements, get an opinion from a barrister, or prepare a case to help you appear before a tribunal. But before 1980 the solicitor could not personally represent an assisted person in court or before a tribunal. Since then such representation has been made possible in a limited range of situations:

(1) Whenever a solicitor successfully applies for the approval of the Law Society to represent a client in certain civil proceedings in a magistrates' court (domestic cases, debt or land cases and some welfare cases); the Law Society will grant its approval only if it is shown that there are reasonable grounds for taking, defending, or being a party to the proceedings and that the application is not unreasonable in the particular circumstances of the case; this "merits" test distinguishes this variant of the legal advice and assistance scheme from situations not involving representative work.

(2) If a person appearing before a magistrates' court or a county court is unrepresented, a solicitor who is within the precincts of the court may be asked, or may apply, to represent that person; this enables "duty solicitor" schemes to be set up, whereby a solicitor happening to be on duty may be called in to help unrepresented persons. Such a scheme has operated in Belfast's magistrates' court since 1982. A similar scheme has been running in Craigavon since 1986, but is now on a "call out" basis only, not "in court" as well.

(3) Proceedings before the Mental Health Review Tribunal (see 7.4), provided the application is reasonable, and disciplinary hearings before the Boards of Visitors at prisons (see 1.6).

Representation under the legal advice and assistance scheme - or indeed under the legal aid schemes to be described shortly - is still not possible in any other kind of tribunal except the Lands Tribunal. The Legal Aid Advisory Committee (see below) has argued for the extension of the representation scheme to industrial tribunals, but the Government has not yet acceded to this. However, a solicitor can still give you advice and assistance (short of representation) on a case which is due to come before any sort of tribunal.

In cases of ABWOR the disposable capital limit for eligibility is the same as for legal aid in civil proceedings (£3,000; see below). But the rule still applies that only £86.50 worth of assistance is obtainable unless the Law Society grants an extension.

How the legal costs are recouped in cases of assistance

The difference between the value of the work done for a client under the advice and assistance scheme and the amount of contributions which the client may have to pay is recoverable by the solicitor out of (in order of priority): (a) the costs which the other side agrees, or is ordered by the court, to pay to the assisted person; (b) the property which is recovered or preserved for the assisted person in the case, unless it is exempted property such as a house or maintenance payments; (c) the Legal Aid Fund, which is an account established and administered by the Law Society. The debt owed to the solicitor constitutes a "charge" on these three funds, but the charge may not be enforced against (b) if, on the application of the solicitor, the Law Society so authorises. The solicitor can make such an application whenever he or she thinks that enforcing this so-called "clawback" provision would cause grave hardship or distress to the client or would be unreasonably difficult because of the nature of the property.

In short, under the green form scheme if you win your case you will normally end up paying little or nothing towards the overall costs involved: any contributions you have already paid will be recouped by the award of costs made in your favour by the judge; if you lose, the cost to you should normally not exceed the amount of the contribution payable under the scheme. If a person who is assisted by representation is ordered by the court to pay the costs of the proceedings, he or she does not have to pay more than what the court thinks is reasonable having regard to all the circumstances. The other side may recover the balance of the costs from the Legal Aid Fund.

The Law Society's Legal Aid Committee has issued guidelines (not rigid rates) for the assessment of costs for work done under the green form and ABWOR schemes. At present these suggest that letters and phone calls should be remunerated at £3.35 each. A domestic case in a magistrates' court would typically attract payment of £190.50 if an interim order is also sought (see 5.2). A debt case would cost £62.

As can be seen from Table 5 (which compares figures for all the legal aid schemes over the last five years), in 1991-92 the Law Society approved the payment of legal fees in 56,508 cases where oral or written advice was provided by solicitors under the green form scheme. This represents a 12 per cent increase on the number of claims paid in 1990-91, though the number of applications for assistance increased by 24 per cent. Almost one-third of the cases involved criminal matters (16,803), the next largest categories being claims for negligence (5,501) and PACE cases (5,113). In addition, as many as 8,807 claims were refused on financial or other grounds (an annual increase of over 300 per cent). During the same year 9,409 payments were made in excess of the statutory limit on the value of advice being given (including 1,898 PACE cases); only 324 requests for this to occur were refused. Contributions were paid in just 1,607 cases (less than 3 per cent), the amount received totalling a paltry £31,642. This meant that the average contribution was a mere £19.69, and the average claim was £53.57, which compares with £81.62 for claims in England and Wales. Payments made to solicitors out of the Legal Aid Fund totalled £3.03 million.

Also in 1991-92 there were 13,861 applications for authority to proceed by way of representation; 11,320 were granted, all but 50 involving family law matters. Again only 1,242 applicants paid a contribution towards the cost of the legal assistance (11 per cent), £32.75 being the average contribution per case and £40,678 being the total amount received as contributions. The average claim was for £124.58, compared with £345.55 in England and Wales. Approximately £1.41 million was paid to solicitors out of the Legal Aid Fund.

The civil legal aid scheme

Legal aid for court proceedings in civil cases was not introduced in Northern Ireland until 1965, 16 years after its introduction in England and Wales. The details of the civil aid schemes are now very similar in both jurisdictions.

If you are honestly contemplating civil court proceedings, whether as plaintiff or defendant, you should contact a solicitor. He or she can help you to fill in the relevant legal aid forms, but the decision whether to grant civil legal aid in any particular case is taken not by the solicitor but by officials of the Law Society, to whom the forms will be sent. Persons living outside Northern Ireland can apply for legal aid for civil proceedings which are to take place within Northern Ireland, but persons living inside the province who want aid for proceedings elsewhere - whether England, Scotland, the Republic of Ireland, or further afield - must apply to the authorities in those countries.

The "merits" test

An important difference between the civil legal aid scheme and the legal advice and assistance scheme (apart from ABWOR) is that for the former there is not only a financial eligibility test to be satisfied but also

STATISTICS ON LEGAL AID IN NORTHERN IRELAND, 1987-92

	Legal advice and assistance	ABWOR	Civil legal aid	Criminal legal aid
Applications received				
1987-88	42,155	11,068	19,251	25,802
1988-89	48,824	10,728	18,893	22,520
1989-90	50,671	11,426	20,461	23,250
1990-91	58,322	11,536	19,078	21,887
1991-92	72,591	13,861	22,016	23,879
Payments made or certificates issued				
1987-88	41,445	9,108	15,283	21,195
1988-89	48,504	10,605	14,099	30,704
1989-90	57,424	8,806	24,332	21,783
1990-91	50,448	9,710	15,655	20,029
1991-92	56,508	11,320	14,585	20,666
Number of contributions				
1987-88	1,023	n/a	1,205	-
1988-89	1,158	1,069	1,868	-
1989-90	1,842	1,109	2,523	-
1990-91	1,512	1,319	1,962	-
1991-92	1,607	1,242	1,601	-
Average contribution				
1987-88	£12.59	n/a	£274.16	-
1988-89	£12.82	£24.28	£265.40	-
1989-90	£15.39	£28.51	£276.92	-
1990-91	£17.33	£27.45	£313.09	-
1991-92	£19.69	£32.75	£322.82	-
Average cost of claims				
1987-88	£29.57	n/a	n/a	n/a
1988-89	£33.00	£124.32	£698.44	£225.02
1989-90	£38.44	£129.35	£711.08	£288.00
1990-91	£46.61	£137.99	£746.61	£295.87
1991-92	£53.57	£124.58	£760.56	£337.23

Table 5

a "merits" test. As regards the financial limits, you will be eligible for civil legal aid from April 1993 if your disposable capital is not more than £6,750 and your disposable income does not exceed £6,800 per annum. For cases involving personal injury claims these limits are increased respectively to £8,560 and £7,500.

As the capital limit is quite high, more people qualify under this scheme than under the legal advice and assistance scheme. If your disposable capital is more than £6,750 you may still be granted aid if you cannot afford to proceed without legal aid because the costs of the case are likely to be too great, but the £6,800 limit on disposable income is absolute. Your disposable capital and income are calculated in similar ways to those already described for legal advice and assistance, except that the calculation is performed by the Legal Aid Assessment Office of the Department of Health and Social Services. In calculating disposable capital no allowances are made for dependants, but allowances are made in calculating disposable income: they are the same as for legal advice and assistance claims, though converted from weekly into annual amounts. Thus, for a spouse the allowance is £1,304 and for a child aged 11 to 15 it is £1,155.

Once you have shown that you are within the financial limits, the Law Society's Legal Aid Department must still be persuaded that you have reasonable grounds for being a party to the proceedings and that it is not unreasonable for you to receive legal aid in the particular circumstances of the case. So if the action is a trivial one, or if the cost to the Legal Aid Fund would be disproportionate to the advantage you might gain from the litigation, legal aid may be refused even if you are financially eligible. This is the same "merits" test as needs to be satisfied in applications for representation under the legal advice and assistance scheme (ABWOR), and indeed civil legal aid may be refused if representation under that scheme would be more appropriate. As it can take several weeks for both the financial and merits tests to be considered, there is a procedure for applying for an "emergency certificate", which can be granted at once provided you promise to pay whatever contributions are later assessed (see below). If a civil or emergency certificate is refused on the ground that the merits test has not been satisfied, you may appeal to a committee of the Law Society but not to a court.

Financial contributions

Contributions towards the cost of civil legal aid have to be made by applicants whose disposable capital is between £3,000 and £6,750 or whose disposable income is between £2,294 and £6,800. Any part of the excess capital can be requested as a contribution, but only one quarter of the excess income can be requested. The contributions can be required to be paid in one sum or in instalments, but as yet only for a period of 12 months: in due course the scheme in Northern Ireland is to be brought into line with that in England and Wales, which requires contributions to be paid during the entire life of a civil aid certificate. Further contributions do not usually have to be paid if another application is made in respect of an appeal in the case to a higher court.

Coverage under the scheme

If the Law Society considers that you have fulfilled both the financial and merits tests, it will grant you a civil aid certificate. This will cover legal services by a solicitor or barrister both before and during a court hearing. You are entitled to choose any solicitor (and, if needed, any barrister) to act in your case: you do not have to stick to the one who forwarded your application for legal aid to the Law Society or to the one from whom you may already have received legal advice and assistance. Practically every type of hearing is within the civil aid scheme, with the exception of tribunals (other than the Lands Tribunal), arbitrations (which include proceedings in a small claims court: see 5.3) and coroners' courts (see 6.3). In Northern Ireland "care" proceedings regarding children or young persons are classified as civil matters for this purpose, as in fact are all appeals in the Court of Appeal on a case stated by a magistrates' court (even in what is otherwise undoubtedly a criminal case). The cost of taking proceedings in the Enforcement of Judgments Office (see 3.4 and 5.7) or of referring an issue to the European Court of Justice (see 2.6) is also covered by the scheme. Particular types of case are excluded in all courts, such as libel and slander claims, admitted debts, and claims relating to elections. People who take cases under the European Convention on Human Rights can benefit from a special legal aid scheme administered in Strasbourg (see 2.6).

While the case is progressing, your solicitor will be in regular contact with the Law Society. Before certain steps can be taken, such as the engagement of a barrister in a magistrates' court or a Queen's Counsel in a county court or High Court case, the permission of the Law Society must be sought. But there is no £86.50 limit on the value of the legal work that can be done for you as there is under the advice and assistance scheme.

How the legal costs are recouped in legally aided cases

The solicitor will be paid for the work, as will any barrister involved in the case, out of the Law Society's Legal Aid Fund. In proceedings at or above High Court level the work will generally be paid for at 95 per cent of the normal rate for work not legally aided. In county court proceedings the full rate will be paid if the costs are "taxed" (see 3.4); if the costs are not taxed, and in all magistrates' court proceedings, the sums paid will be in accordance with scales of remuneration laid down in regulations (see 3.4). At the moment these allow for payment of, for instance, £756 (plus outlays) to a solicitor acting for a plaintiff in a county court case who is claiming between £2,000 and £3,000. In exceptional cases a judge can order that these scales should not apply.

Once the case is over, any sums recovered by the assisted person by virtue of a court order (or agreement) for costs must be paid to the Legal Aid Fund. If these exceed the sums paid out of that Fund on the assisted person's behalf the excess is retained by the Fund; if they are less, the balance is recouped from the assisted person's contributions, the amount unused, if any, being returned. If even the contributions are not enough to satisfy the debt owed to the Legal Aid Fund, a "charge" may be imposed on any property recovered or preserved by the proceedings. This charge is similar to the solicitor's charge in connection with legal advice and assistance mentioned above, but unlike that charge it cannot be waived. The Law Society can, however, take its time over enforcing it and may accept an alternative charge on substitute property; certain forms of property, such as maintenance payments, are in any event exempt from the charge. If an assisted person happens to be insured against the legal expenses incurred, the insurance money received must be paid to the Legal Aid Fund. If the Fund is still owed money after all this, the loss must be borne out of the public purse.

If an unassisted party wins a case against an assisted party the court may order the former's costs to be paid out of the Legal Aid Fund, provided that this is just and equitable in all the circumstances and that (except in appeals) the unassisted party would otherwise suffer severe financial hardship.

As Table 5 above shows, during the year ending 31st March 1992 there were 22,016 applications for civil legal aid. This is a 15 per cent increase on the previous year's figure. Civil aid certificates issued totalled 14,585, which represents a drop of nearly 7 per cent on the 1990-91 figure; there were also fewer "emergency" certificates than the year before (2,811 as opposed to 2,931). Only 19 certificates were issued for magistrates' courts, largely because solicitors preferred to use the ABWOR scheme when working in those courts. In almost nine out of every ten cases no financial contributions were required from the aided person, with only £516,841 being contributed altogether; the average contribution was £322.82. Solicitors and barristers were paid a total of £14.35 million under the civil legal aid scheme in 1991-92, though more than £10.75 million was recouped for the Legal Aid Fund by costs won in court or obtained in settlements - a reflection of the fact that 68 per cent of all aided cases were won or satisfactorily settled. This means that the net expenditure on civil legal aid in Northern Ireland in 1991-92 was less than £3.6 million.

The criminal legal aid scheme

Criminal legal aid has been available in one form or another for decades. The two distinguishing features of the present scheme are that the decision whether or not to grant aid is taken by the court itself (not by a solicitor or by the Law Society) and that, if it is granted, the aid is free; unlike the scheme in England, no contributions are required from the aided person. However, if it transpires that the oral or written statement of means provided to the court by the applicant for legal aid is incorrect, the court may then take action to recover some or all of the costs from the applicant.

The scheme allows for a criminal aid certificate to be granted to persons who have been charged with a criminal offence (see 4.5) or who have been brought before a criminal court on a summons (see 4.3). It operates in the juvenile courts too, where parents or guardians can apply for aid on behalf of children or young persons. People who bring private prosecutions, however, cannot rely on the scheme, except when after winning their case the other side appeals against the decision. The introduction of ABWOR (see above) has provided an attractive alternative to criminal legal aid in some situations.

Applications are best made through a solicitor and preferably before the case is due to be heard in court. They can be made by letter addressed to the clerk of the petty sessions for the relevant district; if unsuccessful at that stage a later application can be made at the hearing itself. In practice in Northern Ireland most applications are made orally at the hearing. The applicant will usually be asked to fill in a form (a copy is reproduced in Appendix 4) stating his or her means, although there is no rigid financial eligibility test as there is for legal advice and assistance or civil legal aid. Having received an application the court may ask the Department of Health and Social Services to inquire into the applicant's means and report back to the court; in that event the case will obviously be a little delayed. For aid to be granted it must simply appear to the court that the applicant's means are insufficient to obtain legal help in preparing and conducting a defence. In appeals from the Crown Court to the Court of Appeal (or, further, to the House of Lords) legal aid is obtainable under provisions in the Criminal Appeal (NI) Act 1980.

Conditions of aid

As a "merits" test it must also appear to the court that it is desirable in the interests of justice that the applicant should have free legal aid. The sorts of factors which the court will take into account in applying this merits test (the so-called "Widgery" criteria because they were laid down in an English case by the Lord Chief Justice of that name) are the gravity of the criminal charge, the ability of the applicant to present his or her own case and the nature of the defence. If a court has any doubts whether the applicant qualifies for aid these must be resolved in favour of granting it, even when the applicant intends to plead guilty to the criminal charges. In cases where the charge is murder, or in situations where a court intends to sentence the defendant to imprisonment, detention in a young offenders' centre or a period in a training school, criminal legal aid *must* be offered.

The aid comes in the form of a "criminal aid certificate". A solicitor and, where necessary, a barrister are assigned to the case by the court after it has taken into account any representations which the applicant may want to make on this matter. In a Crown Court trial the judge may request a solicitor or barrister to undertake the defence of a person who has not been granted a criminal aid certificate, in which event the case proceeds as if a certificate had in fact been granted.

From January 1993 the costs payable to lawyers involved in cases where a criminal aid certificate has been issued are governed by the Legal Aid in Criminal Proceedings (Costs) Rules (NI) 1992. These replaced the rules which had been in place since 1966 and which provided for the creation of a Criminal Costs Assessment Panel. Committees of this Panel awarded costs on the basis of all relevant circumstances including the complexity and duration of the case and the experience of the lawyer involved. It set a bottom, middle and top fee for various types of work, and in many cases solicitors were awarded costs as high as those of senior counsel because the committees recognised that solicitors have much greater overheads than barristers (who do not have an office to run). The 1992 Rules have abolished both the Assessment Panel and its Committees. In their place there is a new Panel appointed by the Lord Chancellor and including non-lawyers; its committees comprise one barrister, one solicitor and one non-lawyer and their function is to award costs on the basis not only of the fees laid down in the 1992 Rules but also of directions issued by the Lord Chancellor.

The 1992 Rules specify how much is to be paid to both solicitors and barristers, whether in magistrates' courts proceedings, appeals to the county court, High Court bail applications or Crown Court proceedings; different fees are listed for different types of work (preparation of the case, advocacy, travelling and waiting, etc). In magistrates' courts fees will usually be assessed on the basis of prescribed hourly rates. In the Crown Court fees will either be standard or non-standard, the latter being assessed on the basis of higher hourly rates than in magistrates' courts; whether standard or non-standard fees are paid will depend on whether the criminal offence charged is serious and whether the court hearing lasts more than two days. Most cases where the defendant pleads guilty (and most appeals to the county court) will attract standard fees. When the assessment committee is awarding non-standard fees it has a degree of discretion to award an amount between an upper and lower limit. By way of examples, a senior solicitor is entitled to £41.25 per hour for attending a barrister at a Crown Court trial while an apprentice solicitor can receive £12 per hour for waiting at the Crown Court for a case to begin; a junior counsel can be awarded up to £256 for handling a defendant's plea of guilty in the Crown Court while a Queen's Counsel can receive up to £400 per day as a "refresher fee" after the first day of a Crown Court trial.

If a solicitor or barrister is not satisfied with a committee's assessment of the costs due, he or she can, in most cases, require the committee to look again at the case. There can then be an appeal to the Taxing Master (see 3.4) and, if the Taxing Master certifies that the case involves a point of principle of general importance, there can be a further appeal to the High Court.

Solicitors doing criminal legal work in Northern Ireland were unhappy when the 1992 Rules came into force. They felt that the Rules would result in significantly lower awards to solicitors than in the past, partly because many assessments were to be based on an hourly rate for the work undertaken. In July 1993 the solicitors refused to appear in legally aided criminal cases, thereby delaying the start of some cases and lengthening the periods some defendants were having to spend on remand in custody. At the time of writing the dispute has still not been resolved to the satisfaction of all concerned, though a decision in a test case by MacDermott LJ has confirmed that when an assessment committee is deciding what would be fair remuneration for work done in the Crown Court by solicitors and barristers it should take cognisance of the fees paid under the pre-1993 method.

Referring again to Table 5 above, during the year ending 31st March 1992 the courts granted 20,666 criminal aid certificates, of which 80 per cent were for magistrates' courts and 5 per cent for the Crown Court. More than 80 per cent of all the defendants were nevertheless found guilty. About one-quarter of the cases involved charges of theft and 16 per cent involved charges of violence. There were also 1,002 applications for criminal legal aid during an appeal and 1,017 applications related to bail hearings. Of all the applications submitted a meagre 405 were turned down. A total of £7.17 million was paid out to lawyers for fees and outlays, making the average cost per case £337.23, an increase of 14 per cent over the previous year's figure.

The administration of the state schemes

Since 1982 Ministerial responsibility for legal aid, advice and assistance has rested with the Lord Chancellor rather than the Secretary of State for Northern Ireland. It is the Law Society of Northern Ireland, however, which administers the schemes on a day-to-day basis. It carries out most of its functions through an annually appointed Legal Aid Committee, which consists of six to nine solicitors nominated by the Law Society, two barristers nominated by the Bar Council, and one barrister or solicitor nominated by the Lord Chancellor. There is also what is termed a Certifying Committee, whose main task is to consider applications for civil legal aid which have been turned down by the legal officers in the Legal Aid Department; if it does not want to grant the aid, the application can then be considered by the Legal Aid Committee, whose decisions can in turn be subject to judicial review proceedings (see 7.1).

The Law Society submits an annual report to the Lord Chancellor on the operation of the legal advice and assistance scheme and on the civil and criminal legal aid schemes; the Lord Chancellor in turn lays this report before Parliament. An advisory committee exists to advise the Lord Chancellor on such questions relating to these schemes as may be referred to it and to comment on the Law Society's annual report. At the moment the Advisory Committee on Legal Aid comprises 11 persons under the chairmanship of a county court judge (Judge Petrie). Each year the report of the Advisory Committee is bound and published together with the Law Society's reports as a House of Commons Paper.

3.4 Lawyers' Fees

The cost of employing a professional lawyer can be very high. In cases of genuine hardship some form of legal aid may be available, as the previous section has explained, but the truth remains that our legal system is still a long way from ensuring free or subsidised legal help in all situations. If you do not qualify for legal aid or legal advice and assistance, or if your case is one for which the £5 fixed-fee interview is inadequate, the choice is stark: you must either try to conduct your legal affairs in person or else engage a solicitor and run the risk of incurring significant expenditure.

Generally speaking it is inadvisable for a person who is untrained in the law to attempt to conduct his or her own legal affairs, or even to help a friend to do so. Rather drastic errors may be made, with the result that much greater expense is eventually incurred than it was originally hoped could be saved. In addition, in many situations it is actually a criminal offence for untrained persons to do legal work on other people's behalf if they ask payment for it. Some committed individuals do get as far as handling the conveyance of their house or conducting their own legal cases in court, but unless you have lots of free time and spare cash you could well find this to be so inconvenient as to be counterproductive. "Litigants in person", as such individuals are called if cases come to court, are few and far between.

The alternative of engaging a solicitor will not, however, always be unattractive! In particular, if the legal matter is one which involves a dispute with another person, rather than one (like drafting a will) which purely affects yourself, you may well stand a chance of getting back from the other person most of what you have to pay to your solicitor - provided you win the dispute. As regards the solicitor's charges, the basic principle, as you would expect, is that the more work a solicitor does, the more he or she will require you to pay. The cost of a first visit should not be very high (perhaps £10 or £20), and if the solicitor has to take any further action on your behalf you can ask to be kept informed about how much the work is going to cost. The bill, when it is finally received, should itemise all the work carried out and the corresponding charge. It will be made up differently depending on whether the work done was contentious or non-contentious, though there are no hard-and-fast rules as to when work becomes contentious.

Non-contentious work

Generally speaking, a solicitor's non-contentious work consists of all jobs done excluding those which concern proceedings in court. It may be work of a more or less routine nature - like conveying a house or drafting a will - or work concerning a dispute which is settled before a date is fixed for a court appearance. The solicitor's bill in such non-contentious cases will be made up as follows:

(1) a charge for disbursements, or outlays, such as the stamp duty on the value of a house or the fee for obtaining probate of a will;
(2) a professional fee; and
(3) VAT, at 17.5 per cent, on those items liable to it (which include the professional fee).

The size of the professional fee will depend on such factors as the time involved in handling the affair, the complexity of the affair, and the value of the property concerned. It is not unusual for a solicitor to charge at a rate of about £40 per hour for time spent on a case. In some matters, though not often, the fee is determined in accordance with guidelines laid down either by the Law Society, which is the governing body of the solicitors' profession, or by a local solicitors' association: the Belfast Solicitors' Association, for example, has guideline prices for the conveying of houses. The typical charge for the conveyance of a house priced at £50,000 will be in the region of £450 (which is somewhat more than in England); the charge for administering a deceased person's estate could be greater, perhaps around 2 per cent of the estate's total value. Without going into the details of each case, which will vary greatly, it is impossible to be more precise in indicating likely charges. Remember that help with the initial costs involved may occasionally be available under the legal advice and assistance scheme described in the previous section.

Challenging a solicitor's bill

If a client is dissatisfied with a bill provided by a solicitor for non-contentious work, two things can be done. He or she can require the solicitor to obtain what is called a Remuneration Certificate from the Law Society. This will state the charge which would be a fair and reasonable one for the work done in the case and the client will have to pay that amount. The Certificate has to be sought within one month from the date when the solicitor informs the client of the right to apply for one (as the solicitor is bound to do). It is supplied free of charge, but experience shows that only about one in every five applications will result in a reduction of the bill.

Alternatively, or in addition, the client can apply to have the costs officially assessed (*i.e.* "taxed") by an official of the Supreme Court called the Taxing Master (see 1.5). Applications must be made within three months of delivery of the bill to the client. The time limit can be extended - and this will usually be necessary if the client has first taken time to ask for a Remuneration Certificate - but the absolute limit is six months. The initial fee for applying to the Taxing Master, in the case of bills relating to non-contentious work, is a flat £20, though after the Taxing Master has dealt with the case the person who loses the argument over the bill must pay an additional 10 per cent of the amount in dispute by way of a fee to the Taxing Master's office. There are only a handful of these "solicitor and client" applications each year.

For further details ask the Law Society for a copy of its leaflet entitled *Unhappy about your bill.*

Contentious work

A solicitor's contentious work consists of all the business which eventually leads to appearances in court. If judicial proceedings are begun, for example by the issuing of a writ or a summons (see 5.6), but are settled before the date fixed for the trial, all the work done up to then is usually classified as non-contentious. In considering how much a client will have to pay for contentious work it is essential to distinguish between criminal proceedings and civil proceedings. In both it is also essential to bear in mind the implications of the legal aid schemes.

Criminal proceedings

If you find yourself defending a prosecution for a criminal offence you will need to consider whether to apply for a criminal legal aid certificate (see 3.3). If a certificate is granted the costs are eventually met in the way described in the previous section. If you do not succeed in obtaining a criminal aid certificate it is not possible to appeal against the refusal to grant one, except during the course of an appeal in the case itself, and you yourself must therefore pay for the services of any solicitor or barrister whose services you engage. You can, of course, conduct your own defence, but in serious cases this is not at all wise. You can also have a friend in court to help you with your case (such people are called "McKenzie friends" after the name of the case where their appearance was first approved), but he or she is not usually permitted to speak on your behalf. If you lose the case, however, it is very rare for an order to be made compelling you to contribute towards the prosecution's costs as well as paying your own. On the other hand, if you win the case and are acquitted it is also very rare in Northern Ireland for the prosecution to be ordered to pay your costs. It is only when the prosecution, or the defence, has been outrageously unsubstantiated that the costs will be ordered "to follow the event", that is, paid by the losing side.

If an order as to costs is made by a magistrates' court, the precise amount of costs will be calculated by the court in accordance with the Magistrates' Courts (Costs in Criminal Cases) Rules (NI) 1988. These allow for up to £75 per lawyer per day, although the court can order payment of a greater sum if the proceedings are exceptionally long, difficult or complex. The recipient of the award will also be reimbursed the court fees which have had to be paid during the proceedings, these too being fixed by regulations. If an order as to costs is made by the Crown Court or, in appeals, by a county court or the Court of Appeal, the precise amount in the absence of agreement between the parties will usually be assessed by the Taxing Master, who is obliged by statute to allow such sums as are reasonably sufficient to compensate the party for the expenses properly incurred. The costs actually awarded to a party may not be in line with those charged by the solicitor or barrister; the client is then left to bear the difference, though, as explained earlier, he or she can always apply to the Taxing Master for a reduction in the solicitor's bill. If a criminal case has been legally aided then the 1992 rules discussed in 3.3 apply. An allowance is usually also made for the compensation of witnesses who, if they are professional people, can be allowed a professional fee in addition to out-of-pocket expenses. The allowances are changed annually but at the moment a witness appearing in a magistrates' court is entitled to £21.95 if attending for less than four hours and to £43.90 if attending for longer than four hours; £4.25 is allowed for food if attendance is between five and 10 hours. The court can award higher amounts for attendance if it thinks the claim is reasonable (and provided any loss of wages is certified by the employer).

Civil proceedings

A person involved in civil proceedings, whether as plaintiff or defendant, should also consider whether to apply for a civil legal aid certificate (see 3.3). The costs, whether borne by the litigants themselves or by the Legal Aid Fund, are calculated differently according to the forum in which the proceedings are brought.

Proceedings in a magistrates' court

The amounts which can be in issue in civil cases in magistrates' courts are small (see 5.2). The fees for issuing a summons and for the various pieces of work which a solicitor or barrister might do are laid down in regulations (the Magistrates' Courts Fees Order (NI) 1989, as amended, particularly in March 1991). The fee for issuing a "process" for the recovery of a debt is just £5, service of a summons by post costs £5 and by hand £7, and the application fee for the renewal of a liquor licence is £60. Parties are usually left to bear their own fees and lawyers' costs even if they win the case, but in a case involving family disputes it is more normal for the court to award costs against the loser of the case. In a typical case these might amount to £150.

Proceedings in a small claims court

From November 1992 the maximum sum which can be claimed in these so-called "arbitration" proceedings, which take place before a district judge (formerly called a "circuit registrar"), is £1,000 (see 5.3). Since the end of 1992 the application fee for claims less than £75 has been £10, for claims between £75 and £300 it has been £22, for claims between £300 and £500 it has been £30 and for claims between £500 and £1,000 it has been £36. The other party (the "respondent") does not pay any fee for defending the case, unless he or she makes a counterclaim (in which event the fees are £5, £11, £15 or £18 depending on the size of the counterclaim). Once again each side is usually left to bear his or her own costs, including the cost of providing witnesses and (unless arranged by the district judge) expert reports; only the application fee itself will be recoverable by the winner from the loser. If a plaintiff makes a claim in a county court for a fixed amount less than £1,000 and the defendant insists upon fighting it in a small claims court but loses, the district judge may award to the plaintiff such costs as he or she would have received if the case had been heard in the county court.

Proceedings in a county court

Up to £15,000 can be claimed in most civil cases in a county court . However, for claims concerning matrimonial property or compensation for criminal injuries or criminal damage to property there is no financial limit (see 5.4 and 5.5). The fees for commencing the proceedings (*i.e.* issuing and serving a "civil bill") and for summoning witnesses, as well as the costs for the work done by solicitors and barristers, are laid down in regulations (see the County Court Fees Order (NI) 1989, as amended, and the County Court (Amendment No. 3) Rules (NI) 1992).

The amount payable (except in the case of a witness summons) depends on the amount of money or the value of the property being claimed. For example, the cost of issuing an ordinary civil bill for a claim amounting to £4,500 is £75, and a further fee of £6 will be exacted for serving this document on the other party (and £6 for serving each witness summons). A solicitor's costs for work done in a case where £4,500 is claimed will be £1,050 or £997 and the barrister's costs will be £222 (plus £11.84 if he or she has had to draft a reply to a notice from the defendant's side requesting further particulars of the claim). The reason why two figures are given for the solicitor's costs is that a slightly lower sum is payable if the solicitor was acting for a defendant rather than a plaintiff. Counsel is also entitled to an allowance for travelling to the court (*e.g.* £7.46 for a trip of 20 to 50 miles from the Head Post Office in Belfast). For each day or part of a day on which a trial or hearing is continued after the first day, counsel can get one-third of the scale fee for the first day and a solicitor in attendance can claim the same. In cases where the claim relates to a personal injury the Bar Council suggests that the "going rate" for brief and negotiation fees is £300 for any claim up to £5,000.

It is important to note that in a county court case the loser will have to pay the winner's costs unless the judge orders otherwise, but even this may not be enough to reimburse the winner completely for his or her outlay: the bill received from the solicitor will include an amount for the time and responsibility involved, which will not be wholly reflected in the fixed scale laid down in the regulations. In such instances the winner must bear the balance of the expense; this could be a significant fraction of the total expense, especially if what was claimed in the case was much more than he or she actually succeeded in winning.

To encourage settlements out of court the scales of costs in county court cases are greatly reduced if a defendant agrees to satisfy a claim within 14 days of the service of the plaintiff's civil bill or if he or she fails to defend the action. A defendant can also safeguard the position on costs by "paying into court" so much of the plaintiff's claim as the defendant is prepared to concede. If the plaintiff does not accept this payment but then does not succeed in getting a higher award from the court, he or she will have to pay virtually all the costs, both his or her own as well as the defendant's.

A plaintiff's costs in the county court may also be reduced if the amount recovered is less than £2,000. In that event the case should have been brought before a district judge and not a county court judge, so only half the scale cost for the amount of the successful claim is allowed. If the recovery is less than £1,000 then, whether the case was heard by a county court judge or by a district judge sitting in a county court, no costs at all will be allowed; the matter should have been dealt with by arbitration in a small claims court (see above and 5.3). Only in cases of misconduct by one party or in proceedings for a fixed amount of money may costs up to the county court scale be awarded. For further details on legal costs incurred in county courts see the County Court Rules (NI) 1981, Order 55 and Appendix 2 to the Rules, as amended in 1992.

Proceedings in the High Court

Any amount of money can be claimed in High Court proceedings. The court fees are again set out in regulations but lawyers' costs are not specified to the same extent as in county court proceedings. Appendix 3 to Order 62 of the Rules of the Supreme Court (NI) 1980 lays down fixed costs only for cases where, in effect, the defendant does not submit a defence to the claim; thus if the amount recovered is more than £3,000 the costs should be £97.50 (plus the fees payable on issuing the writ in the first place). Naturally both fees and costs are higher than in county courts. Senior counsel (i.e. QCs) are more likely to be involved; their charges are high, and the junior counsel who assist them usually get one-half to two-thirds of the fee paid to "the silk". In claims involving personal injuries the Bar Council recommends what the barrister's brief and negotiation fee should be (e.g. £1,500 if the claim is for a sum between £50,000 and £60,000 and £4,000 if the sum is between £150,000 and £200,000; more should be payable if there have been pre-trial consultations between the barrister and the client and if the case is fought for a day or more). If a plaintiff recovers less than £15,000 in the High Court proceedings he or she will be restricted to costs on the county court scale.

The decision as to which side is to bear the costs in High Court proceedings is in the complete discretion of the judge, but in the vast majority of cases the loser will be ordered to pay most, if not all, of the winner's costs. (An exception is often made in Northern Ireland in cases where a husband successfully petitions for divorce against his wife.) Once the judge has ordered who is to pay the costs, the actual amounts to be paid will be agreed between the parties or, in the absence of any agreement, assessed by the Taxing Master. The Master will allow costs only for work which was essential, or proper; any "extra" work must be paid for by the party requiring it to be done. This is termed the assessment of costs on a "party and party" basis. (If the winner of a case is legally aided, the costs will be taxed on what is called a "common fund" basis, which allows the winner to recover a reasonable amount for all expenses reasonably incurred.) A litigant in person in the High Court - someone who is unrepresented by a lawyer - can be allowed up to two-thirds of what the costs would have been if he or she had engaged a solicitor.

Proceedings in a tribunal

Tribunals (see Chapter 7) do not normally have the power to order one side to pay the other side's costs. As legal aid is not available for tribunal proceedings (except in the Lands Tribunal and for representation under the advice and assistance scheme in the Mental Health Review Tribunal and in some prison disciplinary hearings: see 3.3) the parties usually end up paying their own costs. In some situations, however, the tribunal can make payments to cover travel expenses and loss of earnings. Exceptionally (*e.g.* if the respondent's arguments are considered frivolous or vexatious) a tribunal may order the respondent to pay the applicant's costs. This occurred in *Johnston* v *Chief Constable of the RUC* (1988), the case where female police reservists successfully complained of sexual discrimination.

Enforcement of judgment proceedings

As is explained in 5.7, the cost of enforcing a judgment, if the losing side refuses at first to comply with it, can be quite substantial in relation to the size of the judgment itself. The fees payable to the Enforcement of Judgments Office are laid down by the Judgments Enforcement Fees Order (NI) 1992 and to these must be added the solicitor's fee for acting on the winner's behalf. The fee for lodging notice of intent to apply for enforcement of a judgment is just £7, but the fee for an actual application for enforcement grows with the size of the judgment in question. For instance, enforcement of a judgment between £3,000 and £10,000 will cost £367 plus £2 per every £100 by which the judgment exceeds £3,000.

If there is no judgment because the debt is admitted, the fee is reduced by approximately 25 per cent. If the losing side can afford to pay the judgment debt, the enforcement costs are added to it; otherwise the enforcement costs must be written off by the "winning" side as another bad debt.

Challenging costs for contentious work

After any contentious proceedings a party may apply to the Taxing Master for his or her solicitor's bill to be officially examined, provided that the application is made within 12 months of the bill's delivery. (In non-contentious cases, as we have seen, the time limit is usually just three months.) A party who is ordered to pay the other side's costs may, rather than agree them, insist on those being taxed too, this time within six months of the court order.

The Taxing Master will arrange a date for a hearing to take place. He will then assess the costs at what he takes to be a reasonable amount in the light of all the relevant circumstances, referring of course to any appropriate regulations on the matter. A party, whether solicitor or client, who is dissatisfied with the Taxing Master's assessment may ask for a second review by the Master and for yet a further review by a judge. The costs of the taxing process are usually borne by the party paying the bill being taxed.

4

Proceedings in Criminal Courts

4.1 Types of Criminal Offences

The criminal law of Northern Ireland, like that of England, rests on two fundamental principles. The first is that any kind of behaviour is criminal only if it is *expressly* prohibited by the criminal law. The second is that no-one can be convicted of a crime unless the behaviour in question was prohibited at the time it occurred. In recognition of these principles most of the criminal law has been embodied in statutes. Only a few offences - the most prominent of which is murder - are still regulated primarily by judge-made law, though of course the judges do still have to interpret the criminal law statutes whenever their provisions are ambiguous or unclear. It is occasionally a difficult legal question to decide if all the required elements of a crime are present in any particular case, but in most cases the issue is simply whether the prosecution has proved sufficient facts to establish the defendant's guilt.

With rare statutory exceptions, no accused person can be convicted of crime unless the prosecution has proved his or her guilt "beyond a reasonable doubt": since the accused person must be presumed innocent until proved guilty, he or she must be acquitted if the court is not sure that he or she is guilty. There are rare occasions when, once the prosecution has proved certain basic facts, the burden of proving that he or she is not guilty rests on the accused. In such cases, however, it is usually enough for the accused to prove this on a balance of probabilities. This is a lower degree of proof than beyond a reasonable doubt and it really means that the accused must prove that what he or she is saying is more likely true than not. Examples of this occur when the accused claims to have an impaired mental responsibility or to be insane (Criminal Justice Act (NI) 1966), or when he or she has been charged with possession of certain types of prohibited goods. This is the same standard of proof as is required in all civil cases.

The law recognises that not all crimes are equally serious by providing two different forms of procedure and trial. Less serious offences are dealt with by a summary trial in a magistrates' court (sometimes called a court of petty sessions or a court of summary jurisdiction), and they involve no jury. More serious offences are tried on indictment in the Crown Court by a judge and jury (though there is also a preliminary step which takes place in a magistrates' court). However, during the present emergency in Northern Ireland some offences are tried on indictment without a jury; these trials take place in the so-called Diplock courts - it was a Committee chaired by Lord Diplock which in 1972 recommended a trial by judge alone in such cases. Some offences must always be tried summarily and some always on indictment; others (called hybrid offences) may be tried either way. In addition, while some offences must always be tried in Diplock courts, others may at times be tried either in Diplock courts or under the normal procedures. We will now examine all these categories of offences in a little more detail. The differences between the procedures adopted in summary trials and in trials on indictment are explained more fully in 4.6 to 4.8; some special features of the emergency laws and Diplock courts are described in 4.9. A diagram summarising the criminal court system can be found at the end of 4.8 (Table 10).

Offences which must be tried summarily

These are relatively minor offences which have to be tried in a magistrates' court by a resident magistrate (an RM) sitting without a jury (see 1.5 and 4.6). They have all been made triable in this way by a statute, not by the common law, and for most of them proceedings must be begun within six months of the offence being committed. All the offences in this category are considered to be not serious enough to merit the extra time and expense required for a trial on indictment. A common example is careless driving, which is an offence under article 153 of the Road Traffic (NI) Order 1981.

Even some offences under the emergency laws have to be tried summarily, such as refusal to answer a soldier's questions concerning a recent explosion, which is an offence under section 23 of the Northern Ireland (Emergency Provisions) Act 1991.

Offences which must be tried on indictment

These are serious offences which have to be tried in the Crown Court by a judge and jury, though like all cases heard in the Crown Court they are originally dealt with at committal proceedings in a magistrates' court (see 4.7). There is usually no time limit on the commencement of proceedings. Murder, manslaughter, rape and robbery are all offences in this category. There are no circumstances which would justify trying adults for such offences at the level of a magistrates' court.

Offences which may be tried summarily or on indictment

For three kinds of crime there is a choice of proceedings. (The position in Northern Ireland differs from that in England, where significant changes were introduced by the Criminal Law Act 1977.)

(1) A handful of offences which are normally tried summarily can be tried on indictment if two conditions are satisfied. First, the offence must be one for which a person, if convicted, can be sent to prison for more than six months. Secondly, the defendant himself must ask to be tried on indictment. An example of this type of hybrid offence is the improper importation of goods, which is a crime under section 45 of the Customs and Excise Act 1952.

(2) Some offences which are normally tried on indictment can be tried summarily if the resident magistrate who first hears the case at the committal stage (see 4.7) considers that it is not a serious one and if the prosecution and defendant have no objections to a summary trial. The RM can take the initiative to try the case summarily at any stage of the proceedings, but he or she must first give the defendant 24 hours' written notice (or procure a waiver of this requirement). Examples of such offences are theft, indecent assault and assault occasioning actual bodily harm.

(3) In many cases the statute which creates a crime expressly states that it can be tried summarily or on indictment. It is then up to the prosecution, bearing in mind the seriousness of the particular case, to decide which form of trial to use. Examples of these "hybrid" offences are reckless driving, a crime under article 139 of the Road Traffic (NI) Order 1981 and criminal damage, a crime under the Criminal Damage (NI) Order 1977.

Scheduled offences under the emergency laws

These are the offences which are listed in Schedule 1 to the Northern Ireland (Emergency Provisions) Act 1991. They are the ones most commonly committed by terrorists in Northern Ireland and for which the United Kingdom Parliament has considered it necessary to establish emergency procedures. The distinction between scheduled and non-scheduled offences overlies that between summary and indictable offences; that is to say, not all of the scheduled offences will be tried on indictment. One or two of them are in the category of offences which must be tried summarily, and many of them, such as membership of a proscribed organisation or threats to destroy property, are in the category of hybrid offences and will be tried summarily if the conditions outlined in (3) above are fulfilled. But the procedures for dealing with the summary trial of scheduled offences do not differ to any great extent from the ordinary procedures in magistrates' courts (see 4.6). The main differences are that the Director of Public Prosecutions must consent to the prosecution, there are special arrangements for holding young persons in custody (whether on remand or after a finding of guilt), and after the trial of a scheduled offence a resident magistrate must, if finding the accused guilty, give a reasoned judgment, not just a decision. Trials on indictment of scheduled offences, on the other hand, are more extraordinary (see 4.9).

To complicate matters further, some of the offences listed in Schedule 1 to the 1991 Act may be "de-scheduled" if the Attorney-General certifies in a particular case that the offence is not to be treated as a scheduled offence. Amongst these offences are murder, manslaughter, assault occasioning actual bodily harm, assisting prisoners to escape, arson, kidnapping, intimidation and bomb hoaxes. They should be de-scheduled if no element of terrorism was involved in their commission, but if the Attorney-General refuses to de-schedule it is not possible to appeal against that decision to a higher authority or even, probably, to challenge it by way of judicial review proceedings (see 7.1). A few of the offences which cannot be de-scheduled are, however, to be treated as scheduled only in particular circumstances: robbery, for example, is a scheduled offence only where it is charged that an explosive, firearm, imitation firearm or weapon of offence was used in its commission. The offences which under all circumstances must be dealt with as scheduled offences include rioting, causing grievous bodily harm by explosives and withholding information about acts of terrorism.

In 1991 (a typical year) the Attorney-General considered applications from 531 accused persons to have a total of 1,045 offences de-scheduled; in the event 619 of these offences (59 per cent) were de-scheduled. However, it is not possible to tell from the published statistics how many of the accused persons involved did not therefore have to undergo trial in a Diplock court. This is because section 2(2) of the Northern Ireland (Emergency Provisions) Act 1991 requires an accused person to be tried by a Diplock court so long as just one of the charges against him or her remains scheduled.

4.2 The Level of Crime in Northern Ireland

Statistics on offences committed in Northern Ireland are made available through the annual reports of the Chief Constable of the Royal Ulster Constabulary. The Northern Ireland Court Service also distributes a booklet called *Northern Ireland Judicial Statistics* which deals mainly with the level of court business (criminal and civil) each year. The Northern Ireland Office publishes an annual *Commentary on Northern Ireland Crime Statistics*, where trends are identified and comparisons drawn. Also worth consulting is the *Law and Order* chapter of the *Northern Ireland Annual Abstract of Statistics*, published by the Policy Planning and Research Unit of the Government's Department of Finance and Personnel. At all stages it is necessary to bear in mind the distinctions between indictable and summary offences and between adult and juvenile defendants.

Table 6 reproduces parts of Tables 2.1 and 3.2 in the *Commentary on Northern Ireland Crime Statistics* for 1991 and Appendix 4 in the Chief Constable's 1992 Annual Report. It indicates the number of various types of indictable offences recorded during each of the last three years. Attempting, conspiring, inciting, aiding, abetting, causing or permitting an offence is generally included under the heading of the offence itself. It must be remembered that recorded crime is not the same thing as actual crime: for various reasons many offences never come to the notice of the police. Alongside the number of recorded crimes in Table 6 is the percentage which were "cleared" by the police. This means that they are offences for which a person has been charged, summonsed or cautioned, or which a court has taken into consideration when sentencing someone for other crimes, or which cannot be proceeded with because, although there is enough evidence of someone's guilt, the person is too young to be prosecuted or is dead.

Table 7 (which is drawn from Table 2.2 in the 1991 *Commentary on Northern Ireland Crime Statistics*) compares the rate of commission in 1991 of a variety of offences per 100,000 of the population in Northern Ireland, the Republic of Ireland and England and Wales. "Homicide" refers to murder, manslaughter and infanticide. The overall crime rate in Northern Ireland continues to be lower than in almost all other Western European nations, but unfortunately much of the crime is of a serious nature.

RECORDED CRIME AND CLEAR-UP RATES 1990-1992

	1990		1991		1992	
Crime	*Number recorded*	*% cleared*	*Number recorded*	*% cleared*	*Number recorded*	*% cleared*
All personal violence	3374	62	3955	62	4102	64
Murder	71	28	114	60	108	51
Attempted murder	225	28	360	27	311	34
All sexual offences	790	92	877	87	973	80
Rape	94	88	117	80	116	80
All burglary	14817	22	16563	22	17117	19
Burglary in a dwelling	6505	20	7206	18	7461	16
All robbery and hijacking	1630	18	1848	17	1851	19
Armed robbery	579	20	686	18	866	17
All theft	29267	36	32033	34	34256	32
Car theft	7042	31	8455	29	9376	28
Shoplifting	3984	89	3737	92	4549	85
Fraud and forgery	4177	74	4811	67	5486	61
All criminal damage	2191	36	2394	32	2502	33
Arson	691	22	805	20	860	22
Explosive offences	90	37	112	33	117	12
Offences under the Emergency Provisions Act	133	97	151	101*	103	97
Firearms offences	119	84	114	73	73	79
All indictable offences	57198	38	63492	36	67532	34

* Includes offences recorded in previous years

Table 6

CRIME RATES PER 100,000 PERSONS, 1991

	Northern Ireland	Republic of Ireland	England and Wales
Homicide	8	1	1
Rape	7	3	8
Robbery	116	58	89
Aggravated assault	240	40	372
Burglary	1039	941	2392
Theft	1480	1396	4278
Car theft	529	80	1143

Table 7

It can be seen from these two tables that approximately three-quarters of all recorded crime in Northern Ireland is either burglary or theft, though the rate of commission of these is two to three times less than in England and Wales. The clear-up rate for burglary is amongst the lowest for any crime, whilst that for shoplifting is amongst the highest. Across the board in Northern Ireland the clear-up rate rose from 19 per cent in 1982 to 45 per cent in 1988 but fell back to 34 per cent by 1992. It has never been as high as it was in 1969. When the Northern Ireland crime rate is compared with that of police force areas in England with a comparable population (*e.g.* Merseyside), it is clear that Northern Ireland has a lower crime rate than any of them, except for certain offences such as homicide, sexual offences and robbery.

Table 8 (compiled from figures in Chapter 4 of the 1991 *Commentary on Northern Ireland Crime Statistics*) provides details of the proceedings taken in the criminal courts in Northern Ireland between 1988 and 1991. Motoring offences have been excluded from the figures for both summary and indictable offences and have been given a separate entry because of their numerical significance. In all but one category of case around 90 per cent of the defendants were found guilty; only in Crown Court trials of juveniles for non-scheduled offences does the acquittal rate sometimes rise to around 20-25 per cent, though the numbers of defendants involved in such cases each year is always comparatively small. The overwhelming majority of defendants in criminal cases, whether adults or juveniles, are male and most plead guilty, thereby avoiding a full trial. In 1991, as in previous years, more than half of the

CRIMINAL PROCEEDINGS IN NORTHERN IRELAND, 1988-91

Numbers proceeded against

	1988	1989	1990	1991
Adults (aged 17 or over)				
Magistrates' courts				
Indictable offences	9291	8928	9525	9084
Summary offences	6872	5940	4998	4859
Motoring offences	29855	27320	28611	21392
Crown Court				
Scheduled offences	504	456	461	417
Non-scheduled offences	956	875	932	887
Juveniles (aged 10 to 16)				
Magistrates' courts				
Indictable offences	985	808	802	763
Summary offences	222	225	170	126
Motoring offences	110	88	100	72
Crown Court				
Scheduled offences	11	10	9	6
Non-scheduled offences	15	26	20	32

Table 8

persons convicted of crimes had previous convictions against their name; predictably, previous convictions are more likely to exist for persons convicted in the Crown Court than for those convicted in magistrates' courts and, in both types of court, for males when compared with females.

Table 9 gives a picture of the level of "terrorist" crime in Northern Ireland since 1969. The figures are from the annual reports of the Chief Constable of the RUC. A total of 3,059 people had died by the end of May 1993. The worst years have been 1971-76.

TERRORIST CRIME IN NORTHERN IRELAND, 1969-1992

Year	Deaths			Shootings	Bombs and incendiaries
	Police	Army	Civilians		
1969	1	0	12	73	10
1970	2	0	23	213	170
1971	11	48	115	1756	1515
1972	17	129	321	10628	1853
1973	13	66	171	5018	1520
1974	15	35	166	3206	1383
1975	11	20	216	1803	691
1976	23	29	245	1908	1228
1977	14	29	69	1081	1143
1978	10	21	50	755	748
1979	14	48	51	728	624
1980	9	17	50	642	402
1981	21	23	57	1142	578
1982	12	28	57	547	368
1983	18	15	44	424	410
1984	9	19	36	334	258
1985	23	6	25	237	251
1986	12	12	37	392	275
1987	16	11	66	674	393
1988	6	33	54	537	466
1989	9	14	39	566	427
1990	12	15	49	559	320
1991	6	13	75	499	604
1992	3	6	76	506	497
Totals	287	637	2,104	34,228	16,134

Table 9

4.3 Summonses and Arrests

Criminal proceedings are begun in one of three ways: by the issue of a summons, by the issue of a warrant of arrest, or by an arrest without a warrant. A sizeable proportion of persons appearing in court do so after having been originally arrested but then released and later summonsed. Being summonsed and being arrested are, however, quite distinct processes.

Summonses

If the police (or anyone else for that matter) believe that a person is guilty of a summary offence, or a not very serious indictable offence, they can give the details in a "complaint" to a Justice of the Peace or to a clerk of petty sessions. If the JP or clerk of petty sessions is satisfied that there is sufficient evidence to suspect the person of having committed the offence he or she will issue a summons giving details of the alleged offence and ordering that person to appear at a magistrates' court on a particular date to answer the complaint. If the offence allegedly committed is a summary one, a summons should not be issued more than six months after the date of its commission; if the offence is indictable, a summons can be issued at any time. The forms used as summonses are reproduced in Appendix 4.

The summons will usually be served by the police on the defendant (as the person being summonsed is called) a reasonable time before the case is to be heard in court. The summons will tell the defendant the nature of the complaint being made against him or her, but will not set out the evidence on which the police intend to rely. It is usually the only document which the defendant receives, besides perhaps a statement of his or her previous convictions and a copy of any written statements which the prosecution intends to use at the trial. The defendant must prepare a defence before appearing in court, though of course he or she may consult a solicitor and obtain legal representation. The cost of advice or representation may be allowed to the defendant under the legal aid schemes described in 3.3.

Arrests

In more serious cases, or where a magistrate is satisfied that a person suspected of a summary offence cannot for some reason be served with a summons, the police may arrest a person, that is, take him or her into custody. Arrests can lawfully be made in two different ways: either with a warrant or without. The latter are sometimes called summary arrests.

Arrests under warrant

Like a summons a warrant of arrest can be issued by a JP (but not a clerk of petty sessions) provided he or she is satisfied that there is reasonable evidence to suspect a named person of a serious offence. The complaint to the JP must, however, be in writing and substantiated on oath. The warrant is an order by the JP to the police to arrest the person named in the warrant and to take him or her before a court to answer the charges which may be brought.

A magistrate or judge has power to issue a warrant when a person who has been summonsed does not appear in court when ordered to. Such a warrant is known as a "bench warrant". Also, if a warrant is issued in one part of the United Kingdom (*e.g.* Northern Ireland) but is to be executed in another part (*e.g.* England), it is valid only if "backed" (*i.e.* indorsed) by a Justice of the Peace in the jurisdiction where it is to be executed. A similar rule applies when a warrant is issued for the extradition of a suspect from the Republic of Ireland. In such cases judges usually take great care to ensure that the letter of the law is meticulously complied with before ordering a person's further detention.

Arrests without a warrant

The law on summary arrests is now contained in the Police and Criminal Evidence (NI) Order 1989 (the PACE Order) which brought the law in Northern Ireland largely into line with that in England and Wales as laid down by the Police and Criminal Evidence Act 1984. In both legal systems there are special powers to deal with terrorist offences and in some respects these powers are more extensive in Northern Ireland than in Great Britain; some of their features are outlined in 4.9 below.

By article 26 of the PACE Order a police officer may arrest without a warrant in the following circumstances:

(1) where a person is in the act of committing or is about to commit what is called an "arrestable offence";

(2) where the officer has reasonable grounds for suspecting a person to be in the act of committing or to be about to commit an arrestable offence;

(3) where, provided that the officer has reasonable grounds for suspecting that an arrestable offence has been committed, the officer has reasonable grounds for suspecting a person to be guilty of that offence;

(4) where a person is guilty of having committed an arrestable offence which has actually been committed or is someone whom the officer has reasonable grounds for suspecting to be guilty of that offence.

The concept of "arrestable offence" is defined in the same article as meaning:

(a)   any offence for which the sentence is fixed by law (*e.g.* life imprisonment for murder);

(b)   any offence for which a person aged 21 or over may be sentenced to five years' imprisonment (this would embrace all crimes of theft, including shoplifting, as well as cases of criminal damage where the value of the   property destroyed or damage caused is more than £2,000);

(c)   the specific statutory offences listed in article 26(2) of the PACE Order (these include taking a motor vehicle without authority and going equipped for stealing).

There are two other categories of offence for which a person can be arrested without a warrant but which are not, strictly speaking, arrestable offences within the definition of article 26. These are the statutory offences listed in Schedule 2 to the PACE Order, which include breaking a personal protection order (see 5.2), illegal immigration, impersonation at a polling booth, riotous and disorderly behavior at marches and meetings, driving with excess alcohol and loitering and importuning by a prostitute. The police can also arrest for the common law (*i.e.* judge-made) offence of breach of the peace. The statutory offences often require particular conditions to be satisfied before the power of summary arrest can legitimately be exercised. For an arrest to occur for breach of the peace it is enough if harm is likely to be done to any person or to his or her property in his or her presence.

A police officer may also arrest without a warrant for a non-arrestable offence if it appears to him or her that service of a summons is impracticable or inappropriate because, for instance, the name of the person to be arrested cannot be readily ascertained by the constable. But it seems that the PACE Order has not preserved the power of the police in Great Britain to arrest a person there and return him or her to Northern Ireland for prosecution.

As far as the powers of private citizens to make arrests are concerned, article 26 of the PACE Order makes it clear that they are in two respects more limited than those of the police: (i) only if an arrestable offence has in fact been committed can a person arrest someone who is reasonably suspected of being guilty of the offence; (ii) a person has no power to arrest someone who is reasonably suspected of being about to commit an arrestable offence.

Persons who are arrested have four important rights. In the first place, they must be told at the time of their arrest why they are being arrested;

secondly, after their arrest they must be allowed access to a solicitor (although in certain circumstances access can be delayed for as long as 36 hours); thirdly, they can require a friend or relative to be informed of their arrest (again this can be delayed for up to 36 hours); fourthly, they must be released from custody as soon as it becomes apparent to the police that grounds for detaining them no longer exist.

If it appears to the police that it may be necessary to keep an arrested person in police detention for more than six hours, he or she must be taken to one of 20 "designated" police stations in Northern Ireland where "custody officers" will be responsible for their welfare. Detention without charge is permissible for 24 hours but this can be extended to 36 hours if the authority of a police superintendent is obtained and if the offence in question is a "serious" one: the PACE Order defines "serious" in terms of the loss or harm caused by the offence and lists some offences as always being in this category (*e.g.* rape or kidnapping). Detention beyond 36 hours is permissible only on the authority of a magistrates' court; it can be extended by that court up to 72 hours, and then again to 96 hours, but that is the absolute maximum.

Arrest and questioning

We cannot here go into all the complexities of the law on arrest and questioning, but the following general points should be noted. In several respects the provisions of the emergency laws are different (see 4.9).

Attendance at a police station

No person is under a legal obligation to accompany a police officer to a police station unless that person has been formally arrested (with or without a warrant). People who are simply "helping the police with their inquiries" are present at the police station of their own free will and must be allowed to leave if they want to (article 32 of the PACE Order).

Use of force

The police may use reasonable force to effect an arrest (article 88 of the PACE Order). The use of excessive force will make the arrest unlawful which, although not necessarily requiring the arrested person's immediate release, will justify a claim for compensation for assault.

Citizens' powers

Although ordinary citizens can arrest people under certain circumstances, they can detain them only if a breach of the peace would be likely. The persons should be taken to a police station as soon as possible, otherwise the arresting citizen may be committing the civil wrong of false imprisonment and may be sued for compensation.

Right to silence

The general rule is that no-one is legally obliged to volunteer information or to answer questions put by the police (or army). But by virtue of the Criminal Evidence (NI) Order 1988 this right to silence has been qualified in that prosecutors, judges and juries are now permitted to draw inferences about guilt from an accused's silence in the face of questioning. The inference alone cannot be enough to convict the accused, but it can "corroborate" (*i.e.* back up) other evidence implicating the accused in the alleged offence. It should also be noted that under road traffic legislation there is a duty to report certain accidents and under section 23 of the Northern Ireland (Emergency Provisions) Act 1991 there is a duty to answer certain police or army questions (see 4.9). It is also a criminal offence under section 5(1) of the Criminal Law Act (NI) 1967 to fail to give information about an arrestable offence committed by some other person.

Police cautions

Until December 1988 the questioning of persons by the police in Northern Ireland was regulated by the so-called Judges' Rules dating from 1976. These did not have the full force of law but they were meant to be adhered to in practice. Answers to questions asked in contravention of the Rules were still admissible as evidence in a court, subject to the judge's discretion to exclude them. As a consequence of the making of the Criminal Evidence (NI) Order 1988, which altered the law on a suspect's right to silence, the judges rescinded the 1976 Rules and to replace them the Secretary of State for Northern Ireland issued written guidance to the RUC Chief Constable. This guidance requires the police to caution a person being questioned in the following terms: "You do not have to say anything unless you wish to do so but I must warn you that if you fail to mention any fact which you rely on in your defence in court, your failure to take this opportunity to mention it may be treated in court as supporting any relevant evidence against you. If you do wish to say anything, what you say may be given in evidence."

Under the PACE Order, a Code of Practice has been issued dealing with the detention, treatment and questioning of persons by police officers, and there is soon to be a similar Code concerning questioning under the emergency laws. These Codes require the new caution to be given to all persons who are arrested but again, although a breach of the Codes will render a police officer liable to disciplinary proceedings, it will not of itself render the officer liable to criminal or civil proceedings and evidence obtained as a result of the breach will not automatically be declared inadmissible as evidence in later court proceedings brought against the victim of the breach.

Tape-recording of interviews

The PACE Order requires the Secretary of State to issue a Code of Practice governing the tape-recording of interviews. A draft of this Code is currently in existence for use during experimental tape-recording in selected stations. When tape-recording becomes standard practice it should help to eliminate disputes over whether a detained person was physically or verbally abused while being questioned as well as over the precise content of statements made by the detainee. At the moment there are no plans to introduce video-recording of interviews between the police and detainees.

Fingerprinting

Under the PACE Order fingerprints can be taken without the consent of the detained person if he or she has been arrested and if a police officer of at least the rank of superintendent gives written authorisation for them to be taken. If the detained person ceases to be a suspect, or if a decision is taken not to prosecute him or her, or if he or she is cleared of the offence, the fingerprints must be destroyed as soon as practicable (article 64).

Searches of detained persons

The PACE Order regulates in detail the searching of detained persons and distinguishes between intimate and non-intimate body searches. Intimate searches are physical examinations of body orifices. They can be carried out without consent only if there are grounds for believing that the person may have a concealed weapon or drug.

Taking samples

The PACE Order also distinguishes between the taking of intimate and non-intimate body samples. The former can be taken only with the person's consent; they include blood and urine samples. Non-intimate samples, such as hairs from the head or footprints, do not require the person's consent. In Northern Ireland, but not in England, saliva and mouth swabs are classified as non-intimate samples. Special rules apply to persons suspected of road traffic offences.

Confessions as evidence

If a person makes a statement confessing to a crime, this is admissible as evidence in a court only if, when challenged to do so, the prosecution prove beyond reasonable doubt that the confession was not obtained by oppression or in consequence of anything said or done which was likely to render it unreliable (article 74 of the PACE Order 1989). But even if a confession is declared inadmissible under this rule any facts discovered as a result of the confession *can* be admitted in evidence. Judges also have a discretion to refuse to consider any prosecution evidence which they feel "would have such an adverse effect on the fairness of the proceedings that the court ought not to admit it" (article 76 of the PACE Order).

Suing the police

A person who has been arrested unlawfully, or unlawfully treated while in detention, can bring a civil action for compensation against the police (see Chapter 5). The police (or indeed army) will be guilty of the civil wrongs (known as "torts") of false imprisonment and/or assault. But the wrongful police behaviour is not of itself a defence to a criminal charge brought against the victim of that behaviour: the person arrested can still be found guilty of an offence.

The Royal Commission on Criminal Justice

A Royal Commission on Criminal Justice was set up in 1991 in the wake of several much publicised miscarriages of justice such as the Birmingham Six and the Guildford Four. Unfortunately its remit extended only to the law in England and Wales and when the Commission reported in July 1993 none of its 352 recommendations were designed to address particular problems in the criminal justice system of Northern Ireland. The Northern Ireland Office has said, however, that it will look closely at whether any of the recommendations should be implemented in Northern Ireland; it has also issued its own discussion paper entitled *Crime and the Community*. Possible changes in the near future include the video-recording of all activities in a police station's custody area, allowing solicitors to have access to the tapes of police interviews with suspects which occur before the solicitors arrive at the station, giving the police a power to release suspects on bail subject to conditions and the laying down of statutory guidelines for the administering of official cautions to suspects whom it is decided not to prosecute.

It seems likely, moreover, that the Northern Ireland Office will in the near future set up a Criminal Justice Consultative Council, headed by a senior judge. Like the equivalent Council in England and Wales (in existence since January 1992) this will address strategic issues affecting the variety of agencies currently involved in running the criminal justice system, but will have no executive powers.

4.4. Bail and Remand

Usually a person arrested under warrant is held in custody pending a first appearance in court, but when issuing the warrant the Justice of the Peace may authorise the police to release the accused on bail once he or she has been arrested. This means releasing the accused in exchange for a promise to return to the police station, or to attend at a magistrates' court, on a certain day. This promise, or the money which may have to be forfeited if the promise is broken, is called a recognisance. Persons arrested with or without a warrant may also be released on what is called police bail. This is available when the police officer in charge of the station to which the arrested person is brought is satisfied that the offence charged is not of a serious nature and that the arrested person's release would not tend to defeat the ends of justice or cause injury or damage to any person.

When a person who has been charged (see 4.5) eventually appears in a magistrates' court, the prosecution or the defence may still not have fully prepared its case and the resident magistrate will then be asked to "adjourn" (*i.e.* postpone) the hearing. In such circumstances the RM also has to decide whether to release or to "remand" the accused, and, if the latter, whether to remand him or her in custody or on bail. In practice the views of the police are highly influential on these points. The factors which are meant to be taken into account include the character of the accused, the nature of the alleged offence and the strength of the evidence against the accused. Having considered such factors the court should grant bail if it is satisfied that the accused will not fail to turn up again at court, will not commit another offence, and will not try to obstruct the course of justice by, for example, putting pressure on witnesses. (The law in England, under the Bail Act 1976 as amended, is slightly different; see also 4.9.)

Remands in custody

Remands in custody cannot normally be for more than eight clear days, but they can be for 28 days in a case where the accused and the prosecution agree to this, or where the accused is already serving a prison sentence or is detained in a young offenders' centre. Before the end of each period of remand the defendant must again be brought before a court; he or she can then reapply for bail but this will usually be refused unless there has been a significant change of circumstances.

When a magistrate refuses bail the defendant can exercise a common law right to apply to a judge of the High Court for bail, but again there is great reluctance to overturn a magistrate's previous refusal. If the magistrate has awarded bail but at such a sum or on such conditions as to make it impossible for the defendant to accept release on those terms, the defendant can apply to the High Court to have the sum or conditions altered: excessive bail was made unlawful by the Bill of Rights 1689. In such circumstances the defendant can also apply for a writ of *habeas corpus*, which is a declaration that the continued detention of the accused is unlawful. *Habeas corpus* may nowadays also be available if access to a solicitor is denied or if a suspect is mistreated while detained. All applications to the High Court for *habeas corpus* are considered as civil, not criminal, proceedings. A person who has already been convicted can apply for bail to the court which is hearing an appeal in the case.

4.5 Charge and Prosecution

Being charged

When the police officer in charge of the police station believes that there is enough evidence to show that the suspected person has committed an offence the officer should either prefer a charge against that person or tell him or her that he or she may later be prosecuted for that offence (*e.g.* by the issue of a summons). At that time the accused should again be cautioned in the following terms: "You are charged with the offence(s) shown below. You do not have to say anything unless you wish to do so but I must warn you that if you fail to mention any fact which you rely on in your defence in court, your failure to take this opportunity to mention it may be treated in court as supporting any relevant evidence against you. If you do wish to say anything, what you say may be given in evidence". Questions relating to an offence should not be put to a person after he or she has been charged with committing it, unless the questions are necessary to prevent harm to some other person or to clear up an ambiguity in a previous answer. Before such extra questions are put the accused must once again be told of the "right" to remain silent.

Even a person who has not already been arrested can in this way be charged, or informed that he or she may be prosecuted, though if the police want to detain him or her in custody they should formally arrest the person immediately before notifying the charge.

If the police decide not to charge or prosecute a suspect he or she can instead be formally cautioned by a senior police officer and will not then have to appear in court. Such a caution will usually only be administered if the suspect has admitted guilt of an offence and if the police believe that the person's own interests as well as those of society can just as well be served by a formal caution as by forcing an appearance in court. If the police decide not to charge or formally caution the suspect, he or she should be released.

Being prosecuted

Once a person has been charged or summonsed for an offence the process of prosecution has begun. If at any stage it becomes clear that it is not going to be possible to prove the accused's guilt beyond reasonable doubt the charge should be dropped or ordered by a court to be withdrawn.

In Northern Ireland the Royal Ulster Constabulary acts as the prosecuting authority for many minor criminal offences. Its own officers will do all the paperwork and present the case in court. But the prosecution of major criminal offences and certain types of less serious cases is the responsibility of the Office of the Director of Public Prosecutions. This is an independent office created in 1972 as a further safeguard against unjustified prosecutions and to relieve the RUC of some of its workload. As explained in 1.5, the main function of the DPP is to consider any information brought to his notice with a view to initiating or continuing any criminal proceedings.

In all but minor cases then, when the police have completed their investigations into an offence, during which time the accused may have been remanded in custody or on bail (see 4.4) or may not have been charged at all, they will pass the investigation file to the DPP's Office. It will be considered by a member of that Office under the supervision of an Assistant Director, and a decision will be taken as to the offences, if any, for which the accused should be prosecuted. The DPP's Office itself cannot carry out more investigations into the case but it can ask the police to do so and it can consider information from sources other than the police if it is sent directly to the Office.

If the DPP's Office decides that no prosecution is justified a direction is issued to the RUC that no evidence should be offered against the accused and the charges must then be dropped. If the DPP's Office decides that a prosecution is justified it will direct which charges are to be pressed (usually these will be similar to those which may already have been preferred by the police) and (if a choice is available - see 4.1) whether the trial is to be summary or on indictment. If a trial on indictment is directed, the committal proceedings (see 4.7) will be arranged and conducted on the prosecution's side almost entirely by the DPP's Office. If the accused person is then committed for trial to the Crown Court the committal papers (including all the evidence submitted at the committal proceedings) and the police investigation files are sent by the DPP's Office to Crown Counsel. It is this barrister who will draw up the required form of indictment (see 4.8) and act as the chief representative of the prosecution in the trial on indictment. In less serious cases a junior barrister alone will be employed; in more serious cases he or she will be led by senior counsel. The DPP's Office will serve as the prosecuting solicitors in the case.

In theory there is not meant to be any bargaining between the prosecution and the defence as to the offences, if any, to which the accused should plead guilty. In practice it is acknowledged that such "plea bargaining" does occur (as it does quite openly in the United States), but the rule is maintained that a judge is not allowed to tell the accused, or a lawyer acting for the accused, that a plea of guilty will ensure a lighter sentence than conviction following a plea of not guilty. It is common knowledge, though, that a guilty plea will often lead to a sentence discount.

Private prosecutions

In addition to "public" prosecutions by the police and the DPP's Office, it is theoretically possible to bring a "private" prosecution. Any individual can pursue a private prosecution but legal aid is not available for the process and it is believed that to date only one such case has ever reached the Crown Court in Northern Ireland (where it failed). In Great Britain, however, there have recently been successful private prosecutions for manslaughter and rape.

The DPP has the power to take over or abort a private prosecution if he thinks fit to do so at any stage of the proceedings, and any prosecution, whether public or private, can be brought to an end by the Attorney-General entering what is called a *nolle prosequi* ("unwilling to proceed"). This has the effect of preventing further consideration of the charge against the accused in that particular trial but it does not operate as a formal acquittal, so in theory the accused could be prosecuted later for the same offence.

It must be remembered, of course, that whoever is called the prosecutor, the actual representations in court will in the vast majority of cases be made by solicitors or barristers engaged by the prosecutor. Many official bodies and private companies employ staff to detect and investigate offences; when they think that they have sufficient evidence against a suspect they pass the case to the police or the DPP's Office. This happens, for instance, in cases of shoplifting, where large stores employ detectives but suspected culprits are dealt with by the RUC. Other common examples are the so-called "departmental" prosecutions, though in England many of these are prosecuted entirely by employees of the government departments concerned. Examples commonly occurring in Northern Ireland are prosecutions instigated by the Department of Health and Social Services (for non-payment of national insurance contributions or making false claims for social security benefits), the Department of the Environment (for failure to license motor vehicles), the Department of Economic Development (for breaches of the Trade Descriptions Act 1968), the Inland Revenue (for non-payment of taxes), HM Customs and Excise (for failure to make VAT returns) and the National TV Licence Records Office (for non-payment of TV licence fees).

4.6 Summary Trial in a Magistrates' Court

Usually the official name for a magistrates' court is a court of petty sessions, that is, a court of summary jurisdiction which sits at regular specified times and is presided over by a resident magistrate (see 1.5). But a magistrates' court may also be constituted by a resident magistrate or JP sitting "out of petty sessions". Magistrates' courts deal with criminal cases in two different ways: they try persons accused of summary offences or indictable offences being dealt with summarily (see 4.1) and they undertake an initial examination of the case against persons accused of offences being tried on indictment. This latter sort of hearing is called "committal proceedings" because its object is to decide whether the defendant should be "committed" (*i.e.* sent) for trial on indictment in the Crown Court; it is discussed in the next section. In the present section we concentrate on summary trials.

The vast majority of all criminal offences dealt with in Northern Ireland (as in England and Wales) are tried summarily in magistrates' courts (see Table 8 in 4.2 for details). About two thirds of all the charges tried summarily are motoring offences. Even where the defendant has a choice between summary trial and trial on indictment (see 4.1), approximately three out of every four cases are dealt with summarily. Some 20-25 per cent of the charges dealt with by magistrates' courts each year are for indictable offences being tried summarily. Summary trial is quicker, less expensive and subject to less publicity - advantages which usually outweigh the fact that in a summary trial there is no jury and the defendant has no prior knowledge of the strength of the evidence to be tendered by the prosecution. Furthermore, if the defendant pleads guilty or is convicted, the sentence which the RM can impose is likely to be much less severe than the sentence which could be imposed by a judge in the Crown Court. If the case is one which is being tried summarily but which might have been tried on indictment, the RM can send the accused to the Crown Court for sentencing if he does not think that his own powers are sufficient in this regard, but this is a very rare occurrence.

Pleading

A criminal trial in a magistrates' court begins with the clerk of the court (the clerk of petty sessions) explaining to the defendant (if he or she is present) the details of the offence for which he or she has been summonsed or charged. If the offence is one for which the defendant can choose to be tried by a jury in the Crown Court the defendant must be there in person to indicate his or her choice to the magistrate. Similarly, if the case is one which the prosecution can claim to have tried by jury this claim must be made immediately. If the summary trial is to go ahead, the clerk of petty sessions will then ask whether the defendant wishes to plead guilty or not guilty.

If the defendant has been summonsed for an offence which must be tried summarily - but in no other situation - a plea of guilty can be entered by post. The defendant can then be tried without having to appear in court, and unless a custodial sentence is to be imposed he or she can even be sentenced while absent. A plea of not guilty cannot, technically, be accepted through the post, but if no plea of guilty is received it will be assumed that the accused is not admitting the offence. If the accused does not turn up in court on the day in question, a warrant can be issued for his or her arrest; there can even be a trial in the defendant's absence.

Procedure in a summary trial

If the defendant chooses to plead guilty, the prosecutor will outline the facts of the case to the resident magistrate and hand to him a list of the defendant's previous convictions, if any. After listening to defence arguments for leniency - "a plea in mitigation" - the magistrate will pronounce sentence.

If the defendant chooses to plead not guilty, the prosecutor will outline the facts and then call witnesses to give their evidence. This is called "evidence-in-chief". All witnesses give "sworn" evidence (*i.e.* on oath), except that under the proposed Criminal Justice (NI) Order 1993 all children under the age of 14 will give evidence unsworn and in some cases a video recording of an interview with a child involved in a case of violence may be admitted as the evidence-in-chief. The defendant or the defendant's lawyer can cross-examine any of the prosecution witnesses (except child witnesses in some cases of violence).

At the end of the prosecution case the defendant can "apply for a direction", that is, submit that he or she ought to be acquitted because the prosecution has failed to produce any evidence to establish an essential element of the offence or because the evidence adduced is so weak that no reasonable jury (if one had been involved) would convict the accused. If the RM grants the direction, that is the end of the case and the defendant is free to go. He or she is not, however, formally acquitted, and so may be prosecuted later for the same offence. If the application is rejected, the defence can either rest its case on that point or go on to call its own witnesses including, usually, the defendant.

The defendant no longer has the right to make an unsworn statement from the dock, a right taken away by the Police and Criminal Evidence (NI) Order 1989. By virtue of the Criminal Evidence (NI) Order 1988 an accused person must indicate at the start of his or her defence that he or she intends to give evidence or, if this is not done, the defendant must be told that he or she will be called upon to give evidence for the defence. If the defendant then refuses to testify or without good cause refuses to answer any question, the court or jury may use this as corroborative evidence against the accused.

The prosecution can cross-examine all the defence witnesses (including of course the defendant) but if it wants to introduce any new evidence to contradict anything proved or said on behalf of the defence it must first ask the magistrate's permission to do so. With the consent of the other side either party to the proceedings can also submit written statements made by any person; if necessary, the maker of the statement can be called to give oral evidence to supplement what is related in the written statement. When all the evidence has been given, the defence may make a final address to the magistrate outlining its arguments.

Criminal proceedings (whether in magistrates' courts, the Crown Court or appeal courts) are "adversarial" in nature. This means that each side is engaged in a battle against the other with the magistrate or judge acting as a neutral umpire. In continental Europe a much more investigative (or "inquisitorial") function is given to the judge.

The magistrate's decision and sentencing powers

The RM may give a decision on the spot or take a few hours or days to make up his mind. If he decides that the defendant is guilty he considers the defendant's previous convictions, if any, and listens to a plea in mitigation by the defence before passing sentence. The defendant may also ask for other offences which he concedes he committed to be "taken into consideration" (TICs). To await reports, or to see how the defendant behaves in the meantime, the RM can defer sentence for up to six months. Generally speaking the most serious punishment which a magistrate has power to impose is a fine of £2,000 or six months in prison, or both, though if the offence is an indictable one being tried summarily (see 4.1) the maximum prison sentence is 12 months, and this may extend to 18 months if consecutive terms of imprisonment are imposed for more than one indictable offence. Prison sentences may be suspended for between one and three years (only two years in England), which means that they may be "activated" only if the convicted person commits another imprisonable offence within that period. In 1992, 3,890 adults were sentenced to immediate imprisonment by magistrates' courts (over four times the number sentenced in this way in the Crown Court). Periods spent on remand in custody are counted as part of a sentence imposed later.

The commonest punishment in magistrates' courts is a fine. In 1991 it was imposed in 31 per cent of the cases where indictable offences were tried summarily, in 63 per cent of the non-motoring summary cases and in 94 per cent of the summary motoring cases. Since 1984 there have been five scales for fines, the limits of these being set by secondary legislation from time to time. Under the proposed Criminal Justice (NI) Order 1993 the limits are to rise to £200 for Scale 1, £500 for Scale 2, £1,000 for Scale 3, £2,500 for Scale 4 and £5,000 for Scale 5. The maximum fine which a magistrates' court can impose on a child aged 10 to 13 is (under the proposed Order) £250; for a young person aged 14 to 16 the maximm is £1,000. If legislation says that a person can be fined "the prescribed sum" this means £5,000 unless a different amount is specified. Community service orders are also becoming popular with magistrates: about 500 are issued each year.

Under the Criminal Justice (NI) Order 1980 magistrates have the power, rarely exercised, to make compensation and restitution orders against a convicted person. These require a person to pay compensation for any personal injury, loss or damage resulting from any offence for which the court has convicted that person or from any other offence which the court took into consideration when sentencing him or her. The maximum which can be ordered to be paid in respect of any one offence is currently £2,000 and losses arising out of a road accident, except where the vehicle has been stolen, are excluded from the scheme. Sums paid are deducted from any award of damages later obtained by the victim of the crime in civil proceedings but are additional to any sum ordered to be paid by way of a fine. Under the Theft Act (NI) 1969 any property which has been stolen, or its proceeds, can be ordered to be restored by the defendant to the victim of the theft and under the 1980 Order property used for the purposes of crime can be ordered to be forfeited. Under the proposed Criminal Justice (NI) Order 1993 the maximum amount which a magistrates' court can order to be paid in compensation is to be increased to £5,000 and the restrictions on making a compensation order after a traffic accident are to be removed. In many cases magistrates will have to give reasons for *not* making a compensation order.

Compensation, restitution and forfeiture orders, as well as fines, are all enforceable in the same way, namely by issuing a warrant of distress or a warrant of commitment to prison. Distress is the process whereby property belonging to the defendant is seized and sold in order to pay the sums owing. Imprisonment is a last resort, but one which is quite often needed. The duration of the imprisonment will depend on the amount of the sums owing. Under the proposed Criminal Justice (NI) Order 1993 a person fined by a magistrates' court can, for example, be sent to prison for seven days if the unpaid fine is up to £200, or 28 days if the unpaid fine is between £500 and £1,000, or three months if the unpaid fine is between £2,500 and £5,000. As pointed out in 1.6, more than half the people sent to prison in Northern Ireland receive that punishment because they have failed to pay a court fine.

It was partly to avoid fines which defendants could not afford to pay that, in England and Wales, the Criminal Justice Act 1991 created the system of "unit fines". This was meant to ensure that a fine would be related to a defendant's own personal financial circumstances. But the system was so severely criticised by magistrates and others in England and Wales that in 1993 the Home Secretary announced that it was to be replaced. In Northern Ireland the magistrates' court in Newtownards made experimental use of a unit fine system for the first six months of 1992; it will probably not now be introduced province-wide.

Two further types of "sentence" which a magistrate might impose are those for the conditional discharge or absolute discharge of the convicted person. The former is like a probation order: the convicted person is released without punishment but may be sentenced at a later date if he or she breaks the conditions of the discharge. An absolute discharge means no punishment at all: it is not an acquittal, however, so technically the defendant still stands convicted of the offence.

It is worth noting at this point that if a person serves time in prison, after having been convicted of an offence, and it is later shown that he or she did not in fact commit the alleged offence, there may then be the possibility of claiming compensation from the state. The Criminal Justice Act 1988 sets up a limited statutory scheme for the whole of the United Kingdom. It applies whenever a convicted person is pardoned or the conviction is quashed after an appeal beyond the normal time limit for appealing. A specially appointed assessor decides how much compensation should be paid and usually this takes months if not years to calculate.

For further details on a magistrate's sentencing powers in cases involving juveniles, see 6.1.

Appeals by the defendant

When a criminal case is tried summarily and the defendant is convicted, as the vast majority of them are, the defendant has the right to appeal within 14 days. A notice of appeal must be given to the prosecution and a copy of the notice to the clerk of petty sessions of the court where the defendant was convicted. (Appeals are not the same as applications for judicial review, for which see 7.1.)

The defendant may wish to appeal against conviction, sentence, or both - though obviously there cannot be an appeal against conviction if the defendant pleaded guilty at the trial. If the defendant pleaded not guilty at the trial and wishes to appeal against conviction, or if (whether or not he or she pleaded guilty) the defendant wishes to appeal against sentence, there is a choice of two procedures: he or she can appeal to a county court, or by way of case stated to the Court of Appeal.

Appeals to a county court

An appeal to a county court will be heard by the county court judge who sits for the area in which the magistrates' court itself sits. If it is against conviction the appeal takes the form of a complete rehearing of the case: witnesses are called again and all the written statements are reconsidered. The facts, in other words, have to be re-established. The county court judge (sitting without a jury) can reverse the conviction or confirm it - even on grounds different from those given by the magistrate. In these proceedings the judge can also increase or decrease the accused's sentence, even though this was not specifically appealed against. If the appeal to the county court is only against sentence, all that is required is a review of the accused's previous convictions, if any, and a reconsideration of his or her plea in mitigation. In 1992 the county courts disposed of 3,629 appeals from magistrates' courts in criminal cases; 86 per cent of these were against sentence only. In 2,144 cases (59 per cent) the sentence was varied on appeal but in only 118 cases (3.25 per cent) was the conviction itself reversed.

Appeals to the Court of Appeal

An appeal by way of case stated to the Court of Appeal can be used only where there is a disputed point of law. If it is the facts which are disputed, the defendant must appeal to a county court. Points of law can be raised in appeals to a county court as well as in appeals by way of case stated to the Court of Appeal, but the latter procedure *must* be used if only a point of law is involved. Applying this distinction between points of law and points of fact to appeals against sentence, it means that a complaint that the magistrate had, for example, no power to order disqualification from driving for the offence which the accused has committed would be an appeal on a point of law, whereas a complaint that the magistrate disqualified the accused for too long a period would be considered as an appeal on a point of fact.

Under the procedure by way of case stated, the resident magistrate is asked by the side appealing (the appellant) to pose a question to the Court of Appeal for its opinion on what the law is on a particular point. The Court of Appeal answers the question and on the basis of that answer affirms, reverses or varies the decision appealed from. It may also consider any points of law not considered in the court below or give directions on what the law is and remit the case to the lower court for a further hearing. But it may not increase the defendant's sentence, least of all in cases where the appeal was only against conviction. All that the Court of Appeal can do to increase a sentence is decide to discount a period spent in custody pending the appeal. There are only a few of these cases stated each year.

Appeals by the prosecution

All the appeal procedures so far considered have been concerned with appeals by the defendant. The prosecution has fewer rights of appeal. If the defendant is acquitted by a magistrates' court, or if a conviction is reversed by the county court, the prosecution cannot appeal against those decisions on the ground that the facts were wrongly found by the resident magistrate or the county court judge. The only avenue open to the prosecution is to appeal directly to the Court of Appeal on a point of law by way of case stated. Even then the appeal can only be against an acquittal, not against too lenient a sentence.

Further appeals

If the accused has appealed to a county court the main way in which the case can be taken further is by either side stating a case from that court to the Court of Appeal. But if the county court acquits a defendant in an appeal, the prosecution may get the original conviction restored if it has grounds for judicial review proceedings (see 7.1).

All decisions of the Court of Appeal are in turn appealable to the House of Lords, the highest court in the land. Before this can happen, however, the permission (or "leave") either of the Court of Appeal or of the House of Lords must be granted, and this leave will not be obtained unless two conditions are satisfied: the Court of Appeal must certify that a point of law of general public importance is involved, and it must appear to the Court of Appeal or the House of Lords that the point is one which ought to be considered by the latter. All appeals to the House of Lords are therefore on points of law only. Understandably, it is very rare for a case which has been tried summarily in Northern Ireland's magistrates' courts to travel as far as the House of Lords, but two examples are *McEldowney* v *Forde* (1971) (see 2.3), and *Seay* v *Eastwood* (1976).

4.7 Committal Proceedings in a Magistrates' Court

The other type of criminal case which a magistrates' court deals with is committal proceedings. These are held for persons charged with indictable offences which are not triable summarily or which, although triable summarily, the defendant or prosecution has elected to have tried on indictment (see 4.1). The purpose of committal proceedings is to decide if there is a *prima facie* case (*i.e.* a case "on the face of it") for the accused to answer. A finding that there is simply means that the defendant is then committed for trial to the Crown Court: it does not imply any presumption that the accused is guilty.

Committal proceedings take the form of either a preliminary investigation (a PI), where witnesses attend and give their evidence by word of mouth on oath in court, or a preliminary enquiry (a PE), where copies of witnesses' written statements are simply presented to the court and, if either side so requests, read out aloud. When evidence is given by word of mouth on oath it is written down in court and is then called a deposition. Witnesses are then "bound over" to attend and give evidence if required at the main trial. In all cases the defendant can opt for either form of proceeding, though in practice he or she rarely objects to a preliminary enquiry. Occasionally there can be a mixture of both types of committal proceedings - a preliminary enquiry where the defendant nevertheless insists that the evidence of certain witnesses be taken down by way of deposition.

In the committal proceedings the prosecution does not have to reveal all its evidence and the accused will usually reserve his or her defence by saying nothing at all but trying to assess the strength of the prosecution's case by cross-examining some of the Crown's witnesses. The only situation in which a defendant is obliged to disclose any part of his or her defence in advance of the main trial is where he or she intends to rely on an "alibi", that is, a defence that the defendant was somewhere else at the time the offence was committed: if the defendant is committed for trial, the particulars of such a defence must be given to the prosecution within seven days of the end of the committal proceedings, provided that the prosecution has told the defendant of the need for this period of notice.

Discharging the accused

If the resident magistrate considers that there is not enough evidence to require the accused to answer the charge brought by the prosecution, he will not commit the accused for trial. This is called "discharging" the accused or "refusing an information". The defendant is then free to go, though because there has not been a formal acquittal he or she may be charged again with the same offence at a later date. The prosecution cannot appeal against a discharge but it can apply to a judge of the Court of Appeal, High Court or Crown Court for permission to present an indictment notwithstanding the absence of any committal by a magistrates' court.

This is known as a "voluntary" indictment and is very rare in Northern Ireland. It has been used in cases where no committal proceedings at all have taken place (because, for example, the chief prosecution witness was an alleged accomplice of the defendant and the prosecution wished to protect him before the main trial), but it may also be used where there have been committal proceedings and the magistrate has discharged the defendant. In either case, it is then a matter for the judge to decide whether or not there is a *prima facie* case against the defendant and, if so, to permit a "voluntary" indictment to be presented to an appropriate Crown Court. Under the proposed Criminal Justice (NI) Order 1993 committal proceeedings can be by-passed in cases involving violence, sex or cruelty where children have been victims or witnesses; the Director of Public Prosecutions will serve a "notice of transfer" on the magistrates' court and the case will then be proceeeded with without delay in the Crown Court.

Reviews of committals

If a resident magistrate does commit the accused for trial the accused or his or her barrister can, before arraignment in the Crown Court (see 4.8), apply to the trial judge to have the committal reviewed or the proposed venue changed. Under this procedure, if the judge is satisfied that the evidence does not disclose a sufficient case to justify trying the accused for an indictable offence, he can order an entry of "No Bill" in the Crown Court book, thereby discharging the accused without requiring any further answer from him or her. From the accused's point of view this is not as good as a formal acquittal because he or she can still be indicted again in the future on the same facts or evidence. The same applies if the accused successfully brings judicial review proceedings on account of some irregularity at the committal hearing. If the review application is unsuccessful the trial will proceed.

4.8 Trial on Indictment in the Crown Court

Trial on indictment involves two distinct court stages. There must, first, be committal proceedings in a magistrates' court or leave given for the presentation of a voluntary indictment (see 4.7). There is then the main trial in the Crown Court, which is the stage described in this section.

When a person has been committed by a magistrates' court for trial, it is the responsibility of the Office of the Director of Public Prosecutions (see 1.5 and 4.5) to prepare a formal document known as "the form of indictment", sometimes referred to inaccurately as "the bill of indictment". This contains details of the specific charge or charges against the accused arising out of the committal proceedings (see the blank example in Appendix 4). Each offence charged in the indictment is known as a "count", and each count must contain a statement of the offence and particulars indicating the person indicted, the person (if any) injured, and the necessary ingredients of the offence. A copy of the indictment must be given to the defendant to let him or her know precisely for what offences he or she is being tried. The case is then ready to proceed to trial at the sitting of the Crown Court identified by the magistrate who committed the accused. The trial should take place no sooner than eight days and no later than 14 weeks (eight weeks in England) after the date of the accused's committal. During 1992 the average delay between committal and trial was seven weeks (but 10 weeks in Diplock cases; see 4.9)

The Crown Court

The Crown Court was created as a branch of the Supreme Court of Judicature of Northern Ireland in April 1979 (see 1.3). It sits at nine different places in the province and often there are several sittings occurring at the same time. The court can be presided over by the Lord Chief Justice, a judge of the Court of Appeal, a High Court judge or a county court judge, but the Lord Chancellor has directed that some offences (*e.g.* murder) must be tried by at least a judge of the High Court. In 1992 the Crown Court disposed of 921 cases, which involved 1,325 defendants; 811 defendants (61 per cent) pleaded guilty to all charges against them, which meant that only 190 cases were actually tried. Only

162 defendants (12 per cent) were acquitted of all charges by the Crown Court judge.

In all cases there will be a jury of 12 persons, except when the offence being dealt with is a scheduled offence (*i.e.* one liable to be committed by terrorists), which is tried by a judge sitting alone (see 4.9). The trial of non-scheduled offences takes place at the sitting of the Crown Court determined by the magistrate who committed the accused, though this venue can be altered by a ruling of the Crown Court itself. Usually, non-scheduled offences are tried at the Crown Court acting for the county court division in which the offence is alleged to have been committed, but a different venue can be arranged on account of special circumstances such as the convenience of witnesses, security reasons or the need to speed up the proceedings.

Arraignment

Proceedings in a Crown Court commence with the "arraignment" of the accused, that is, with the court clerk reading the indictment to the accused and asking the accused personally how he or she pleads on each count. If the accused pleads guilty to all counts there will be no need for a jury to be sworn: the prosecution will outline the facts and the judge will pass sentence after considering the accused's previous convictions, if any, and any plea in mitigation by his or her barrister. If the accused pleads not guilty to any count, and if the offence is not a scheduled offence, a jury must be sworn from the panel already summoned to the Court for that day. Technically the trial begins only with the swearing of the jury.

Juries

Under the Juries (NI) Order 1974 jurors are selected from "Area Jurors Lists" by the Juries Officer of each county court division. These lists are drawn up annually from registers prepared by the Chief Electoral Officer for Northern Ireland. Every registered elector aged between 18 and 70 is qualified for inclusion, though certain individuals (persons currently or recently imprisoned) are disqualified from serving and others (by reason of their jobs, for example, lawyers, ministers of religion, doctors, nurses and chemists) are exempt. The Juries Officer selects a jury to serve not just for one particular trial but for all the hearings in a particular court or place over a prescribed period of time. To keep the size of a jury panel manageable the judge of any court may divide the selected jurors into two or more sections and may excuse from attendance jurors whose names appear in any one or more of those sections.

People called for jury service are paid allowances, but these may not fully compensate them for expenses incurred. From August 1993 the financial loss allowance is £43.90 per day if more than four hours are taken up (though this can be doubled if the juror is required to attend for longer than 10 days), the daily subsistence allowance is £4.25 (for periods between five hours and 10 hours), and the basic allowance for travelling by car to and from the court is 23p per mile.

When the members of a jury panel are being "empanelled", or sworn in to serve a particular trial, a defendant can, without giving reasons, object to any 12 of them. This is called the right to a peremptory challenge and those members must then stand down. Such challenges were abolished in England and Wales by the Criminal Justice Act 1988 but are still possible in Northern Ireland. After 12 peremptory challenges the defendant can challenge would-be jurors only if reasons are given, and the jurors will have to stand down only if the judge considers the reasons to be satisfactory. The prosecution has no right of peremptory challenge but can require any would-be juror to "stand by", that is, to wait on one side until the rest of the jury group has been gone through to see if a full jury can be sworn. If by then a full jury has not been sworn the prosecution can prevent a juror who has been stood by from serving only if it provides the judge with good reasons why this should be so. Even if the defence or the prosecution do not object to a particular juror, the judge himself may excuse jurors who have already participated in a trial of an exceptionally exacting nature and a juror may always apply to be excused on the grounds of hardship or ill-health. In England and Wales the Attorney-General has laid down guidelines for what amounts to acceptable "jury-vetting" by either side in particularly sensitive trials. In Northern Ireland, juries would tend not to be involved in such trials anyway.

Procedure in a trial on indictment

Once a jury has been empanelled for the case in hand - and it must be stressed that no jury will be sworn in trials on indictment of scheduled offences (see 4.9) - it is the duty of the prosecution to prove beyond a reasonable doubt that the defendant committed the offence. Only in exceptional cases is there any burden on the defendant to prove his or her innocence: for instance, when he or she claims to be unfit to plead, or to be of impaired mental responsibility, these matters must be proved by the defendant "on the balance of probabilities". Examination, cross-examination and re-examination of witnesses take place as in a magistrates' court, but will usually be conducted in more detail and with the utmost attention to the law's many rules of evidence. All witnesses may remain in court during the hearing of evidence, unless a special application to exclude some of them is granted by the judge. This differs from the practice in England, where, more sensibly, witnesses remain outside the courtroom during the taking of other evidence. Proving the accused's guilt beyond a reasonable doubt means that the jury has to believe that the evidence produced shows that the accused committed the offence and that there is no real doubt about that.

Trials within a trial

If at any stage of the trial either side wishes to produce evidence which may not, according to the strict rules of evidence, be admissible, the judge will ask the jury to withdraw while he himself hears the evidence and decides whether or not it is admissible. Technically it is for the defendant to decide whether the jury should be present or not, but in practice the judge controls this. This is an example of what is called a "*voir dire*" hearing, or a trial within a trial. If the judge decides that the evidence is admissible the jury will be recalled and the trial will proceed with the evidence being presented. If the judge decides that the evidence is not admissible the jury will be recalled and the trial will proceed with no mention being made of the inadmissible evidence. In this way the jury is protected from hearing evidence which for one reason or another the law considers to be improper.

Hearsay evidence, which is evidence given by A about what B said, rather than direct evidence given by B, is generally inadmissible because it tends to be inaccurate. Another commonly recurring example of questionable evidence is a confession extracted by dubious methods. As explained in 4.3, in trials of non-scheduled offences such a confession is inadmissible if it may have been obtained by oppression or as a result of anything said or done which was likely to render it unreliable. The defendant's previous convictions will not be made known to the jury unless the prosecution is allowed to refer to them because the precise manner in which the earlier offences were committed bears a striking resemblance to the offence now alleged against the accused.

The verdict in trials on indictment

After all the evidence in a Crown Court trial has been presented, the lawyers representing prosecution and defence make final speeches summarising their case. The judge must sum up the whole case for the jury by drawing its attention to the rival versions of the relevant facts and directing it on the relevant law to be applied to those facts. In long trials the judge's summing-up may last for days.

The jury's verdict should be unanimous, but if it has been deliberating for at least two hours and cannot come to a unanimous decision, the jury is allowed to return a majority verdict by 11 to 1 or 10 to 2 (but not by 9 to 3 or some smaller majority). If the jury finds it impossible even to arrive at a majority verdict the judge may discharge that jury and order a new trial before a different jury. If the jury's verdict is "not guilty" the accused must be acquitted and cannot be held in custody or tried again in connection with the offence charged. If charged again for the same offence the accused is said to have the defence of "*autrefois acquit*" (*i.e.* formerly acquitted) and to be protected by the principle which forbids a person being subjected to "double jeopardy". If the verdict is "guilty", the judge will pass sentence. Before doing so the judge will consider the defendant's previous convictions, if any, and may be addressed by the defence on points of mitigation as well as being assisted by reports from probation officers, welfare officers, doctors, etc.

Sentencing in the Crown Court

The sentencing powers of the Crown Court embrace all of those exercisable by resident magistrates (see 4.6) but include as well other powers conferred by the common law and statutes. The commonest sentence is immediate imprisonment, which, if we include detention in a young offenders' centre (see 6.1), was imposed in 52 per cent of Crown Court cases in 1991 (631 out of 1,209). In a further 24 per cent of cases (238) a suspended prison or detention sentence was given. A suspended sentence must not exceed seven years and the period of suspension must be between one and five years; the sentence *may* be activated if the offender commits another imprisonable offence during the period of suspension. Until recently Crown Court judges in Northern Ireland (like their counterparts in the Republic of Ireland, but not in Great Britain) also exercised a self-professed power to impose what were known as "recorded" sentences. This allowed a prison term of *any* length to be suspended for *any* period and to be activated automatically if there was *any* breach of the suspension. However the Treatment of Offenders (NI) Order 1989 abolished this power. It still exists in the Republic of Ireland.

The precise sentence which a convicted person will receive will depend on a number of factors. Some of these relate to the nature of what the accused actually did at the time of or immediately after the crime - whether it was particularly brutal, malicious or dishonest, whether he or she acted with premeditation, whether there was a degree of co-operation with the police investigation, etc - while others relate to the kind of person the defendant is - whether he or she has an otherwise unblemished record, is genuinely remorseful, is easily influenced by others, is mentally unstable, etc. Each crime is subject to a maximum possible sentence, but not to any minimum. A judge will know from experience what is the normal "tariff" for a certain kind of offence and in all cases will adjust this in the light of the factors referred to above. An important influence might be the wish to deter others from perpetrating similar crimes. It is notoriously difficult to compare sentences in different cases because the precise factors to be taken into account are unique to each case.

There are many offences for which the maximum punishment laid down by statute is life imprisonment, but the only offences for which that sentence *must* be imposed are murder and torture. The death penalty was to all intents and purposes abolished in Northern Ireland in 1973 (the last execution having taken place in 1964), though, as in England, hanging still exists for one or two obscure offences (including high treason). When judges impose life sentences they are at liberty to state that in their view the accused should serve at least a certain number of years in jail before being released. This recommendation will be respected by the Secretary of State (who has the responsibility for the continued detention of prisoners) but is not binding on him. "Lifers", as such prisoners are called, are in any event subject to a special review system which may lead to their release after, say, 12 or 15 years (see 1.6). Their release can then only be "on licence": they are liable to be recalled to prison at any time; in practice the vast majority of persons released on licence in this way do not re-offend.

People who are under 17 years of age when they commit a serious crime cannot be sentenced to life imprisonment. Instead they must be detained "at the Secretary of State's pleasure". This means that, like lifers, they do not have a definite release date, but unlike lifers they do not benefit from a formalised review system for assessing their suitability for release. There are about a dozen so-called SoSP's in Northern Ireland at the time of writing.

In 1991 only 2.5 per cent of all Crown Court defendants were fined, 7 per cent were given community service orders and 9 per cent probation orders. Every offence tried on indictment can carry an unlimited fine as well as, or instead of, a prison sentence (Criminal Law Act (NI) 1967, section 7(3)), but in practice the power to fine is not frequently exercised. If a fine is unpaid a sentence of imprisonment can be imposed (under the Criminal Justice Act (NI) 1945, section 35, as amended by the proposed Criminal Justice (NI) Order 1993); an unpaid fine between £5,000 and £10,000, for example, can lead to imprisonment of up to six months.

Appeals by the defendant

When a criminal case is tried on indictment the accused person can appeal against conviction on a point of law alone without obtaining the permission of any court. If he or she wishes to appeal against the conviction on a question of fact alone, or on a question of mixed law and fact, the permission, or "leave", of either the Crown Court judge or the Court of Appeal is required. As a general principle appeal courts are very reluctant to interfere with the findings of fact made by a lower court, though it can often be a nice question whether a disputed point is indeed one of pure fact, or of mixed law and fact, rather than one of pure law. If a convicted person wishes to appeal only against sentence again the leave of the Court of Appeal is required.

There is also a power vested in the Secretary of State for Northern Ireland (under section 14 of the Criminal Appeal (NI) Act 1980) to refer a conviction, or a decision of not guilty on the ground of insanity, to the Court of Appeal either as a proper appeal or for the Court's opinion on a point of law. There is no case stated procedure (see 4.6) for trials on indictment, nor is the judicial review procedure (see 7.1) available, because it lies only in respect of proceedings in tribunals or "inferior" courts (*i.e.* magistrates' courts and county courts). This power to refer a case to the Court of Appeal may be exercised (as in the *UDR Four* case in 1992) even though there has already been an unsuccessful appeal by the defendants in the case. Its exercise is not wholly dependent on there being new evidence to consider.

Appeals by the prosecution

As far as the prosecution is concerned there is no right of appeal against the acquittal of a defendant who has been tried on indictment. All that can be done is for the Attorney-General (under section 15 of the Criminal Appeal (NI) Act 1980) to refer a point of law to the Court of Appeal for its opinion. This is only a reference and not an appeal as such. Even if the Court of Appeal considers that the trial judge made an error of law which resulted in an undeserved acquittal, the acquittal still stands; once a person has been formally acquitted he or she cannot be tried again for the same offence. The Court of Appeal's opinion will guide the prosecution in the trials of other defendants in the future.

The Criminal Justice Act 1988 (section 36) has also conferred on the Attorney-General in both Northern Ireland and England and Wales the power to refer a case to the Court of Appeal if he believes that the sentence imposed by the Crown Court was "unduly lenient". This provision was provoked by highly publicised cases in England where violent sex offenders were given comparatively light sentences by trial judges. In 1992 the Attorney-General successfully applied to the Northern Ireland Court of Appeal to have increased the sentence originally given in the Crown Court to a woman convicted of the manslaughter of her lover's wife (*R* v *Christie*).

The powers of the Court of Appeal

Pending the determination of an appeal the Court of Appeal can permit the defendant to be released on bail, though this rarely occurs. When it has heard the defendant's appeal against conviction the Court of Appeal can take one of five courses of action. It may:

(1) straightforwardly dismiss the appeal;
(2) dismiss the appeal by "exercising the proviso" (*i.e.* the proviso in section 2(1) of the Criminal Appeal (NI) Act 1980); this means acknowledging that an error occurred at the trial but deciding that no miscarriage of justice has ensued because a reasonable jury would still, despite the error, inevitably have convicted;
(3) allow the appeal but substitute a verdict of guilty of one or more offences;
(4) allow the appeal but order a retrial because, for example, new evidence has come to light since the first trial or (a ground for retrial not existing in England) because there has been a wrong decision on a question of law or a material irregularity in the course of the trial;
(5) allow the appeal and acquit the defendant.

If it adopts any of the first three courses the Court of Appeal may also (even on its own initiative) reduce, vary or even increase the appellant's sentence. It can do likewise in any appeals against sentence.

In 1992, 136 appeals in criminal cases were dealt with by the Court of Appeal - 63 of these were appeals by defendants in ordinary cases, 66 by defendants in "Diplock" cases (see 4.9), four were references by the

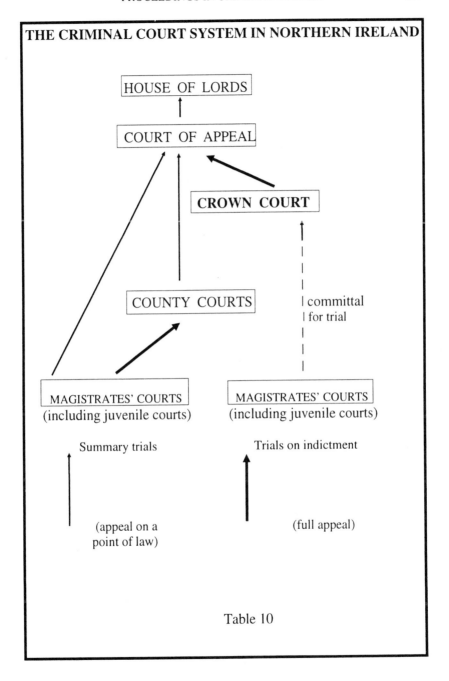

THE CRIMINAL COURT SYSTEM IN NORTHERN IRELAND

HOUSE OF LORDS

COURT OF APPEAL

CROWN COURT

COUNTY COURTS

committal
for trial

MAGISTRATES' COURTS
(including juvenile courts)

MAGISTRATES' COURTS
(including juvenile courts)

Summary trials

Trials on indictment

(appeal on a
point of law)

(full appeal)

Table 10

Secretary of State (the *UDR Four* case) and three were references by the Attorney-General. About two-thirds of the appeals lodged were against sentence only. The success rate for defendants in ordinary cases was 22 per cent; in Diplock cases it was just 12 per cent.

Further appeals

Decisions of the Court of Appeal relating to trials on indictment can be further appealed *by either the prosecution or the defence* to the House of Lords. But, as with appeals after summary trials, the leave of either the Court of Appeal or the House of Lords is first required, and this is granted only if the Court of Appeal certifies that a point of law of general public importance is involved and if the Court of Appeal or the House of Lords thinks that the point is one which ought to be considered by the House. There are on average only one or two such appeals each year from Northern Ireland. A "reference" under section 15 of the Criminal Appeal (NI) Act 1980 (see above) can also be further referred by the Court of Appeal to the House of Lords, but the decision of that House can still not reverse the original acquittal. Likewise a decision by the Court of Appeal under the Criminal Justice Act 1988 in relation to an "unduly lenient" sentence (see above) may be referred to the House of Lords if there is a point of law of general public importance at issue.

The appeal system for criminal proceedings is resented diagrammatically in Table 10.

Pressure is mounting, especially in the wake of the Report of the Royal Commission on Criminal Justice in July 1993 (see 4.3), for the establishment of some kind of Miscarriage of Justice Authority to review those cases where a doubt about a person's guilt remains unquelled in the public's mind. The Authority would investigate the doubt and, in place of the Secretary of State, decide whether the case should be referred back to the Court of Appeal.

4.9 Special Features of the Emergency Laws

As mentioned in 4.1, the United Kingdom Parliament and, when it existed, the Parliament in Belfast, have enacted emergency laws for Northern Ireland to help deal with "the troubles". The most important is now the Northern Ireland (Emergency Provisions) Act 1991 (the EPA 1991), a successor to the Civil Authorities (Special Powers) Acts (NI) 1922-33 and to the previous EPAs of 1973, 1978 and 1987. Some comparable provisions are to be found in the Prevention of Terrorism

(Temporary Provisions) Act 1989 (the PTA 1989), a statute applying throughout the United Kingdom. Both the Emergency Provisions Act and the Prevention of Terrorism Act are the subject of annual reviews (between 1987 and 1993 these were prepared by Viscount Colville of Culross QC); the reports are considered by Parliament before it decides whether to renew the Acts for a further year. As well as these supposedly "temporary" laws, which in any event cannot persist for longer than five years without being completely replaced, some permanent measures have been enacted, such as the Protection of the Person and Property Act (NI) 1969 (dealing with, amongst other things, the offence of intimidation), the Public Order (NI) Order 1987 (which allows meetings and demonstrations to be re-routed or banned) and (as explained in 4.3) the Criminal Evidence (NI) Order 1988, which alters the law on the right to silence. It is worth noting that there are no special laws dealing with the use of force by security forces in Northern Ireland or with the status of prisoners. In the area of civil law there are special laws dealing with discrimination in employment on religious or political grounds (see 8.2 and 8.6).

The EPA 1991 confirms the existence of scheduled offences and the juryless Diplock courts, but as well it contains special powers and procedures for nearly every stage in the ordinary criminal process whenever a scheduled offence is being dealt with. A few of these special rules apply even when a scheduled offence is being tried summarily, but clearly it is in relation to trials on indictment that the emergency procedures have their greatest impact. The following points are particularly important.

Powers of arrest and detention

As regards powers of arrest, under section 14 of the Prevention of Terrorism (Temporary Provisions) Act 1989 the police may arrest without a warrant any person whom they reasonably suspect to be guilty of certain specified offences or of being concerned in the commission, preparation or instigation of acts of terrorism. Terrorism is defined as the use of violence for political ends. In addition, section 18 of the Northern Ireland (Emergency Provisions) Act 1991 allows any soldier on duty to arrest without a warrant any person whom he or she reasonably suspects of committing, having committed or being about to commit *any* offence. The police remain under the common law duty to give a reason for an arrest at the time it is effected, but by section 18 the army do not. In 1991, 1,690 people were arrested under the PTA 1989 in Northern Ireland, of whom 383 (23 per cent) were charged with some kind of offence; in the same year 108 were arrested under the EPA 1991, of whom exactly half were charged.

As regards powers of detention, persons arrested by the police under section 14 of the PTA 1989 may be detained for up to 48 hours and the Secretary of State may extend this by a further period not exceeding five days. A person arrested by the army under section 18 of the EPA 1991 may be detained for up to four hours, but may then be passed to the police for detention under section 14. Approximately one-third of those arrested under the PTA 1989 are detained beyond the initial 48 hour period. The powers of detention are obviously designed to enable the security forces to place arrested persons under sustained questioning, but there is still no legal obligation on such persons to answer any questions and the ordinary law on cautioning and charging must still apply (see 4.3 and 4.5). There is an obligation under section 23 of the EPA 1991 to answer questions about your identity, your movements and what you know concerning any recent explosion or any recent incident endangering life, but this arises only after you have been stopped in the street by the police or army.

Persons arrested under section 14 of the PTA 1989 may be forcibly photographed and fingerprinted by the police in the same situations where this could occur under the Police and Criminal Evidence (NI) Order 1989, namely when a police superintendent is satisfied that it is necessary. But, unlike under the PACE legislation, the fingerprints taken under the PTA 1989 do not later have to be destroyed if no charge is brought against the person concerned. The detained person may also be denied access to a solicitor for up to 48 hours, which is 12 hours longer than in ordinary cases, and the grounds upon which such denial may be permitted are more numerous. The same variations exist in relation to the right to have a friend or relative informed of the arrest. Once access to a solicitor is granted it does not stretch to allowing the solicitor to be present during the periods when the detained person is being interrogated by the police; nor are these interrogation sessions tape-recorded. Again this is contrary to the practice in ordinary cases.

Bail, committal and juryless courts

For scheduled offences tried on indictment the law on bail is altered by section 3 of the EPA 1991 so as to permit only a judge of the High Court or of the Court of Appeal, or the judge at the trial itself, to grant bail. Resident magistrates have no power to grant bail in these cases, presumably in order to confine the judicial function to a small number of judges (whom it is easier to defend against terrorist attack).

In committal proceedings for scheduled offences the prosecution is entitled to insist on a preliminary enquiry rather than a preliminary investigation (see 4.7), unless the court is of the opinion that in the interests of justice a preliminary investigation should be conducted into the offence. In practice nearly all committals are conducted through the shorter preliminary enquiry process, which apart from anything else avoids a witness having to attend on two separate occasions to give evidence in court (once at the committal proceedings and again at the trial itself).

Trials on indictment of scheduled offences take place before one judge sitting without a jury. It is felt that the risk of perverse verdicts, either through jury bias or the intimidation of jurors, is too great to allow continued use of jury trials. One implication of this is that when scheduled offences are involved, trials within a trial (see 4.8) are not very different from the main trial: the judge who decides the *voir dire* issues will usually be the one who goes on to decide the issues of fact at the main trial. If the judge has held certain evidence to be inadmissible during the *voir dire* he is meant to put that evidence out of his mind when deciding the main issues; occasionally, because he realises how difficult this will be, he directs the main trial to be re-commenced before a different judge.

In 1992, of the 190 Crown Court trials which took place in Northern Ireland (*i.e.* ignoring the cases where the defendant pleaded guilty) 53 (28 per cent) were held in the absence of a jury and they involved 195 defendants. A total of 418 people were processed through the Diplock Court system in that year: 223 (53 per cent) pleaded guilty and a further 57 (14 per cent) were found guilty after a trial.

Confessions and the burden of proof

One of the commonest reasons for holding a trial within a trial is to assess the admissibility of a confession. The test for admissibility in non-scheduled cases (set out in 4.3) has been significantly altered for scheduled cases: the confession is inadmissible only if made by a defendant who was subjected to torture, violence, threats of violence, or inhuman or degrading treatment inflicted in order to induce him or her to make the confession, though as always the confession may still be excluded from the evidence at the judge's discretion even if this test is not satisfied (section 11 of the EPA 1991). Once the defendant raises a *prima facie* case that the confession was obtained in this fashion the burden of proving beyond a reasonable doubt that it was not is on the prosecution.

In trials on indictment of non-scheduled offences the burden of proving the defendant's guilt is on the prosecution. In some trials on indictment of scheduled offences this principle has been qualified in that section 12 of the EPA 1991 appears to place the burden of proving their innocence on persons found to be in possession of explosives, firearms or ammunition. In actual fact, the judges in Northern Ireland have mostly interpreted this provision in a way which equates it with the ordinary law.

Appeals

All persons convicted of a scheduled offence tried on indictment in Northern Ireland can appeal against conviction to the Court of Appeal *on any ground and without any leave*. This is largely because there is no jury in the case, an absent safeguard which the automatic right of appeal is intended in part to replace. Moreover, because the judge in a Diplock Court, unlike a jury in an ordinary trial, is obliged to give reasons for his decisions, it should be easier for a defendant to establish grounds for appeal. In 1992, 66 appeals in scheduled cases were disposed of; the appeal was allowed in 8 of these cases (12 per cent).

5

Proceedings in Civil Courts

5.1 The Nature of Civil Proceedings

Civil proceedings have to be distinguished from criminal proceedings (see also 2.1). The best way to understand the difference is to consider the legal action that may be taken after a road accident, where one person's careless driving damages another person's car. The careless driver may receive a summons from the police, which means that criminal proceedings are being taken in a magistrates' court with the object of punishing the driver if he or she is found guilty of the crime of careless driving (see 4.6). But this will not help the other person to pay for the repairs to the car. Even if the careless driver is fined by the magistrates' court, the money paid will go to the state and not to the other car-owner. Unless the careless driver or an insurance company pay up voluntarily, the other car-owner must commence civil proceedings against the careless driver in a county court or in the High Court (depending on the amount involved), claiming "damages" (*i.e.* compensation) to cover the cost of repairing the car. The same distinction is apparent whenever some property is stolen. The owner of the property may well sue the culprit for the recovery of the property or its value, but the state - in the shape of the police or the Director of Public Prosecutions - may also prosecute the defendant for the crime of theft.

It can be seen, therefore, that one incident can give rise to both civil and criminal proceedings, but the person initiating the proceedings and the object of those proceedings are different, and the courts hearing the cases are also different (though the judges may be the same). Criminal courts do have some powers to award civil law remedies in the course of criminal proceedings, but these powers are limited and are not frequently exercised (see 4.6). Furthermore, the right to claim compensation from the state for losses suffered through violent criminal action is a civil right and must be processed through the civil courts; it is described in more detail in 5.5 below. A diagram illustrating the civil court system in Northern Ireland appears in Table 11. The workload of the various courts over the past four years is reflected in statistics given in Table 12.

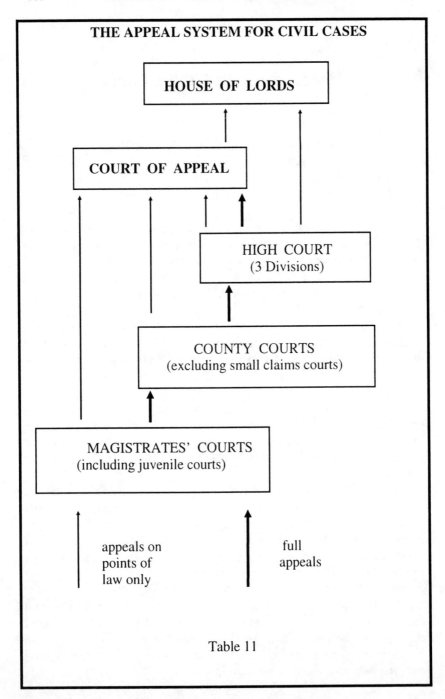

THE APPEAL SYSTEM FOR CIVIL CASES

HOUSE OF LORDS

COURT OF APPEAL

HIGH COURT
(3 Divisions)

COUNTY COURTS
(excluding small claims courts)

MAGISTRATES' COURTS
(including juvenile courts)

appeals on
points of
law only

full
appeals

Table 11

STATISTICS ON CIVIL CASES IN NORTHERN IRELAND, 1989-92

	1989	1990	1991	1992
Court of Appeal				
Appeals from the High Court	39	33	56	36
Cases stated	30	18	32	27
Queen's Bench Division				
Appeals from county courts	686	525	484	286
Actions begun	9,797	11,156	12,354	13,078
Actions tried	193	198	209	191
Actions settled	3,487	3,619	3,642	3,940
Judicial review hearings	50	115	191	192
Chancery Division				
Total cases begun	3,220	3,415	4,000	2,979
Company liquidations begun	142	134	205	155
Bankruptcy cases begun	265	342	416	843
Family Division				
Divorce decrees *nisi*	1,310	1,315	1,419	1,350
Adoption orders made	176	108	168	176
County courts				
Criminal appeals heard	3,261	2,985	3,862	3,629
Civil appeals heard	294	310	276	272
Criminal injury cases	2,450	3,313	3,728	3,526
Defended civil bills	7,739	7,976	7,857	7,143
Divorce decrees *nisi*	719	675	925	1,036
Small claims courts				
Cases defended	859	1,022	1,017	1,043
Cases undefended	9,836	9,786	8,967	9,403
Magistrates' courts				
Family cases dealt with	8,885	8,899	8,778	8,712
Debts and ejectments	32,429	37,973	36,481	33,500
Licence applications	4,563	4,895	4,746	4,549
Enforcement of judgments				
Notices of intention	26,967	29,250	31,932	28,178
Money judgment orders	8,374	8,513	9,255	10,852
Cases of unenforceability	1,102	996	851	898
Money recovered	£2.69m	£2.69m	£2.57m	£2.90m

Table 12

Settlements

Once criminal proceedings have begun they must go to court unless the charges are dropped, even if the defendant pleads guilty, and there is therefore no trial, the court must impose the appropriate sentence. But in civil proceedings (with some rare exceptions, most notably divorces) the plaintiff and the defendant can at any time - even after the court has started to hear the case, or when the case has reached an appellate court - decide between themselves that they want to "settle" (*i.e.* compromise) the case by agreement; once they so decide, the civil proceedings are usually terminated. The vast majority of civil actions are in fact settled before they ever see the inside of a courtroom. Once court proceedings have actually started, the court must be officially notified of any settlement (so that "judgment by consent" can be decreed) and it must grant its approval before a civil action involving a person under 18 years of age can be settled. The question of who is to bear the costs of a settled action is usually made part and parcel of the settlement agreement, but failing this the court can order the costs to be "taxed" (*i.e.* assessed by a court official: see 3.4).

If the case is not settled there are three types of court for civil proceedings, depending largely on the amount of money or value of property at stake. They are magistrates' courts, county courts and the High Court. These will be examined in turn, together with the procedures for appealing to higher courts. We shall then consider how judgments in civil cases are enforced.

Reforming the civil justice system

In 1988 a review body set up by the Lord Chancellor issued a report on how to improve the machinery of civil justice in England and Wales. Few of its recommendations have yet been implemented but they may be soon. As well as recommending a shift in workload from the High Court to the county courts by altering the financial boundaries between the two sets of court (a reform which *has* occurred), the report deals in detail with specific types of case such as those involving personal injuries, small claims, debt, housing or commercial matters. There is a proposal that every court should have a "link officer" with the specific job of liaising with advice agencies which are regularly present at the court. Such agencies should qualify for funding from the Legal Aid Board established under the Legal Aid Act 1988. In the review body's opinion the feasibility of allowing a contingency fee system, like that in the United States, where lawyers get paid by results, should also be re-examined and rules allowing a 100 per cent mark -up in selected cases *were* introduced in England in August 1993. Other recommendations are mentioned in passing later in this chapter, for although the report is confined to England and Wales, it is very likely that the changes it brings about will in due course also be made in the civil justice system of Northern Ireland.

In 1993 a working group of the Law Society and Bar Council in England and Wales (the Heilbron Committee) produced a further set of recommendations for reforming the civil justice system; they include the merging of the Queen's Bench and Chancery Divisions in the High Court, the adoption of common rules of procedure for county courts and the High Court and the operation of additional schemes for alternative dispute resolution.

5.2 Civil Proceedings in a Magistrates' Court

The powers and jurisdiction of a magistrates' court in relation to civil proceedings are much less important than its criminal law powers (see 4.6). Resident magistrates spend only about 15 per cent of their time in court on civil work. But in both spheres it is a local court, mainly dealing with *comparatively* unimportant matters arising within the petty sessions district where the court sits. At the moment there are 23 magistrates' courts in the province; they are listed in Table 2 in 1.3. They sit at intervals varying from every day (in Belfast) to once a month. As implied in 4.6, the jurisdiction of these courts is called summary because the procedure used in them is simple, informal and speedy; in civil matters there is none of the elaborate procedure normally found in High Court cases or to a lesser extent in county court cases. When the case comes to court it is decided by a resident magistrate sitting without a jury. The litigants are often represented by solicitors rather than barristers, though witnesses are examined and cross-examined in the same way as in a higher court. Because there is often not a great deal at stake in the case, compared with proceedings in a higher court, the proceedings do not usually take much time and most decisions are announced straightaway.

The main types of civil case which a magistrates' court can deal with are domestic cases, claims to recover small debts, claims to deprive someone of the occupation of land, and applications for licences. Of the 54,916 proceeedings in civil cases dealt with during 1992 some 16 per cent related to domestic matters, while nearly 61 per cent concerned small debts or ejectment. A few words must be said about each type of case.

For further details readers are referred to the intricacies of the Magistrates' Courts (NI) Order 1981 and the Magistrates' Courts Rules (NI) 1984, both as amended.

Domestic cases

Domestic cases are those involving family matters. Many legal remedies (but not decrees of divorce or nullity) are now available in a magistrates' court to a husband or wife whose marriage is not working out very happily. Even cohabitees can sometimes obtain relief. Under the Domestic Proceedings (NI) Order 1980, a resident magistrate may grant any of the following orders; almost 9,000 are issued each year.

Financial provision orders

If things are going badly between husband and wife it is obviously very important that proper financial provision is made for both spouses and for any children. In many instances the court may have to compel these arrangements to be carried out. If the spouses have agreed in writing between themselves that one of them should pay an amount of money to the other, or to a child of the family, the court can confirm this agreement and order the payments to be made. Similarly, if the parties are living apart by agreement and one of them has been paying money to the other or to a child of the family for at least three months, these voluntary payments can be ordered by the court to be continued. Finally, if a person contests his duty to pay anything at all to his spouse the latter can apply for a financial provision order to compel such payment. This last course of action is possible, however, only if certain grounds are first satisfied: these are (i) that the spouse has failed to provide reasonable maintenance for the applicant or a child of the family, (ii) that he has committed adultery, (iii) that he has deserted the applicant, or (iv) that he has behaved in such a way that the applicant cannot reasonably be expected to live with him. In all of these situations the financial provision which a magistrate can order to be made may take the form of a regular weekly or monthly sum, or one single lump sum not exceeding £1,000.

Personal protection orders

These may be granted if the magistrate is satisfied (i) that one party has used, or threatened to use, violence against the other or a child of the family, and (ii) that an order is necessary for the protection of that other party or child. The order restrains the violent party from "molesting" the other party or child, which means not only that he must not use or threaten violence but that he must not cause trouble to them or pester, vex, annoy or inconvenience them. If the order is disobeyed, a police officer can arrest the guilty party without a warrant. The law was changed in August 1993 so as to make breach of the order a criminal offence.

Exclusion orders

These can be granted on their own or in conjunction with a personal protection order. An exclusion order is available on the same grounds as a personal protection order but its terms will prohibit a party from entering the matrimonial home or other specified premises, or some area in which the matrimonial home or those specified premises are situated. It can remain in force for up to six months or for extended periods of up to six months. If it is disobeyed, the guilty spouse can be arrested.

Orders concerning children

As well as being able to make a financial provision order to ensure that children are reasonably maintained, a magistrates' court can decide who should have the custody of children or access to them, or whether a child should be placed under the supervision or committed to the care of the Department of Health and Social Services. All of these powers concerning children can only be exercised, however, if the court is already considering financial provision arrangements between spouses; they cannot be exercised in isolation from those arrangements. They really exist because the Domestic Proceedings (NI) Order 1980 compels the court, when considering financial provision arrangements between spouses, to regard the welfare of any children of the family as the first and paramount consideration.

It should be noted that magistrates also have the power to make "affiliation orders", which compel a man to pay for the upkeep of illegitimate children whom he has fathered. Magistrates do not, however, have jurisdiction to grant adoption orders: for those the applicant has to go to a county court. The powers of magistrates, and of other judges, in relation to children will be significantly altered when the proposed Children (NI) Order (published in July 1993) comes into force.

The party who wants any of these domestic remedies in a magistrates' court (the complainant) can begin the civil proceedings by stating the facts (in a "complaint") to a JP or clerk of petty sessions and asking for a summons to be issued ordering the other spouse to come before a magistrates' court on a certain day. As in criminal cases the summons is then served on the defendant, who must appear at the time and place stated in the summons. This is all that is required, though of course it will usually be wise to seek proper legal advice before making the complaint to the JP or clerk. The complaint must be made within a year of the action complained about. Domestic cases are heard at different times from other cases and *in camera*, that is, with the general public excluded. For further details on rules of procedure in these cases see the Magistrates' Court (Domestic Proceedings) Rules (NI) 1980, as amended.

Small debts

Claims to recover small debts are a second common type of civil case in a magistrates' court. Generally speaking, the debt in question must be for a fixed amount and less than £100. If you are in arrears with your rent, for example, you are liable to be proceeded against in this way. If the claim is for the balance of an account - say you still owe £120 on a bill for £240 - you can be proceeded against provided that the total bill is for no more than £250. Larger sums are also recoverable, but only if a statute so provides (as the Rent (NI) Order 1978 does in the case of rent). Proceedings for debt recovery are initiated not by way of complaint or summons but by way of a "process", which is a form filled in and served by the creditor or the creditor's solicitor. It can be issued at any time within six years of the debt falling due. The jurisdiction of magistrates' courts to deal with cases of debt overlaps with that of small claims courts, which are really a branch of the county courts (see 5.3).

Land cases

Claims to deprive someone of the occupation of land are in this context known as "ejectment proceedings". They can be brought by landlords to get rid of tenants who are no longer entitled to stay on the premises. But unless a statute provides otherwise, a magistrates' court has jurisdiction in such matters only when premises have been let at a rent which is less than £110 per annum. Most commercial and residential tenancies would therefore not be affected by this procedure were it not for the fact that the Housing (NI) Order 1981 confers special recovery rights upon housing associations and the Northern Ireland Housing Executive. In these matters proceedings are begun by a process, just as in claims to recover small debts. In 1992 there were as many as 33,500 applications for small debt recovery and ejectment in Northern Ireland's magistrates' courts.

Licences and appeals

Magistrates also have the important functions of renewing licences authorising the sale of intoxicating liquor, certifying that premises are suitable for the conduct of the business of bookmaking, judging whether an applicant for a bookmaker's licence is of suitable character, granting bingo-hall, gamekeepers' and general dealers' licences, and granting or renewing registered club certificates. They deal too with appeals against certain decisions taken by bodies such as education authorities. Thus if an Education and Library Board refuses to issue a licence to someone under the age of 16 to allow participation in public performances on the stage, an appeal can be heard by a magistrate. The document which is used to bring any of these applications to a magistrates' court is itself called a "notice" rather than a complaint or a process. In 1992, 4,549 applications for licences were dealt with (and all but 107 were granted).

Appeals from a magistrates' court

If either side is dissatisfied with the civil decision of a court of summary jurisdiction it may appeal against that decision in one of two ways: by way of ordinary appeal (in the form of a complete rehearing of both factual and legal issues) to a county court, or by way of case stated (on a point of law only) to the Court of Appeal. If the first course is taken, there is then a further right of appeal for either side on a point of law - by way of case stated only - to the Court of Appeal. The procedure by way of case stated and the composition of the Court of Appeal are described in more detail in 4.6 and 1.5 respectively. (For the different procedure known as judicial review see 7.1.) In 1992 there were 12 cases stated to the Court of Appeal by resident magistrates.

In these appeals the decision of the Court of Appeal is to all intents and purposes final. The only occasion when a civil case begun in Northern Ireland's magistrates' courts (or indeed county courts) can be taken to the House of Lords is when it involves a question about the validity of a piece of legislation passed by the Northern Ireland Parliament.

5.3 District Judges and Small Claims Courts

The small claims court is dealt with at this stage because it is the popular name given to a type of proceeding which in fact is a special county court procedure. The jurisdiction is exercised by officials called district judges, formerly known as circuit registrars, four of whom have been appointed under the Judicature (NI) Act 1978 to serve in the court circuits into which the province has been divided - the Northern, Southern, Eastern and Belfast (see Table 2 in 1.3). The chief task of the district judges, who must be solicitors of at least seven years' standing, is to deal with claims which are for less than £1,000. They also hear undefended county court claims for sums up to £15,000 and they frequently sit as deputy county court judges to hear other claims. If the value of the money or property claimed is between £1,000 and £3,000 the district judge will deal with the claim just as a county court judge would deal with a larger one, but if the value of the claim does not exceed even £1,000 then a much simpler procedure - known technically, though misleadingly, as "arbitration" - is followed. It is this type of hearing which is popularly called a small claims court.

Some types of dispute involving less than £1,000 cannot be resolved in a small claims court and must still be taken to the county court in the normal way. These "excepted proceedings" are disputes involving personal injuries, road accidents, libel or slander, a gift under a will or an annuity, the ownership of land, the property rights of married couples, and the matters referred to the county court from the High Court. Debt claims up to £1,000 can be brought either as a small claim or as a civil bill, but they must be treated as a small claim if either party so wishes. Moreover no claim can be taken against a person living, or a firm carrying on business, outside Northern Ireland. All other cases involving £1,000 or less *must* now be brought under the small claims procedure (unlike in England, where the procedure is optional and where, incidentally, small claims *can* be made for damages arising out of road accidents or any situation which causes personal injury).

The current procedure

To make a claim in a small claims court the applicant sets out the details of the case on an application form (see Appendix 4 for an example) and sends it with two copies to a county court office. The fee is £10 for a claim not exceeding £75, £22 for a claim between £75 and £300, £30 for a claim between £300 and £500 and £36 for a larger claim. A copy of the application form and a notice as to when and where the hearing is to take place will be returned to the applicant. Another copy is sent to the person against whom the claim is being made (the respondent) to find out if he or she intends to dispute the claim. If the respondent wishes to submit a counterclaim there is a fee of between £5 and £18 depending on the size of the counterclaim (see also 3.4).

About one-quarter of the claims will be settled out of court but if they are not they will be heard by the district judge on the day specified for the hearing; the English practice of holding a preliminary hearing to sort out which documents etc. will need to be produced is not deemed necessary in Northern Ireland. The hearing itself will usually take place within three months of the application being submitted, although recent research conducted for the General Consumer Council for Northern Ireland showed that delays of longer than three months were occurring in as many as 19 per cent of the cases. Two out of every three applicants tend to win their case at the hearing.

The procedure at the hearing itself is intended for use by individual applicants without the need for legal or lay representation; in practice, however, solicitors are present in up to 30 per cent of the cases and advice workers would occasionally represent claimants. Legal aid, though, is *not* available. Compared with proceedings in a proper court, the hearing will be informal; it will sometimes be in private in a small room of the courthouse. If the parties agree, the district judge may even decide the claim on the basis of written evidence only. Witnesses are usually required; there may be no witness box as such, but the swearing of a formal oath is usually demanded. If a witness is reluctant to attend, the party wishing to call the witness can oblige him or her to attend by applying to the district judge for a witness summons compelling attendance.

Neither of the parties can (except rarely) recover their costs from the other in a small claims arbitration (except for the fee payable with the application form), so any travel expenses incurred by witnesses (the "*viaticum*") and the charge of any lawyers who are engaged for the case will have to be borne by the party calling the witness or employing the lawyer. So will the cost of engaging an expert (like a doctor) to report on some matter, but the registrar may ask for a report from an independent expert to clarify a technical point and the cost of this will be borne by the court office and not by the parties. The only occasion on which a district judge may award costs to one party is where the other party's conduct has been unreasonable.

The district judge's decision will usually be announced as soon as the hearing is over. It may be issued even in the absence of the losing party. If the losing party does not comply with whatever order is made, the winner can take the case to the Enforcement of Judgments Office (see

5.7). If one party wishes to appeal against the decision of a district judge, he or she can only ask for a case to be stated to a High Court judge or apply to the High Court to have the arbitration set aside on account of the district judge's misconduct of the case. The rights of appeal are deliberately restricted so as to prevent undue consideration of what are, relatively speaking, fairly minor matters.

During 1992 a total of 13,580 applications were dealt with in the small claims courts, with Belfast accounting for 38 per cent of the business. Almost two-thirds of these were claims by business or commercial organisations, usually in respect of non-payment of hire-purchase instalments or money owed for goods delivered or services rendered. There were just 734 applications by consumers against shops and firms (5 per cent of the cases dealt with). As many as 90 per cent of the small claims which went to a hearing in 1992 would have been undefended; in England such cases do not lead to a hearing at all.

5.4 Civil Proceedings in a County Court

With the establishment of the Crown Court in 1979 (see 4.8) county courts became almost exclusively civil courts. However they still hear appeals from criminal cases tried summarily in magistrates' courts, and judges who sit as county court judges also frequently sit as Crown Court judges (see 4.6 and 1.5).

The civil work of the county courts is much more varied than that of the magistrates' courts, but it is still subject to restrictions as regards both type and size of claim. We shall first of all list the main types of case dealt with in a county court and then look at a few typical procedures. Further details are to be found in the County Courts (NI) Order 1980 and the County Court Rules (NI) 1981, as amended. From September 1993 significant changes were made by the County Courts (Financial Limits) Order (NI) 1993 to the sizes of claims which could be brought in the county courts. At the moment the main types of case, or "action", heard in the county courts in Northern Ireland are the following:

(1)   actions in tort, or for breach of contract, where the amount claimed is less than £15,000 (£3,000 in libel or slander claims); an action in tort is what lawyers call a claim for compensation for personal injury or damage to property caused by the defendant - the kind of legal action taken by the victims of assaults, thefts or accidents at work

or on the roads; libel and slander (together forming the tort of defamation) allow compensation for damage to a person's reputation;

(2) actions for the recovery of land or involving disputed claims to the ownership of land where, generally speaking, the land does not have an annual rateable value of more than £1,000 (this covers, for example, disputes between landlords and tenants or between neighbours);

(3) Chancery work, such as the management of funds held in trust, the enforcement of mortgages, the ending of partnerships, and the supervision of contracts for the sale of land, provided that in all these cases the sum of money or value of property involved is less than £45,000 or the annual rateable value of any land involved is less than £1,000 (in the county courts, Chancery work is always referred to as Equity business: see 1.3);

(4) disputes as to the validity of a will and as to who is to act as executor under a will, or administrator of the estate of someone who dies without making a will, provided that in such cases the estate does not exceed £45,000 in value after payments of all taxes, etc.; this heading includes disputes over "legacies" in wills, where the legacy claimed is less than £15,000;

(5) undefended petitions for divorce, and certain applications for a share in matrimonial property (regardless of the value of the property);

(6) applications to adopt children;

(7) equality of opportunity and sex discrimination cases brought under the Equal Pay Act (NI) 1970, the Fair Employment (NI) Acts 1976-89 and the Sex Discrimination (NI) Order 1976, though cases alleging sex discrimination in employment practices are dealt with by industrial tribunals (see 7.3.);

(8) applications brought under the Consumer Credit Act 1974, for example, to reopen a credit agreement of less than £15,000 on the ground that its terms are extortionate;

(9) applications for licences to sell intoxicating liquor (applications to renew or to transfer licences are made to a magistrates' court);

(10) actions to recover rates under the Rates (NI) Order 1977 and applications to determine the proper rent for a protected tenancy under the Rent (NI) Order 1978;

(11) appeals against decisions of the Secretary of State for Northern Ireland on applications for compensation for criminal injuries and criminal damage (these are considered to be civil claims even

though they arise out of the commission of a crime; they can be for any amount: see also 5.5).

It is to be noted that the county courts can deal with any debt cases (*i.e.*, a claim for a "liquidated", or certain, amount of money) even though the sum involved is greater than that laid down as the normal upper limit, provided that the parties themselves agree to this. The county courts must also deal with any cases which for one reason or another are transferred to them by the High Court. And they hear appeals from civil as well as criminal cases heard in magistrates' courts, with the criminal workload being by far the more demanding: in 1992 there were 272 civil appeals and 3,629 criminal appeals. In over half of the civil appeals the magistrate's order was reversed or at least varied.

Undefended divorce cases

County court cases concerning family matters are begun either by issuing a summons (as with domestic cases in magistrates' courts: see 5.2) or by lodging a "petition". Since 1981 county courts have been able to grant divorces, but only in undefended cases. From 1992 it has not even been necessary for the petitioner to appear personally in court; like petitioners in England since much earlier, he or she can in effect get a divorce by post. Legal aid is available to cover all divorce cases whether defended or undefended (see 3.3). In 1992 there were 1,036 divorces granted by the seven county court divisions; 64 per cent were at the request of women. Of all divorce decrees granted in Northern Ireland in 1992 almost 43 per cent were obtained in the county courts and about 57 per cent in the High Court.

Civil bills

Other county court cases are usually begun by the plaintiff, or the plaintiff's solicitor, issuing a document called a "civil bill" (see Appendix 4 for an example). The civil bill is a way of proceeding which is peculiar to Ireland and dates back to mediaeval times. It is more straightforward than the procedures used in county courts in England, requiring much less resort to "interlocutory" (*i.e.* preliminary) proceedings and there being no need for carefully worded pleadings (see 5.6). The case raised by the civil bill is dealt with by a judge sitting without a jury and the emphasis is on speed and cheapness. During 1992, 7,143 defended civil bills were dealt with by the county courts (6,083 ordinary bills and 1,060

Equity bills, the latter being reserved for the Equity business described in (3) above).

In all debt cases, if the defendant decides not to defend the civil bill or fails to return to the court the documents sent out attached to the civil bill, the county court judge can deal with the claim "summarily", relying on the case presented by the plaintiff alone and not hearing the defendant at all. In 1992 this occurred in no fewer than 3,647 cases, which is more than half the number of civil bills which *were* defended. In all other cases, even if the defendant does not appear for the trial, the plaintiff must call witnesses to prove his or her case and allow the defendant (if appearing) the opportunity both to question them and to call others.

Generally speaking, as you would expect, the proceedings in county courts are more formal than in magistrates' courts but less formal than in the High Court. It must also be remembered that at any stage the parties to a civil dispute can agree to sink their differences and settle the action between themselves. If this does not happen a county court judge usually delivers a judgment as soon as the parties have completed the submission of their arguments. In only a few cases will judgment be "reserved" until a later date.

Appeals from a county court

A person aggrieved by a decision of a county court in the exercise of its "original" (*i.e.* non-appellate) civil jurisdiction may appeal either by way of a full rehearing to the High Court or by way of case stated on a point of law to the Court of Appeal. The High Court can itself then state a case on a point of law for the opinion of the Court of Appeal. Whichever path is followed the decision of the Court of Appeal is final. In 1992 there were 286 county court appeals disposed of in the High Court, a drop of 41 per cent on the 1991 figure; 69 per cent of these appeals were either settled or withdrawn before the second trial could occur. (For details of appeal and case stated procedures, see 4.6; for the procedure known as judicial review, see 7.1.)

5.5 Compensation for Criminal Injuries and Criminal Damage

This section deals with one particular type of claim which can often end up being dealt with by a county court. As pointed out in 2.1 and 5.1 the law makes a basic distinction between civil wrongs and crimes. The former are acts for which private individuals can seek redress, whereas crimes are acts by which the state is offended. Even though one and the same act can constitute both a civil wrong and a crime the two forms of misbehaviour are processed quite differently in the legal system. The victim of a civil wrong *sues* the perpetrator of the act for *damages*; the state *prosecutes* and *punishes* him or her for the crime. In a perfect world both the victim and the state would be satisfied and the offender would pay his or her debt to the individual and to society alike.

For a number of reasons things may not work out so neatly, certainly from the point of view of the victim. In the first place the perpetrator of the act may never be caught; secondly, even if caught, the perpetrator may not be convicted because he or she is very young, mentally handicapped or immune from prosecution, or because the evidence is insufficient; thirdly, whether or not caught and convicted for the crime, the perpetrator may not be able to afford to compensate the victim. In these circumstances it would be unjust to expect the victim to bear the loss alone. For a very long time, therefore, the state has operated compensation schemes to which the victim of violent crime can have recourse, and these can be used even if no-one has been prosecuted or convicted for the crime.

In Northern Ireland, because of the heavy incidence of violent crime, there are two such schemes; each is long-established, though the legislation now applicable is the Criminal Damage (Compensation) (NI) Order 1977 for criminal damage and the Criminal Injuries (Compensation) (NI) Order 1988 for criminal injuries. In addition there is a scheme for compensating persons whose property is damaged under the emergency powers legislation. In England, under the Criminal Justice Act 1988, there is a statutory scheme for compensation for criminal injuries, with claims being made to the Criminal Injuries Compensation Board, but the provision for property damage compensation - the Riot (Damages) Act 1886 - is different from and less extensive than that in Northern Ireland. In June 1993 there was increasing speculation that from October 1994 the government was planning to make the Northern Irish criminal injuries scheme more like the English scheme by creating a Criminal Injury Board to decide claims on a tariff basis and removing the right of appeal to the courts and access to legal aid.

It should be stressed that the claims made under all the schemes are civil, not criminal, claims. They are not like the compensation and restitution orders which can be made during criminal proceedings (see 4.6) but are direct actions against the state. Until April 1992 the claims were dealt with by the Criminal Compensation Division of the Northern Ireland Office, but in that month the Division became the Compensation Agency, the first Executive Agency to be set up in Northern Ireland. The Agency employs approximately 150 staff under a Chief Executive and each year it publishes both a business plan and an annual report. Table 13 sets out some of the most important statistics appearing in those publications.

If you think you are entitled to make a claim you should immediately contact a solicitor. Pay close attention to the time limits involved - the injury or damage must have been reported to the police within 48 hours - and bear in mind that help under the civil legal aid and legal advice

STATISTICS ON CRIMINAL COMPENSATION CASES, 1989-93

	1989-90	1990-91	1991-92	1992-93
Criminal injury claims				
Cases cleared	7,566	9,461	10,001	11,773
Payments made	£16.5m	£19.5m	£25.0m	£26.6m
Average payment	£2,181	£2,061	£2,500	£2,259
Criminal damage claims				
Cases cleared	4,862	5,062	4,382	5,336
Payments made	22.1m	£22.7m	£33.1m	£75.9m
Average payment	£4,545	£4,484	£7,554	£14,224
EPA claims				
Cases cleared	3,167	3,438	4,233	4,615
Payments made	£1.1m	£1.6m	£1.9m	£2.8m
Average payment	£347	£465	£449	£607
Appeals to the courts				
Cases cleared	2,176	2,319	3,282	3,139

Table 13

and assistance schemes may be available to you (see 3.3) and that, if your claim is successful, your reasonable legal expenses will be paid for you by the Compensation Agency.

Criminal injuries compensation

To qualify for compensation for personal injuries resulting from a crime of violence in Northern Ireland the victim, or the relatives of a victim who has died from injuries received, must report the crime to the police within 48 hours and serve on the Secretary of State for Northern Ireland, usually within 28 days, a document known as "a notice of intention to apply for compensation". This must fully and truthfully disclose all the facts which are within the applicant's knowledge and belief and which are material to the application. If such disclosure is not made, compensation can be refused outright; or if compensation has been paid and the Northern Ireland Office then discovers that full and true disclosure was not made, the Secretary of State can apply to a county court for reimbursement by the recipient.

Within a further three months of serving the notice of intention to apply, the application for compensation must itself be made. These time limits may be extended in special cases, but no compensation can ever be paid if the application is made more than three years after the injury was suffered. This is in line with the general legal rule that all civil claims for compensation for personal injuries, even those brought directly against the person who caused the injury and not involving a criminal offence, must be brought within the "limitation period" of three years. After three years the claims are said to be "time barred".

For present purposes a "criminal injury" is defined as an injury or death which is directly attributable to a violent offence, the arrest of an offender or the prevention of an offence. "Injury" is taken to include mental illness caused by reaction to a violent crime (called in law "nervous shock"), but in most cases only if the mental illness is a serious one and the person was actually present when the crime was committed. A "violent offence" is defined quite broadly: it is by no means restricted to terrorist offences, so "ordinary" crimes such as street-mugging or causing injury during the course of a burglary are covered. Traffic offences are excluded, however, and where the violence has occurred within a household (*e.g.* wife-battering) certain further conditions must be satisfied before compensation can be claimed.

Although the coverage of the scheme is wide, there are many situations in which compensation will be refused or reduced because of the conduct or background of the victim. This will happen where the victim has been negligent or provocative, where there has been a failure to co-operate with the police, where the victim has at any time been a member of an unlawful organisation, or where the applicant or victim has a criminal conviction which is "indicative of a certain character or way of life". A compensation award will in no case be reduced because the applicant has already received money from an insurance company, but to help keep down administration costs the scheme does not allow compensation to be paid at all if it amounts to less than £1,000, while "nervous shock" is compensatable only if it is worth more than £2,500. There is also a general power to take into account any relevant circumstances.

The method of calculating how much compensation, if any, should be paid differs according to whether the victim was merely injured or was killed. In the former case the compensation will cover pecuniary loss (*i.e.* loss of earnings minus social security benefits, sick pay, pension money etc.), reasonable expenses, pain and suffering, and "loss of amenities" (the ability to enjoy life). A woman who has been raped, gives birth to and keeps a child conceived as a result of the rape is entitled to up to £5,000, but no compensation is payable for the maintenance of such a child. If the victim of a violent crime has died from injuries received, the compensation paid to the relatives will cover pecuniary loss and expenses, but instead of an award for pain and suffering and loss of amenities a bereavement sum of up to £7,500 is payable to the victim's husband or wife or (if the victim was under 18 years of age) to the parents. The Secretary of State has a discretion to "top up" an award made to a widow or widower. Of course no amount of money can fully compensate a person for things such as pain, suffering, grief or the loss of an ability to undertake certain leisure activities, but the law requires some sort of estimate to be made and these estimates must be as consistent as possible in all cases.

If the Secretary of State (as represented by the Compensation Agency) makes no decision within six months of an application having been lodged, the applicant may ask a county court for a declaration that the Secretary of State has had sufficient information and a reasonable time to come to a decision. Such declarations are in practice very rarely sought, but once obtained they will certainly speed things up. Much more importantly, any person who is aggrieved by a decision of the Secretary of State can appeal against it within 10 weeks to a county court (see 5.4). This is a matter on which there is no financial limit to a county court's jurisdiction. Further appeals lie to the High Court and the Court of Appeal. If someone is later convicted of the criminal offence which caused the criminal injury, the Compensation Agency can apply to a county court for an order that this person must reimburse to the Agency the whole or a part of the compensation already paid to the victim.

During the year ending 31st March 1993 the Compensation Agency cleared 11,773 applications for criminal injuries compensation and almost £26.57 million was paid out (including applicants' costs). In 1992 there were 3,526 criminal injury appeals disposed of in Northern Ireland's county courts, a 5 per cent decrease on the 1991 figure. Over 3,700 cases were outstanding at the year's end - an indication that this area forms a very important part of the county courts' workload.

Criminal damage compensation

The scheme for compensating people who have suffered criminal damage is a little more technical than the criminal injuries scheme. Except in relation to agricultural buildings and property, compensation for damage is available only if it has been caused by three or more persons who have "unlawfully, riotously or tumultuously assembled together", or by an act committed maliciously by a person acting for an organisation engaged in terrorism. Compensation for the unlawful removal of property (i.e. "looting") is restricted to situations where the removal takes place in the course of a riot causing more than £200 worth of damage to the building where the property was located.

To qualify for compensation a person must again serve on the Secretary of State (as represented by the Compensation Agency) and on the police, within 10 days of the damage being caused, a notice of intention to apply for compensation. This notice must fully and truthfully disclose certain facts. Within a further four months the application itself must be made. The Compensation Agency decides what amount of compensation, if any, should be paid having regard to all such circumstances as are relevant and in particular to the conduct of the applicant and whether all reasonable precautions were taken to reduce or avoid the loss. As with the criminal injuries scheme, anyone who at any time has been a terrorist or a member of an organisation engaged in terrorism is barred from recovering compensation, with the exception that the Secretary of State may in any particular case make an *ex gratia* payment in the public interest. No compensation at all is provided for the first £200 of any loss, and it cannot be paid for lost money or jewellery or for any loss for which the applicant has already received adequate compensation under a statute or at common law (as in a civil action for damages).

There are special provisions for dealing with situations where more than one person with an interest in property suffers loss through its damage or removal (*e.g.* when a house is mortgaged or a car is being bought on hire-purchase), but the provisions relating to appeals and reimbursement are the same as in the criminal injuries scheme (see above).

During the year ending 31st March 1993 the Compensation Agency cleared 5,336 applications for criminal damage compensation and the amount of compensation and costs awarded was nearly £76 million. Naturally most of this money was paid in respect of damage caused by terrorist outrages. The large bombs which exploded in various towns during the summer of 1993 will mean that much more will need to be paid in compensation during the current financial year than was originally estimated.

It is also worth noting that since 1970 a non-statutory scheme has operated under which applications can be made to a Compensation Tribunal by employees who, having been in continuous employment for two years, have been dismissed by their employer or ceased employment voluntarily because of threats or other reasons directly attributable to civil disturbances in Northern Ireland. The scheme is administered by the Department of Economic Development and is applied to only a handful of cases each year.

Compensation under the emergency powers legislation

If any property is taken, occupied, destroyed or interfered with by the security forces acting under the Northern Ireland (Emergency Provisions) Act 1991 (see 4.9), compensation must be paid by the Secretary of State, again acting through the new Compensation Agency (section 63). The only exception is that no person who has been convicted of a scheduled offence (see 4.1) or of any other offence under the 1991 Act has a right to compensation in respect of acts done in connection with that offence. Applications for compensation have usually to be submitted within four months of the act which is the subject of the complaint. Failing acceptance of the amount offered as compensation, the claimant can appeal to a county court. The county court judge will process the application as if it were an Equity civil bill (see 5.4), except that no limit applies as to the amount which can be claimed. In the year ending 31st March 1993 the Compensation Agency dealt with 4,615 applications for this kind of compensation and £2.8 million was paid out to people whose property had been damaged or requisitioned by the security forces. However in his report on the operation during 1992 of the Northern Ireland (Emergency Provisions) Act 1991, Lord Colville states that nearly £5.5 million was paid in that year as compensation for losses caused by the security forces.

5.6 Proceedings in the High Court

Unlike that of the inferior courts (magistrates' courts and county courts), the jurisdiction of the High Court is limited neither geographically nor by the value of the claim. If the matter is one which could also be dealt with in a magistrates' court or in a county court, the proceedings should be begun there because they will be cheaper and quicker; if they are begun in the High Court the judge can transfer them to a lower court and the plaintiff can be penalised as regards costs (see 3.4). The High Court can deal with any subject-matter, though for reasons of administrative convenience its business is roughly distributed between its three divisions as follows.

(1) *Queen's Bench Division:* claims for compensation for personal injury or for damage caused to a person's property or reputation (these are called "tort" claims); claims for breach of contract; claims concerning ships ("Admiralty actions"); all business not specifically assigned to another division (including various appeals);

(2) *Chancery Division:* disputes concerning the distribution of a deceased person's property; difficulties arising out of the management of trust funds, including a charity's funds; the enforcement of mortgages and other securities; problems concerning partnerships and companies; bankruptcies; copyright; the supervision of contracts for the sale of land; the correction of deeds;

(3) *Family Division:* petitions for divorce or nullity; property claims between married couples; disputes over a person's marital status or illegitimacy; applications concerning the wardship, adoption or guardianship of persons under 18; applications for the right to carry out the terms of a person's will or to manage the property of someone who dies intestate (*i.e.* without having made a will); matters affecting mental patients.

The High Court in England is comprised of the same three divisions, but there are in addition some informally organised subdivisions. In Northern Ireland there are only two of these, namely the Companies

Court within the Chancery Division and the Commercial Court within the Queen's Bench Division. The Restrictive Practices Court is a separate court in its own right, on the same level as the High Court. It operates for the whole of the United Kingdom, its members comprising five judges (including one Supreme Court judge nominated by the Lord Chief Justice of Northern Ireland), and 10 lay members, though usually only one judge and two lay members sit in any particular case. When it hears cases originating from the province - an extremely rare occurrence - appeals lie to the Court of Appeal of Northern Ireland.

It is also necessary to note the existence of so-called Divisional Courts, not to be confused with the courts of the three separate divisions. A Divisional Court is a court *within* a division and usually comprises two, or three, judges. It hears special appeal cases or deals with a particular type of case as a court of first instance. In England there are Divisional Courts within all three divisions, two of them carry out the very important task of hearing appeals from magistrates' courts in criminal and family law matters. The Divisional Court of the Queen's Bench Division also deals with applications for judicial review. It is mainly to deal with this last type of case that the Divisional Court of the Queen's Bench Division also exists in Northern Ireland. The decisions of Divisional Courts, being decisions of the High Court, are not as authoritative, according to the system of precedent, as decisions of the Court of Appeal (see 2.4).

Proceedings in the High Court can be begun in a variety of ways, depending on the type of claim being made. We shall first of all look at a typical Queen's Bench action and then briefly consider actions in the Chancery and Family Divisions. It will be clear from the description of the Queen's Bench action that proceedings at a High Court trial can be rather formal and ponderous. Despite all the documentation, great emphasis is still laid on hearing the oral evidence of witnesses in the court-room. The system is designed to ensure that the plaintiff and the defendant feel satisfied that the trial in open court leaves no stone unturned in the dispute between them. It is an "adversarial" system, where the parties fight each other, rather than an "inquisitorial" or "investigative" system (like those on the Continent), where the court itself takes the initiative in seeking the truth. Partly on account of the delays and expense engendered by the present system, the review body on civil justice (see 5.1) suggested that the Lord Chancellor should consider introducing a no-fault scheme of liability for less serious road accidents. This would mean that insurance companies would pay out compensation automatically to people injured in such accidents regardless of whether the policy-holder was negligent or not. The Lord Chancellor's Department has accordingly issued a consultation paper on this topic.

Pleadings in a Queen's Bench action

Proceedings in the High Court can be begun in a variety of ways, depending on the type of claim being made. In the Queen's Bench Division the most typical claim is one made following an accident on the roads or at work. The claimant, who is called the plaintiff, sets the ball rolling by issuing a writ of summons, which warns the defendant that a claim is being made and states the general nature of that claim (see the sample writ in Appendix 4). The writ will be delivered by hand or posted to the defendant.

If the defendant wishes to have a chance to contest the plaintiff's claim he or she should, within 14 days, "enter an appearance" with the court by handing in or posting the appropriate document. If the defendant does not do this the plaintiff can obtain a judgment without further argument, provided it is proved that the writ of summons was properly delivered. This is called "a judgment in default of appearance". Even after an appearance has been entered, the plaintiff may be so confident of the defendant's lack of defence to the claim (except perhaps as to the amount of compensation being claimed) that he or she will apply for what is called a "summary judgment", that is, judgment without a full-scale hearing. (In a few types of action, however, such as those involving libel, slander or fraud, it is not possible to apply for a summary judgment.) Another way in which cases can be brought to a conclusion without a full hearing taking place is if the defendant pays a sum of money into the relevant court office and the plaintiff, within three weeks, decides to accept this amount in settlement of the claim. This "stays" (*i.e.* stops) the proceedings. If a payment into court has been made but not accepted, the judge and jury must not be told about it in case it prejudices their decision on whether and to what extent the defendant is liable.

If the defendant enters an appearance and the plaintiff does not apply for summary judgment, the plaintiff should, within six weeks, send the defendant a document called a statement of claim, which specifies the precise facts and law on which the claim is based and asks for particular remedies. The statement of claim will specify, for instance, where and how the accident occurred, why the defendant is liable and what injury was suffered. The defendant should respond to this, within three weeks, by sending to the plaintiff a defence. This document will deny most of the allegations made in the statement of claim and may well be accompanied by a counterclaim which makes allegations against the plaintiff. Within a further three weeks (14 days in England) the plaintiff produces a reply to the defence and, if necessary, a defence to the counterclaim. All these documents are called "pleadings", and the general rule is that points not raised in the pleadings cannot be argued in court.

At this juncture the pleadings are normally "closed", though further documents can be served with the special permission of the court, and in most cases either side can apply to the court at an earlier stage to have the action tried without the exchange of any further pleadings. Pleadings are meant to serve the purpose of making each side aware, before the case comes to trial, of what exactly the other side is arguing. In practice, however, the lawyers drafting these documents often prefer to hedge their bets, so that when the case does come to court they will not be prevented from arguing a certain point just because it was not mentioned in their pleadings. The time limits for serving the various pleadings are, as well, usually ignored in practice, by agreement of both sides. It is therefore a widely held view that the system of pleadings does little to reduce the length and cost of a High Court action. As explained in 5.2 and 5.4, civil cases in magistrates' courts and county courts are not hampered in the same way. For a Northern Ireland case where the failure of the plaintiff's lawyers to plead certain points ultimately led to rejection of the plaintiff's case, see *Farrell* v *Secretary of State for Defence* (1980).

Interlocutory proceedings

Once the pleadings in a Queen's Bench action have been closed, the plaintiff can apply within six weeks to have the case set down for trial at a date some time in the future. But further pre-trial procedures can still be taken to ensure that when the case does reach the trial stage it will be dealt with as efficiently as possible. These further proceedings are called "interlocutory proceedings". Though well intentioned, they do add to the length, cost and complexity of the action. Examples are applications for the "discovery" of documents or for the serving of "interrogatories": these help a party to prepare for the trial by giving access to certain vital papers or answers to important preliminary questions. There is also a right to apply for disclosure of documents held by persons not involved in the court case (see *O'Sullivan* v *Herdmans Ltd*, 1987). The process known as an application for a summons for directions, where a party seeks a ruling from a judge on a preliminary point, is commonly used in England but is not known in Northern Ireland.

The decision-making process

If the case eventually comes to trial - and this will be many months or even years after the issue of the writ - it will usually be held in the presence of a judge sitting alone. Until June 1987 it was quite common in Northern Ireland for cases to be heard by a judge sitting with a jury (of seven persons), but the province then adopted the English rule whereby trials without a jury are the norm unless special circumstances warrant otherwise. Only actions such as claims for libel will now be heard by a jury, or if the judge accedes to a particular application. In 1991 there were just two jury trials and in 1992 there was only one, compared with a total of 421 non-jury trials (excluding trials which were settled during the course of the hearing). Jury trials, not surprisingly, tend to last a lot longer than non-jury trials: in 1991 the two jury trials took an average of nine hours to complete whereas the average duration of the non-jury trials was just under three hours.

When a judge sits with a jury it is the judge's task to make sure that the trial is properly conducted and that the jury understands what law must be applied to the facts. The jury decides which version of the facts to believe, whom to hold liable, and what amount of compensation is to be paid. This power to decide what remedy to give distinguishes the role of the civil jury from the roles of the criminal jury (see 4.8) and the coroner's jury (see 6.3). However, if there is a need to carry out a detailed assessment of compensation to be paid, the matter will be referred to a High Court Master (see 1.5). There is general agreement that compensation awards are on average slightly higher in Northern Ireland than in comparable cases in England and Wales. In 1992 just over 29 per cent of all Queen's Bench judgments were for up to £5,000 (which means that the claims should really have been brought in a county court); 34 per cent were for between £5,000 and £10,000, and 37 per cent for more than £10,000. Now that claims up to £15,000 can be heard in county courts, the pressure of work in the High Court should be eased.

At present only about 5 per cent of all Queen's Bench cases lead to a full-scale trial; the remaining 95 per cent are settled before or during the course of the trial. In 1992 a total of 13,078 actions were initiated, with default or summary judgments being issued in 3,697 cases. In all, 5,610 Queen's Bench actions were set down for trial and 4,311 were disposed of during the year; the backlog therefore continued to accumulate (standing at about 8,000 cases). Of the 2,560 actions which led to a court hearing 86 per cent resulted in judgment for the plaintiff and 95 per cent concerned claims for negligence, nuisance or breach of a duty imposed by statute. Just over one-half of the actions disposed of during 1992 had been set down for trial within the previous 12 months, but 15 per cent had been set down more than two years previously. Similarly, 55 per cent of the actions disposed of were begun (by the issue of a writ) less than two years previously but 20 per cent were begun more than three years previously.

Actions in the Chancery and Family Divisions

High Court proceedings in the Chancery and Family Divisions may be just as cumbersome as those in the Queen's Bench Division, but because in such cases there is often little argument about the relevant facts giving rise to the action - the dispute being really about whether some legal rule applies - the legal procedures are sometimes speedier and more informal. Again, many such actions are settled out of court. Chancery actions - such as claims that a contract for the sale of a house should be enforced - are usually started by a document called "an originating summons", which does not then lead to an exchange of pleadings. The matter is heard in the absence of a jury by a Master (see 1.5) or by a High Court judge sitting in chambers (*i.e.* his own private office). Witnesses usually do not have to be present at the hearing because the evidence is presented in the form of written statements, called "affidavits", rather than as oral testimony. (Affidavits are documents sworn to be true by the maker in the presence of a Commissioner for Oaths. All solicitors are also Commissioners for Oaths.) During 1992 the number of proceedings begun in the Chancery Division was 2,979 (a drop of 26 per cent on the 1991 figure); 85 per cent of writs and summonses issued were mortgage suits brought by money-lending institutions; only 12 writ actions were actually disposed of in a full court hearing. Of all the proceedings begun, 843 were bankruptcy cases (a 103 per cent annual rise) and 189 were Companies Court cases (*e.g.* for winding-up orders).

An action in the Family Division, such as a request for a divorce, is usually begun by the petitioner lodging a petition with the court (see the sample document in Appendix 4) and serving a copy of it on the respondent by having it handed over personally or posted. The petitioner no longer has to appear in open court in every case in order to give an oral account of the grounds for the petition, though this is usually the case. There will of course be no jury involved. Many family actions are undefended, which obviously allows them to be processed more quickly and cheaply. What might delay the proceedings is the necessity for the judge to be satisfied that, when the parties to the action have children, the welfare of these children is being protected. There may also be complications over the division of the family property, a matter which is usually dealt with by a Master or a judge in chambers. Applications by a married person for an award of money against his or her partner are made by originating summons and not by petition. During 1992, 2,597 divorce petitions were filed in the Family Division (67 per cent of them by wives); 1,350 decrees *nisi* were granted, the vast majority being in undefended cases; a further 1,036 decrees *nisi*, it must be remembered, were granted in county courts.

Appeals

As well as its "original" (*i.e.* non-appellate) jurisdiction, the High Court also functions as an appeal court, most notably for civil cases first heard in the county courts and for matters first dealt with by a Master. In 1992 it disposed of 286 and 250 of these respectively.

For cases begun in the High Court appeals lie directly to the Court of Appeal. The appeal takes the form of a full rehearing, without the re-examination of witnesses but usually with a word-for-word transcript of the evidence being placed before the judges. The Court of Appeal can overturn the decision on whether or not the defendant is liable, but it cannot recalculate the damages to be awarded. That issue has to be sent back to the High Court for retrial. The total number of civil appeals disposed of by the Court of Appeal in Northern Ireland during 1992 was 64, which is less than half the number of criminal appeals dealt with (151); 36 of the civil appeals were originally High Court cases, the others being a mixture of "cases stated" from inferior courts and tribunals (and one case involving punishment for contempt of court).

There is then a further avenue of appeal, provided either the Court of Appeal or the House of Lords gives its permission, to the House of Lords. Only one or two such cases arise each year. An even rarer procedure is that provided for by the Administration of Justice Act 1969, whereby in certain cases there can be a direct appeal straight from the High Court in Northern Ireland to the House of Lords, by-passing the Court of Appeal. This "leapfrog" procedure is possible only if all the parties to the case agree to it and if the proposed appeal raises a question of law of general public importance involving either the interpretation of a piece of legislation or an issue on which the High Court must follow a precedent laid down by the Court of Appeal or the House of Lords (see 2.4).

For the composition of the Court of Appeal and House of Lords, see 1.5; and for the procedure known as judicial review (not to be confused with appeal procedures strictly so called) see 7.1.

5.7 The Enforcement of Civil Judgments

The fact that a court order is issued in favour of the winner of litigation does not necessarily mean that he or she will receive the money (or whatever else is awarded) from the other side. Sometimes the loser does not pay and has to be forced to do so. Ensuring that the loser of litigation complies with a court order can often be as difficult as obtaining that order in the first place. Since 1971, however, the task has been simplified in Northern Ireland through the creation of the Enforcement of Judgments Office (the EJO), which is part of the Northern Ireland Court Service. It handles virtually all types of money judgments, the principal exceptions being most judgments issued in criminal proceedings and those against a spouse ordering him or her to make maintenance payments to the other spouse or to a child. It maintains a register of judgments which can be searched, on payment of a small fee, by anyone who needs to know whether a particular person or company has an unpaid judgment debt against their name. The EJO enforces civil judgments of magistrates' courts and county courts (including small claims courts) as well as of the High Court, whereas in England the judgments of each of these courts are enforced in different ways. For details see the Judgments Enforcement (NI) Order 1981.

The person ordered by a court to pay money to another is called a judgment debtor; there is a duty to pay the money within a reasonable time of the judgment being delivered. If the person who is owed the money (the judgment creditor) thinks that more than a reasonable time has elapsed, he or she may get the Enforcement of Judgments Office to send the debtor a document called "a notice of intent to enforce" (see the sample in Appendix 4). This orders the debtor to pay up within 10 days. If the debtor still refuses to pay after that period has elapsed, the creditor may apply to the EJO for actual enforcement of the judgment. This can cost quite a bit of money (*e.g.* £235 in respect of a £1600 judgment), so before good money is thrown after bad, the creditor should try to ensure that the debtor does in fact have assets out of which the value of the judgment can be realised. Money spent on enforcing a judgment is added to the amount owed by the judgment debtor, so that in the event of success the judgment creditor will get back the fees paid to the Enforcement of Judgments Office. Interest on the judgment debt is also payable.

In furtherance of an enforcement application the Enforcement of Judgments Office will interview the debtor to assess his or her means and will proceed to enforce the award in whichever of a number of ways it thinks fit. It may, for instance, make an order that property belonging to the debtor should be seized and sold, or an order that goods on premises occupied by the debtor should be deemed to be in the custody and possession of the EJO, or an order that the debtor's earnings should be "attached" so that an employer must make periodical deductions from wages or salary and pay them directly to the EJO on the creditor's behalf.

The EJO may postpone enforcement if it thinks that the debtor's property ought to be administered for the benefit of all the creditors and not just those who have applied for enforcement. Or if the EJO thinks that enforcement within a reasonable time is impossible, it must issue a notice to that effect and, after hearing the parties, grant "a certificate of unenforceability". In these circumstances, or if the EJO otherwise fails to extract any money from the debtor, the creditor is not allowed to resort to self-help and must come to terms with the fact that the judgment in his or her favour is worthless.

Against some of the EJO's orders, such as an order for the transfer of possession of land or attachment of earnings, an aggrieved party may appeal to the High Court; against the rest an appeal may be made, on a question of law only, to the Court of Appeal. In both instances the decision of the court in which the appeal is heard is final.

During 1992 there were 28,178 notices of intent lodged with the EJO and 11,106 accepted applications for enforcement. There were 11,556 enforcement orders made (704 of which were for the possession of land or goods, the rest being for money). There were 898 certificates of unenforceability. A total of £2.9 million was recovered from debtors and the fee income was £2.1 million.

Between 1985 and 1987 a Review Committee under the chairmanship of Master Hunter considered what changes should be made to the law and practice in this field. It recommended reforms in every respect: for example, forms should be simplified, an information booklet should be published, persons aggrieved by delay should be able to take the matter to the Director of the Northern Ireland Court Service, and decisions should always be appealable to the High Court and then, on a question of law, to the Court of Appeal. Not all of these proposed changes have yet been introduced.

6

Special Courts

6.1 Juvenile and Family Proceedings Courts

Juvenile courts are courts of summary jurisdiction which deal with persons aged between 10 and 16. They normally consist of a bench of three members, one of whom will be a resident magistrate acting as the chairperson; the others will be lay members, including at least one woman. The lay members are selected for cases by the clerk of petty sessions from panels appointed by the Lord Chancellor for each of the seven county court divisions. There are about 100 names on the panels, each of whom must retire at 70. Many of the lay panellists are in due course appointed Justices of the Peace (see 1.5). They will usually possess no legal qualifications but will have to attend training classes before assuming their responsibilities. The chairperson of the court may sit alone, and has a casting vote if only one lay member is present; otherwise decisions are reached by majority vote.

The court generally sits in the same building as the district's magistrates' court, though it is a district court in its own right and usually sits at different times so that there is little chance of juveniles coming into contact with adult offenders or litigants. The proceedings are held in private, with only court officials, the parties to the case, the parties' representatives, *bona fide* representatives of the press, and other persons directly concerned in the case (such as parents) being present. Unless the court directs otherwise, no report or picture in any newspaper or broadcast can reveal the identity of any juvenile involved, in whatever capacity, in juvenile court hearings.

The jurisdiction of juvenile courts is at present mostly laid down in the Children and Young Persons Act (NI) 1968; procedure is governed by the Magistrates' Courts (Children and Young Persons) Rules (NI) 1969. It must be considered under two heads: proceedings relating to the care, protection or control of juveniles, and criminal proceedings. The Report of the Children and Young Persons Review Group (the Black Report) recommended in 1979 that future reform of the system should preserve a clear distinction between these two types of business. At long last the proposed Children (NI) Order, published in July 1993, implements this recommendation by stipulating that when dealing with any civil matter under that Order a juvenile court may be known as a family proceedings court and there is to be a right of appeal to the High Court. Indeed matters concerning children are to be handled by whichever level of court is most appropriate in the circumstances, the aim being to allow one court to deal with all related problems at one go. The Northern Ireland Office is currently considering the criminal law governing juvenile offenders as part of a wider review of criminal justice policy. The Children (NI) Order, when enacted, will change the law on many other issues relating to the care and supervision of children, some of which are noted in 5.2, 5.4 and 5.6. It will bring the law concerning children in Northern Ireland largely into line with that in England and Wales under the Children Act 1989. One of the key principles is that in any court proceedings the welfare of the child is to be the paramount consideration; courts are to ensure that delay is avoided and they are to issue a court order only if to do so is better for the child than making no order at all.

Care, protection or control proceedings

Typical cases in this category (now representing about one-fifth of all juvenile court cases) are those involving youngsters who fail to attend school regularly or who are suffering or at risk because of a lack of parental care or because a member of their household has committed an offence directly linked to the safety of juveniles. Most of these cases are brought to court by one of the four Health and Social Services Boards in Northern Ireland, which will submit a report on the home surroundings, school record, physical and mental health and the character of the child or young person. In reaching its decision in any case, the juvenile court must take such reports into consideration in fulfilment of its statutory duties to have regard to the welfare of the juvenile and, if appropriate, to take steps to remove the juvenile from undesirable surroundings and to secure that proper provision is made for his or her education and training. The juvenile can be represented at the hearing, with the normal provisions as to legal aid and advice applying (see 3.3).

To deal with such cases, of which there were 863 during 1991, the juvenile court currently has the power to make a number of different orders. These include the following:

(1) *A fit person order*. This is an order, sometimes referred to as a care order, which places the juvenile under the care of someone who is

willing to undertake that care and whom the court thinks is suitable. The fit person may be a relative or friend of the juvenile, but in the vast majority of cases the "person" will in fact be a Health and Social Services Board. It is the duty of these Boards to further the best interests of the child or young person within the limits of the facilities and services available. To allow the fit person to exercise proper care, the juvenile will sometimes be required to reside in that person's home or in a hostel run by the Health Board, but this requirement will usually be relaxed before the order expires (on the juvenile's eighteenth birthday).

(2) *A supervision order.* This is an order which places a child or young person under the supervision of a probation officer or some other person or body appointed for the purpose (including a Health Board). Again, the juvenile need not have to reside away from home during the life of the supervision order but in many cases will do so. The supervisor's function is to visit, advise and befriend the juvenile and where necessary help him or her to find suitable employment. The order can remain in force for up to three years.

(3) *A hospital or guardianship order.* These orders require the evidence of two medical practitioners to the effect that the juvenile is suffering from a mental disorder warranting detention or special care. A hospital order entails specialised expert treatment as a resident in a hospital, while a guardianship order obliges the guardian to receive the patient into his or her care and make arrangements for the patient's training, recreation and good health. The duration of such orders is decided by the Health and Social Services Board, though in the case of hospital orders the juvenile court can restrict discharge of the patient during a specified period.

(4) *A training school order.* Although training school orders can be made during care, protection or control proceedings, they are much more commonly made in criminal proceedings and are therefore described more fully below.

In addition to these four different types of order the juvenile court can require a juvenile's parent or guardian to enter into a promise, called a "recognisance", to exercise proper care and guardianship. This means that the parent or guardian will forfeit some money if the promise is not fulfilled. In cases where a child or young person is considered to be the victim of abuse he or she can be removed to a place of safety and made the subject of a "place of safety order". Such an order can be made on an interim basis for up to two periods of five weeks, during which time the specific needs of the child will be fully assessed; a full order can then be made for a further period of five weeks. Under the proposed Children (NI) Order place of safety orders will be replaced by emergency protection orders, which will last for a maximum of eight days and may be extended once only for a further seven days, and by child assessment orders, which will allow an investigation to be conducted into a child's safety and well-being in situations not deemed urgent enough for the emergency protection procedure.

The Children (NI) Order, when enacted, will enable an Education and Library Board to apply for what is to be called an "education supervision order". This will require the Board to "advise, assist and befriend, and give directions to the supervised child and his or her parents in such a way as will, in the Board's opinion, secure that he or she is properly educated". In all cases involving the child care responsibilities of the DHSS and the Health and Social Services Boards a child will be entitled under the new Order to have an independent person appointed by the court (probably a social worker) to represent the child's interests; this person will be called a "guardian *ad litem*" and he or she will in turn be able to appoint a solicitor to act for the child.

Criminal proceedings

Efforts are made to keep the number of criminal proceedings against juveniles to a minimum. If the police believe that a child or young person may be in need of advice, guidance or assistance they are required to inform the local social services office, and if they suspect children or young persons of the commission of some offence they often prefer to rely on informal words of advice or official cautions rather than bring the matter before a court. Since 1975 the RUC have operated a Juvenile Liaison Scheme as an extension of the practice of cautioning, thereby enabling themselves to supervise informally those young persons who admit to having committed an offence but who have not been made to face a juvenile court. A total of 9,441 cases were referred to the Juvenile Liaison Scheme during 1992; a warning and advice were administered in 4,253 cases, an official caution was given in 2,839 cases and in 1,462 cases no further police action was taken. As a result of such screening the cases which were prosecuted tended to be quite serious.

As Table 8 in 4.2 indicates, the number of juveniles proceeded against in juvenile courts in Northern Ireland has been steadily declining while the number proceeded against in the Crown Court has remained fairly constant. But in 1991 the total number proceeded against was the lowest for 10 years, being less than half the number in 1982. About three-quarters of the indictable charges against juveniles are connected with burglaries, thefts or fraud.

There is a rule of law that a boy or girl under 10 years of age cannot commit a criminal offence: they are said to be *doli incapax* (incapable of wickedness). Care proceedings may be taken in respect of such youngsters, but not criminal proceedings. A child, who in law is someone aged 10 to 13, is also presumed to be *doli incapax* but this time the presumption can be reversed by the prosecution, especially if the child is aware of what it means to be wicked. Children and young persons (14, 15 and 16 year olds) *can* be punished for committing criminal offences, though not in the same way as adults, and even the words "conviction" and "sentence" must not be used in relation to children and young persons dealt with summarily: the expressions "finding of guilt" and "order made on a finding of guilt" must be used instead. There is an exception if a child or young person is charged jointly with a person aged 17 or over: such charges must initially be heard by an ordinary magistrates' court and the ordinary terminology can be employed.

Any juvenile who has been arrested and charged may be released on police bail unless the charge is a very serious one, such as murder or manslaughter, or unless it is necessary in the juvenile's own interest to remove him or her from association with any reputed criminal or prostitute. If not so released, the police must detain the juvenile in a remand home until he or she can be brought before a magistrates' court. A remand in custody during the course of a hearing must also be to a remand home; it can be to a prison only if the court certifies that the juvenile is of so unruly or depraved a character that a remand home would not be a suitable place. Otherwise the same provisions concerning bail and legal aid and advice which apply to suspected adult offenders apply also to juvenile criminal proceedings (see 4.4 and 3.3).

A juvenile court can try juveniles summarily or can conduct preliminary investigations or preliminary enquiries into indictable offences (see 4.7). It can also deal summarily with any indictable offence other than murder if it thinks that such a course is expedient and if the prosecutor and the child's parent or guardian, or the young person, consent. In such a case the juvenile court, on making a finding of guilt, may make any order which might have been made if the case had been tried by the Crown Court on indictment. It may therefore impose a much more serious sentence than an ordinary magistrates' court. Even after Crown Court trials the juvenile may be sent back to the juvenile court for sentencing. In 1991, 80 per cent of the juveniles proceeded against were charged with indictable offences; the equivalent figure for adult defendants was 28 per cent.

Punishment

As in care proceedings, the juvenile court dealing with criminal proceedings must consider all medical and welfare reports relating to the juvenile and can choose from a wide selection of available responses. As the cases brought to court involve the more serious allegations it comes as no surprise to find that in 1992 as many as 25 per cent of the juveniles proceeded against were given an immediate custodial sentence in the young offenders' centre or at a training school (none was sent to prison). The form of punishment most frequently administered, however, is a conditional discharge (25 per cent in 1992). A comparatively small proportion of juveniles (11 per cent in 1992) are fined; in theory a juvenile can be fined for any offence other than murder, although a child cannot personally be made to pay more than £100 (including costs) or a young person more than £400. Under the proposed Criminal Justice (NI) Order 1993 these maxima are to rise to £250 and £1,000 respectively. A parent or guardian may be ordered to pay the fine instead. The court may also order the payment of up to £2,000 in compensation to the victim of the offence and make any of the first three orders which were outlined above in respect of care proceedings. The main features of the other sentencing options available to the juvenile court in criminal proceedings are the following:

(1) *Detention in a young offenders' centre or in prison.* This option, which is available only for persons aged at least 16, can be resorted to if the court certifies that the young person is of so unruly or depraved a character that no other method of dealing with him or her is appropriate. If the offence involved is one which is punishable in the case of an adult with 14 years' imprisonment (or five years if it is a scheduled offence - see 4.1) the detention of the offender may be ordered to be in such place and for such time as the Secretary of State for Northern Ireland may direct. These include the "SoSPs" mentioned in 4.8. Otherwise the maximum permissible period of detention in a young offenders' centre is four years. The only young offenders' centres in Northern Ireland are at Hydebank Wood in

South Belfast and (for females) at Maghaberry near Lisburn. In 1992 there were 146 committals to these centres.

(2) *A training school order.* These orders demand the residence of the juvenile in one of the province's five training schools, the aim being to allow the juvenile to learn how to readjust to society at large and to grow accustomed to the habit of work or school. The order can remain in force for up to two years (or until the young person turns 19 years of age) but the manager of the school is required to review the pupil's progress at regular intervals and will release the pupil at any time after six months if he or she is considered to be ready to return to the community. The parents of a juvenile residing in a training school may be asked to contribute to his or her keep and at the end of the period the juvenile will continue to be supervised at home by a social worker. During 1992 there were 417 training school orders issued.

(3) *An attendance centre order.* Such an order requires the offender to attend the centre at Millfield in Belfast for a fixed number of hours every Saturday. A session of physical education is usually followed by a lecture (*e.g.* on first aid), employment in handicrafts, or other instruction. A juvenile cannot be required to attend for a total of more than 24 hours, but a young person (aged 14 to 16) must attend for at least 12 hours. During 1992, 97 attendance centre orders were made.

(4) *A probation order.* This places the juvenile under the supervision of a probation officer for a period between six months and three years and requires the juvenile to lead an honest and industrious life during that time. Under the Treatment of Offenders (NI) Order 1989 a court can attach an extra condition to a probation order whereby the probationer is required to attend at a specified place for up to a maximum of 60 days. If a probation order is breached, the juvenile may then be dealt with as if found guilty of the original offence for which he or she was placed on probation. If a young person (aged 14 to 16) does not wish to be placed on probation then the juvenile court must resort to some other punishment. There are also some offences which by statute cannot be dealt with in this way. In 1992, 21 per cent of convicted juveniles were either placed on probation or made the subject of the comparable supervision order (described above in the section on care proceedings).

(5) *A community service order.* These orders are available only for persons aged 16 or over. They require a person to undertake a

specified service for a specified number of hours. Only 26 were issued against 16-year-old juveniles in 1991.

Appeals

The system of appeals against decisions of juvenile courts, whether in care proceedings or criminal proceedings, is the same as for appeals against decisions of ordinary magistrates' courts (see 4.6 and 5.2), with the difference that in criminal proceedings lay members from juvenile court panels are appointed to sit as assessors with a county court judge hearing any appeal.

6.2 Courts-Martial

Courts-martial are a relic from the days when in addition to the ordinary courts of law there were many other courts dealing with special matters. Ecclesiastical courts are another example, but they are too specialised to warrant expanded treatment in this book.

Courts-martial apply military law, a special body of rules addressed only to persons serving in the Army, and they apply a similar body of rules addressed to members of the Navy and Air Force. Auxiliary and reserve forces are affected as well, as are civilians employed by the armed forces abroad. The rules are published officially in the Manual of Military Law, but derive ultimately from Acts of Parliament and from Regulations issued under the Royal Prerogative (see 2.2). They provide for many internal disciplinary offences, but all offences under the criminal law of England are also offences under military law if committed by a member of the armed forces. Some very serious offences, such as murder, manslaughter or rape, must be tried in ordinary civilian courts if committed within the United Kingdom. Once a trial has occurred in one of the court systems there cannot be a second trial on the same or a similar charge in the other court system. In practice, in Northern Ireland as well as Great Britain, the vast majority of criminal offences committed by members of the armed forces during peacetime are tried in the ordinary way, or as scheduled offences, by the ordinary courts; only if the defendant has since been posted abroad, or if the incident did not in any way affect civilians, might a court-martial be held.

There is also a system for dealing with complaints against soldiers lodged by members of the public; these should be sent to the Complaints and Civil Courts Department of Army Headquarters in Lisburn. In 1992

Mr David Hewitt was appointed by the government, under the Northern Ireland (Emergency Provisions) Act 1991, as an Independent Assessor of Military Complaints Procedures; his duty is to keep under review the procedures adopted by the General Officer Commanding Northern Ireland for responding to complaints (of which, in 1992, there were 427 alleging a criminal offence and a further 282 not alleging such an offence). In 1992 the DPP directed prosecutions against soldiers in 72 cases, 15 of which developed out of complaints made by members of the public.

Ordinary soldiers and non-commissioned officers can be dealt with summarily by the commanding officer of the battalion or regiment for a number of minor military offences. The severest punishment which can be imposed is 60 days' military detention or the forfeiture of 28 days' pay. The accused is not allowed to have any form of representation at these summary hearings, but if the commanding officer intends to order a fine or detention the accused has the right to call for a court-martial.

Trials

More serious charges must be investigated to see if the accused should be sent for trial by court-martial. The decision is taken by the commanding officer after consideration of an "abstract", or summary, of evidence. This is evidence notified to the accused in proceedings comparable to committal proceedings in ordinary magistrates' courts (see 4.7), though without the accused being entitled to representation. At the court-martial itself there can be representation by a lawyer nominated from civilian life or by a regimental officer; representatives from the forces are often preferred because they are more familiar with service standards and jargon. Legal aid under the Northern Ireland criminal legal aid scheme is not available for military proceedings in the province, but a special Army scheme based on the English civilian scheme has been set up in its place. One consequence of this is that the Army scheme does not ensure free legal aid: the accused may be compelled to contribute an amount depending upon his or her savings and annual income.

In peacetime there are two basic types of court-martial. One is a District Court-Martial, which consists of a bench of three officers usually presided over by a major or lieutenant-colonel. It tries ordinary soldiers and non-commissioned officers, with powers to imprison convicted defendants for up to two years. The other is a General Court-Martial, which has a bench of at least five officers presided over by a colonel or higher-ranking officer. It can try any member of the forces and impose any sentence prescribed by military law. The judges for General Courts-Martial are appointed for one case at a time, but the Presidents of District Courts-Martial (of whom there are five in the United Kingdom) are appointed on a long-term basis for a particular area. The accused has the right to object to a particular officer being appointed to hear his or her case. The trial of civilians in a court-martial must be before Crown servants rather than military officers (with the exception of the court's President). The courts sit at irregular intervals (every four to six weeks) and in makeshift courtrooms. Each year there are about 1,000 District Courts-Martial and between 30 and 40 General Courts-Martial throughout the United Kingdom.

Judge Advocates

No court-martial sits with a jury, but in serious cases the officers on the bench are assisted by a lawyer employed in the Office of the Judge Advocate General. This is an independent civilian office with general responsibility for supervising the handling of legal matters affecting the armed forces. As well as the Judge Advocate General himself, and the Vice-Judge Advocate General, there are (for the United Kingdom) four judge advocates. These are barristers who function in a similar way to the advocates-general in the European Court of Justice (see 2.6); they sum up the evidence and advise the court on questions of law. On some matters the court is bound to follow the judge advocate's advice, but the actual decision in the case must be taken by a vote among only the officers on the bench.

As well as being continuously under the supervision of the Office of the Judge Advocate General, the proceedings of a court-martial can be subjected to the judicial review procedures described in 7.1, and writs of *habeas corpus* can be issued to put an end to any unauthorised detention. In addition, every finding of guilt and every sentence has to be confirmed by a higher ranking officer before it takes full effect; in Northern Ireland this confirming officer will be a brigadier. The confirming officer can refuse to confirm any finding and can reduce any punishment, but in practice this occurs very infrequently.

Reviews and appeals

The court-martial's decision will be to find the defendant guilty or not guilty. By way of punishment it can fine, detain or imprison; it cannot grant a conditional discharge, make a probation order or impose a suspended sentence. If the defendant wishes to query a finding of guilt or the punishment, he or she can first of all ask for a review by the Defence Council (a body which co-ordinates all the armed forces); there can also be a formal petition to the Defence Council. If still dissatisfied, the defendant can ask the Courts-Martial Appeal Court for permission to appeal there.

This Appeal Court was set up in 1951 and is staffed by all the English Court of Appeal judges and by such English, Northern Irish and Scottish judges as are nominated for the purpose. It usually sits in London as a bench of three judges, though it may in fact sit anywhere in the United Kingdom or even abroad. Its powers are similar to those of the Northern Ireland Court of Appeal (see 4.8), though it can order a retrial only where there is fresh evidence to consider (not where there has been a wrong decision of law or a material irregularity in the course of the court-martial), and unless the appellant is a civilian it cannot hear an appeal against sentence alone (in such cases it can only voice disquiet at the harshness of the sentence and hope that the particular Service Board will as a result reduce it). Only a handful of appeals are heard each year.

There is a further channel of appeal for either side to the House of Lords, but one of the two courts must first grant permission for this appeal and the Courts-Martial Appeal Court must certify that a point of law of general public importance is involved. The last such appeal was in 1968.

6.3 Coroners' Courts

In Northern Ireland coroners are appointed by the Lord Chancellor from among barristers or solicitors of five or more years' standing. (In England they are appointed by local authorities.) Before 1959 doctors were also eligible to be appointed. Coroners are meant to act completely independently of the government, the police and the medical profession. At present there are seven in Northern Ireland, with five deputies; only the coroner for Greater Belfast, Mr John Leckey, is full-time. The relevant legislation is the Coroners Act (NI) 1959 and the Coroners (Practice and Procedure) Rules (NI) 1963, as amended.

The chief function of coroners is to investigate unexpected, unexplained, violent or suspicious deaths. Formerly the investigations were carried out with a view to uncovering unsuspected homicide, but with the development of the police service and medical science one of the main objects today is the accurate ascertainment of the cause of death. To assist in determining the cause of death, the coroner can order a *post mortem* examination to be carried out by a government-approved doctor, and this is done in more than half the cases investigated. If the investigation indicates that death was due to an unnatural cause the coroner will usually hold an inquest. An inquest can be held even though the death occurred abroad, provided the body has since been returned to the coroner's area.

Inquests

In 1992 there were 2,958 investigations into suspicious deaths in Northern Ireland and inquests were held in 492 cases. A *post mortem* examination took place in a further 915 cases. The inquests usually take place in recognised courthouses and do not normally involve a jury, but if it appears to the coroner that there is reason to suspect that the death occurred in prison, in an accident, or in circumstances prejudicial to the safety of the public, a jury of between seven and 11 persons must be summoned. (In England a jury must also be summoned if the death results from an injury supposedly caused by a police officer in the execution of his or her duty.) Some of the most controversial inquests occurring in Northern Ireland are those into deaths caused by members of the security forces.

The purpose behind an inquest is to determine who the deceased person was, and how, when and where he or she came to die. It must be held in public. The coroner plays a more leading role than a judge would do in a regular court of law in that he or she has a wide-ranging discretion as to which witnesses should be called, compelling their attendance if necessary, and the coroner will take an active part in examining them. The witnesses are placed under oath and may also be questioned by other interested parties such as the family of the deceased person. There is no absolute right for these parties to be legally represented in the proceedings, neither legal advice and assistance nor legal aid are available, and speeches cannot be made to the jury except by the coroner in his or her summing-up. The proceedings, in short, are more inquisitorial than adversarial (see 5.6).

In Northern Ireland the procedures at inquests differ in some important respects from those in England and Wales (there is an altogether different system in Scotland, where they rely on fatal accident inquiries). In particular, any person who has been, or is likely to be, charged with a criminal offence connected with the death cannot be compelled to give evidence at an inquest in Northern Ireland; nor can any legal objection be raised if such a person decides to submit written evidence but not to appear in the witness box (*Devine* v *Attorney General for Northern Ireland*, 1992). This usually means that at inquests after so-called "shoot-to-kill" incidents the soldiers or police officers involved need not give their version of the events if they do not wish to.

Within five days of the end of the inquest the coroner must send the particulars of death to the appropriate registrar of deaths. Where the circumstances appear to the coroner to disclose that a criminal offence may have been committed the coroner must also, as soon as practicable, furnish the Director of Public Prosecutions with a written report of those circumstances, but neither the coroner nor the jury may express any opinions on questions of criminal or civil liability. Coroners are not judges in a trial, and nothing in proceedings before a coroner should prejudice proceedings which might be taken in another court; for this reason inquests are often delayed until any criminal proceedings connected with the death have run their course. In Northern Ireland these delays often endure for several years.

Until 1981 the coroner or jury had to record the death in one of five ways: natural causes, the result of an accident or misadventure, the deceased's own act (adding, if appropriate, "whilst the balance of his mind was disturbed"), execution of sentence of death, or an open verdict. This last verdict was used when none of the others was appropriate. Since 1981 coroners or juries in Northern Ireland have simply had to list their "findings", a procedure which in theory ought to allow for more informative conclusions but which still precludes any verdict (such as is possible in England) of "unlawful killing". The jurors' conclusions need not be unanimous, provided not more than two of them dissent.

There cannot be any appeal against the decision at a coroner's inquest, but the proceedings can be made the object of an application for judicial review (see 7.1), which might lead to a new inquest if at the earlier one the coroner, for example, failed to call a jury when one should have been called, or failed properly to sum up the evidence to the jury. In 1988 the Northern Ireland Court of Appeal ordered a new inquest to be held in respect of a shooting incident in 1982; at the first inquest the coroner had applied a rule of evidence which the Court of Appeal said was *ultra vires* (*i.e.* beyond the powers conferred by) the Coroners Act (NI) 1959. A year later the House of Lords reversed this decision (*McKerr v Armagh Coroner*). In England, but not in Northern Ireland, the Attorney-General retains a power to refer a coroner's inquest to the High Court, which can order a second inquest to be held.

Treasure trove

Coroners also have jurisdiction to hold inquests into the finding of treasure trove, which is property consisting substantially of gold or silver. If the property was deliberately hidden it qualifies as treasure trove and belongs to the Crown, which then usually makes an *ex gratia* payment of compensation to the finder and donates the treasure to a museum. If the property was merely lost, the finder, his or her employer or the owner of the land acquires a good title to it and can keep it. Naturally enough this type of inquest is very rare.

6.4 Election Courts

The statutes governing elections in Northern Ireland allow for the establishment of election courts to try election petitions. These petitions are challenges to the election of a Member of Parliament or a local councillor on the basis that there was some material irregularity in the course of the election. They must be presented within 21 days of the election or within 28 days of any alleged corrupt practice. Each year the judges of the High Court and the Court of Appeal must select two of their number to be the judges to sit in these election courts, from which (unlike in England and Wales) there can be no appeal. They do not sit with a jury.

Naturally enough election petitions are rare. The most recent example of an election court is that which sat to determine the validity of the election of Mr Joe Hendron as the MP for West Belfast in the April 1992 general election. The court found, as it was entitled to do under the Representation of the People Act 1983, that illegal practices had occurred (*e.g.* spending £782 in excess of the allowed limit) but that they were of too limited a character to justify a report to the Speaker of the House of Commons to the effect that the election must be declared void (*McGrory v Hendron*, 1993).

It is also possible for an elector to appeal against his or her registration or non-registration on the electoral register. The appeal is first heard by an official called the Revising Officer but it can be further dealt with by a county court. There were two such county court appeals in Northern Ireland in 1992, the first since 1976.

7

Tribunals

7.1 Tribunals in General and Judicial Review

In Chapters 4 and 5 we examined the workings of the criminal and civil courts in Northern Ireland. These can be called ordinary courts of law. Elsewhere in the book we have mentioned what might be called special courts of law: the Judicial Committee of the Privy Council (see 1.4), the European Court of Justice and the European Court of Human Rights (see 2.6), the Restrictive Practices Court (see 5.6), juvenile courts (see 6.1), courts-martial (see 6.2) and election courts (6.4). With coroners' courts, in the previous chapter, we encountered an institution which is called a court but which in fact differs markedly in its procedures and powers from all the other courts. At this point it is necessary to turn our attention to other institutions which do not bear the name of courts but which, like coroners' courts, officially adjudicate on certain issues and make pronouncements. These institutions are called tribunals. They constitute a most important sector in our legal system.

The vast majority of tribunals are created by legislation. Among the first to be established were those which settled disputes arising out of the pension, health and unemployment insurance schemes set up by the Old Age Pensions Act 1908 and the National Insurance Act 1911. Since then many dozens of different kinds of tribunal have been formed throughout the United Kingdom, their proliferation during the last 40 years being largely attributable to the development of the welfare state. About 60 different kinds of tribunals operate at the present time, recent creations being the Registered Homes Tribunal and the Curriculum Complaints Tribunal. Given this phenomenon the ordinary law-abiding citizen is much more likely to confront a tribunal than a court of law. The number of cases dealt with by tribunals certainly far exceeds that disposed of at county court level or in a higher court.

There are many reasons why tribunals have become such popular institutions. On the whole they provide justice which is quicker, cheaper, less formal and more private. But essentially they are preferred because the conventional judicial system is ill-suited to dealing with their particular kind of problems, notably those which arise in the administration of a complex statutory scheme. Judges cannot be experts in every walk of life or field of law; some issues demand a particular expertise possessed by other persons which it would be wasteful to ignore when disputes arise. There are also issues which are peculiarly factual in nature and for which it would be both unnecessary and inappropriate to resort to the traditional paraphernalia associated with courts of law. It has to be conceded, though, that there sometimes appears to be little logic in the way in which some issues are allocated to courts of law and others to tribunals.

Tribunals are most often composed of three members, only the chairperson being legally qualified. The pernickety rules of etiquette and of evidence, so beloved by judges and professional lawyers, are for the most part ignored. Representation is usually permitted, but it is often undertaken by someone other that a solicitor or barrister - something unheard of in the ordinary courts. Civil legal aid for representation at tribunals (see 3.3) is generally not available, as the objective is to "de-legalise" proceedings as much as possible. But the legal advice and assistance scheme *can* be used. Decisions are more frequently arrived at on the spot than in courts of law, and the costs are kept to a minimum. Courts do, however, still play a significant background role: they decide questions specifically reserved to them by the legislation governing the administrative scheme involved, they deal with some appeals and they supervise tribunals by hearing complaints that they have denied natural justice to one of the parties or have committed some elementary error of law (such as hearing a case with which they had no authority to deal).

It is this supervisory jurisdiction which is exercised through the granting of applications for judicial review and which has given rise to many of the developments in what is now called "administrative law". The procedure outlined below would have been initiated in only a handful of cases a few years ago, but by 1992 there were 192 such cases in Northern Ireland (see Table 12 in 5.1). A high proportion of the applications have involved claims by prisoners concerning disciplinary hearings in prison; indeed it was a precedent set by the Northern Ireland Court of Appeal in *In re McKiernan* (1985) which persuaded the House of Lords to allow decisions by prison governors to be reviewed in England and Wales (see *Leech* v *Parkhurst Prison Deputy Governor*, 1988).

Applications for judicial review

In general, the judicial review procedure can be applied to all persons or bodies exercising a judicial, quasi-judicial or administrative function. However, as far as courts of law are concerned, the superior courts (Crown Court, High Court and above) are exempt from judicial review; only magistrates' courts and county courts are affected. The orthodox view is that the procedure is also unavailable in respect of some tribunals - those which are predominantly private bodies, such as when individuals are in dispute with trades unions, professional bodies or universities. But a decision of the House of Lords permitting the procedure to be used *vis-à-vis* the City Panel on Mergers and Takeovers has cast doubt on this view (*Ex parte Datafin*, 1987). Tribunals dealing with private disputes (often involving disciplinary matters) are called domestic, as opposed to administrative, tribunals. Many are set up voluntarily, within a company for example. Those which are established by statute, however, such as the Law Society's Disciplinary Committee, *are* subject to the judicial review procedure. For details of the procedure see the Rules of the Supreme Court (NI) 1980, Order 53.

Permission to make an application for judicial review in respect of an administrative tribunal cannot be granted unless the applicant is deemed to have a sufficient interest, or "*locus standi*", in the matter to which the application relates. The law on what constitutes adequate standing for this purpose is still in a state of flux, but in matters directly affecting the general public - such as the levying of rates - it seems that virtually any person may be justified in applying. The application for permission must be made to a High Court judge as soon as is practicable and no later than three months after the proceeding complained of, unless the judge is satisfied that the granting of relief after this time would not cause hardship to, or unfairly prejudice, the rights of any person. If the application for permission is unsuccessful, an appeal can be lodged with the Court of Appeal. Once permission to apply is granted, the judicial review application itself will usually be considered by one judge of the High Court, again with appeals lying to the Court of Appeal. In some cases, particularly those involving criminal matters, the High Court will sit as a court of two or even three judges; this is the Divisional Court mentioned in 1.3 and 5.6. The High Court judge who currently hears most of the judicial review applications is Mr Justice Carswell.

In an application for judicial review the applicant can seek a number of remedies: (1) "*certiorari*", an order that a decision be quashed; (2) "prohibition", an order that a body decline to deal with a matter; (3)

"mandamus", an order to compel the performance of some public duty; (4) an "injunction", an order to stop acting in a certain manner; and (5) a "declaration", an order clarifying someone's legal position or condemning an administrative decision as illegal. The first three of these used to be officially known as "prerogative orders" and are sometimes still referred to as such.

Injunctions and declarations can be obtained not only through applications for judicial review but also through the issuing of a civil bill (see 5.4) or a writ (see 5.6). These conventional processes allow aggrieved persons to query even the private, domestic proceedings which cannot be subjected to judicial review, but the remedy will not be obtained as quickly, directly or cheaply. On the other hand the conventional processes are not so constrained by time limits, they do not require prior judicial permission, they allow for more effective emergency relief, and they provide for a fuller trial of all the issues.

Tribunals in Northern Ireland

Although for most purposes Northern Ireland constitutes an independent legal system with its own laws, courts and tribunals, there are still some fields of law which are uniformly administered either throughout the United Kingdom or at least throughout England, Wales and Northern Ireland. Many of these fields are ones which were never within the domain of the Parliament of Northern Ireland because they were excepted or reserved matters under the Government of Ireland Act 1920 (see 1.2). Any tribunal system existing within such fields will be a nationwide system, so that a tribunal sitting in Belfast will apply the same laws and operate in the same way as a tribunal sitting in Birmingham.

Examples of this phenomenon are the Banking Appeal Tribunals, the Income Tax Tribunals (composed of Special and - from 1989 - General Commissioners of Income Tax), the VAT tribunals, the Misuse of Drugs Tribunal, the Data Protection Tribunal and the Copyright Tribunal. All of these are supervised by the Council on Tribunals, set up in 1958 to keep under review the workings of most tribunals throughout Great Britain. The Council can make recommendations to government Ministers as to who should be appointed to sit on a tribunal and it must usually be consulted before rules of procedure are laid down for a tribunal. If courts need to be involved in such fields, to hear appeals, answer referred questions, or exercise a supervisory jurisdiction, the courts of Northern Ireland will deal with proceedings originating within the province, but the tribunals will still remain part of the United Kingdom system. Most of the general rules concerning the functioning of tribunals are now contained in the Tribunals and Inquiries Act 1992.

Occasionally, as in the case of immigration appeal tribunals and the Foreign Compensation Commission (which deals with claims for compensation regarding British-owned property confiscated abroad), hearings will take place at centres in England even though some of the relevant facts relate to Northern Ireland. If courts have to be involved in these cases they may be English courts.

For most matters, however, Northern Ireland retains its own independent tribunal systems. The law that the tribunals apply may well be virtually identical to the law in the rest of the United Kingdom, and the procedures that they adopt may also be indistinguishable, but they nevertheless constitute separate systems. They are not subject to the supervision of the Council on Tribunals. It would be impossible to examine here the jurisdiction and procedures of all such tribunals, but the remaining sections of this chapter describe those which are most prominent.

The tribunals dealt with in this chapter should be distinguished from the tribunals of inquiry set up on an *ad hoc* basis under the Tribunals of Inquiry (Evidence) Act 1921. These are created by resolution of both Houses of Parliament; they entrust to a judge the task of inquiring into some recent scandal or disaster. An example is the Widgery Tribunal of Inquiry appointed in 1972 to investigate the killing of unarmed demonstrators in Derry on so-called "Bloody Sunday". From time to time a judge or other senior figure is appointed to conduct a less official inquiry and with less extensive powers. Various statutes also allow for the creation of inquiries for which the Lord Chancellor, under the Tribunals and Inquiries Act 1992, can make procedural rules.

7.2 Social Security Appeal Tribunals

These tribunals handle disputes over entitlement to contributory, non-contributory and means-tested social security benefits - such as unemployment benefit, child support or income support. Local offices of the Social Security Agency can provide information as to the conditions to be fulfilled before you are entitled to any of these payments; the conditions change frequently, usually in April of each year. These offices can also explain what precisely to do if you disagree with the assessment of your entitlement; this section gives just an outline of what might happen in such a situation.

Claims for benefits

Most of the law concerning entitlement to social security benefits now derives from the Social Security Contributions and Benefits Act (NI) 1992 and regulations made thereunder. The initial decision as to whether or not a claimant qualifies for a particular benefit is taken by an adjudication officer working in the local social security office or by an adjudicating medical authority. Adjudication officers consider the information passed on by the staff of the office and can ask for more to be obtained. They do not make other inquiries or interview the claimant; although they are employees of the Social Security Agency they are meant to be independent. There is a Chief Adjudication Officer whose functions include advising adjudication officers on how to carry out their tasks; he or she publishes a multi-volume *Guide to Adjudication Officers* and issues an annual report commenting on the way in which adjudication officers have taken decisions. The Social Fund Commissioner likewise reviews the standards achieved by the social fund inspectors.

Adjudication officers decide on eligibility for both contributory benefits (for which you help to pay through subscriptions to the national insurance fund deducted from your wages or salary), non-contributory benefits and means-tested benefits. Contributory benefits include statutory sick pay, sickness benefit, invalidity benefit, statutory maternity pay, maternity benefit, unemployment benefit, industrial injuries benefit, widow's benefit and retirement pensions. Non-contributory benefits include child benefit, one parent benefit, disability living allowance, attendance allowance and invalid care allowance. The best known of the means-tested benefits is income support (formerly supplementary benefit) which is designed to provide income to people who are not in full-time employment and whose income, if any, whether from other benefits or from private resources, is not enough to meet their requirements. Other means-tested benefits include housing benefit, family credit, disability working allowance and social fund payments.

An adjudication officer or adjudicating medical authority is under a legal duty to dispose of a claim, so far as is practicable, within 14 days of its being submitted. However, certain issues must be reserved for consideration by a different body, which may take longer than 14 days. For instance, the questions whether a person satisfies the medical conditions relating to disability living allowance, or which of two people might be entitled to an invalid care allowance in respect of a particular invalid, must be decided by officials in the DHSS. These special matters have their own systems of appeal (*e.g.* decisions on whether contribution conditions have been satisfied can be appealed to the High Court).

In ordinary cases the claimant can ask for the adjudication officer's decision to be reviewed; the review will be automatic if requested within three months of the original decision, otherwise some grounds for the review (such as a material change of circumstances) must be provided. There is then a right to appeal against the decision within a further three months (or 28 days in the case of child support); the appeal will be dealt with by a Social Security Appeal Tribunal, a Medical Appeal Tribunal, a Disability Appeal Tribunal or a Child Support Appeal Tribunal. The appeal must be in writing - you simply fill in a form and return it to your local social security office - and it will usually be heard within two or three weeks of the tribunal receiving the papers. There can be a further appeal, provided that a point of law is involved, to the Social Security Commissioner. In the case of housing benefit and social fund payments there can be no appeal to the Commissioner: final decisions are taken by the Housing Benefit Review Boards and the Social Fund Inspector.

The tribunal hearing

The system for dealing with appeals in social security matters was reformed in 1984. Prior to then there were separate appeal procedures depending on whether the claim in question was for a benefit connected with the national insurance fund or for supplementary benefit. Under the Social Security (Adjudications) Regulations (NI) 1984, most of the features of the former national insurance local tribunals were incorporated into the new tribunal system. Thus, a Social Security Appeal Tribunal consists of a legally qualified chairperson, one member representing employers and the self-employed, and another member representing employees and the unemployed and possessing knowledge of local social conditions. Members of Medical Appeal Tribunals are doctors of consultant status. These "lay" members are drawn from a panel appointed by the President of the Independent Tribunal Service, but the chairpersons are appointed by the Lord Chancellor. The Independent Tribunal Service is the name given since 1992 to the Office of the President of Social Security and Medical Appeals Tribunals.

Tribunals in this sphere are meant to be, as well as to seem, completely independent of the Department of Health and Social Services. For this reason the tribunal hearings are not conducted on DHSS premises. Members of the public can attend tribunal hearings just as they can attend hearings in a court of law, though of course they rarely do so. If intimate personal or financial circumstances or public security considerations are involved, the chairperson can direct the hearing to be held in private. The proceedings in a Social Security Appeal Tribunal are meant to be informal and uncomplicated, with the chairperson having a wide discretion as to how to run things. With a little forethought a claimant ought to be able to conduct his or her own case (it is, after all, a personal problem and no-one knows all the circumstances better than the claimant), but research has shown that claimants stand a far greater chance of winning their cases if they are legally represented. At the very least claimants ought to ensure that they turn up in person at their hearings: cases can be dealt with in their absence but the vast majority of these will be lost.

Most controversially, legal aid is not available for people who are too poor to pay for representation by a solicitor, although the legal advice and assistance scheme (described in 3.3) can make £86.50 worth of solicitor's help available short of actual representation; this would cover most of the cost of the paperwork involved in preparing a case for hearing. Alternatively, or additionally, a welfare rights worker, Citizens' Advice Bureau worker, friend or relative is allowed to represent the claimant free of charge; in tribunals, unlike courts, there are no restrictions on who can act as a legal representative. Some people believe it is a good thing that legal aid is not available for representation because otherwise the proceedings would be bound to become too legalistic; others hold that the denial of legal aid is blatant discrimination against the underprivileged.

A claimant can obtain reimbursement of travelling expenses and compensation for loss of wages incurred through attendance at a tribunal. Witnesses can be called and questioned by both sides, and a tribunal can ask the High Court to compel the attendance of witnesses or the production of documents. Whatever decision the tribunal comes to - whether it be unanimous or by a two to one majority (with the lay panel members perhaps outvoting the legally qualified chairperson) - it must be supported by written reasons. Occasionally decisions will be copied for the information of tribunal chairpersons but formal publication is rarely necessary because points of real substance will almost invariably go to the Social Security Commissioners (see below) for a definitive ruling on the legal issues arising.

The Social Security Appeal Tribunal system is presided over by the President of the Independent Tribunal Service (Mr Conal MacLynn). The President's role is to ensure that chairpersons and panel members are adequately trained and informed, that procedures are kept fair and easy to understand, and that the arrangements for holding tribunals are properly made. In status and salary the President is of equal rank with a county court judge.

Reviews and further appeals

All decisions in social security matters may at any time be internally reviewed by adjudication officers; indeed, in income support and child support cases a review takes place automatically whenever a decision is queried and the original decision may be altered in a way which cures the appellant's grievance before an appeal tribunal hearing takes place. An appeal which has already been lodged will lapse only if the adjudication officer conducting the review grants all the relief which the appeal tribunal could have granted. Even after the tribunal hearing reviews are still possible. They can occur if the decision was based on a mistake as to a material fact or if there has been a change of circumstances since the decision complained about was made.

From the decision of a Social Security Appeal Tribunal there is the opportunity of a full appeal within three months, by either the claimant or the adjudication officer, to the Social Security Commissioner. But the permission of the chairperson of the tribunal is required before an appeal can go ahead and in all cases there must be a question of law in dispute, not just a question of fact. If the chairperson refuses permission to appeal a request can be put direct to the Commissioner. Commissioners have to be barristers of at least 10 years' standing, which also puts them on a footing with county court judges. Apart from the Chief Commissioner there is one other full-time Social Security Commissioner in Northern Ireland. The conduct of the proceedings before the Commissioners is regulated by the Social Security Commissioners Procedure Regulations (NI) 1987.

The Commissioner may or may not hold an oral hearing into the case, but he or she must always fully reconsider the case and give a decision in writing. A new decision can be substituted for that of the tribunal, or the case can be referred back to a tribunal with instructions as to how to determine it. Reports of some Commissioners' decisions are published, and precedents are sometimes cited to, and followed by, tribunals. Another appeal can lie from the Commissioner, though only with permission and on points of unclear law, to the Court of Appeal; only one or two of these arise each year. In 1992 the Social Security Commissioners in Northern Ireland dealt with 150 applications for leave to appeal (48 of these after granting a hearing); they dealt with 92 actual appeals,

51 of these involving a hearing. There were three applications to the Commissioners for permission to appeal to the Court of Appeal.

Reviews of social security decisions can be appealed against in just the same way as an original decision of an adjudication officer. Questions reserved for officials in the DHSS are also reviewable, but only by the DHSS itself. There is also a process known as setting aside, which can occur within 28 days of a decision if the decision-making body made an accidental error or a relevant document went astray in the post; the procedure is the responsibility of the body which took the original decision. The appeal, review and setting aside procedures must, of course, be distinguished from the judicial review procedure described in 7.1.

The Social Security Advisory Committee

The Social Security Advisory Committee (SSAC) was set up in 1980 when the supplementary benefit scheme was being substantially altered. It is an independent body with the task of advising the Secretary of State for Social Services and the Department of Health and Social Services for Northern Ireland on United Kingdom social security matters. Although the chairperson and the dozen or so members are appointed by the Secretary of State, they do not automatically toe the government line when giving an opinion on social security issues, which they may do either at the government's request or on their own initiative. Most social security regulations, when they are at the drafting stage, have to be submitted to the SSAC for its comments; before producing a report on the draft regulations the SSAC usually undertakes a public consultation exercise. The government must publish the report when it lays the regulation before Parliament for consideration.

7.3. Tribunals Dealing with Employment Disputes

Industrial tribunals deal with disputes relating to individual employment contracts. More general collective disputes (those between employers and trade unions) are the concern of the Industrial Court and statutory bodies such as the Labour Relations Agency. To deal with the particular problem of religious and political discrimination in employment the Fair Employment Tribunal has been created. Watchdog bodies with a role to play in matters concerning employment or industrial relations are outlined in Chapter 8.

Industrial tribunals

Industrial tribunals have operated in Northern Ireland since 1965 and are now established under the Industrial Training (NI) Order 1984. Their procedures are governed by the Industrial Tribunals (Rules of Procedure) Regulations (NI) 1981, as amended. They are staffed by a President (Mr J E Maguire), a Vice-President, one full-time and 11 part-time chairpersons, and approximately 130 lay members. A full-time chaiperson earns £54,035 per year. Industrial tribunals sit all year round in six different venues in Northern Ireland, the headquarters now being in Waring Street in Belfast. The chairpersons and lay members are appointed by the Department of Economic Development, and of course they are meant to act completely impartially.

The various employment rights which industrial tribunals protect are enshrined in many different pieces of legislation and are subject to varying conditions and qualifications. The most frequently recurring types of case are those which concern redundancy, unfair dismissal, discrimination or activities on behalf of a trade union. One important employment right - to a minimum period of notice of dismissal - is at present protected not by means of a complaint to an industrial tribunal but through an action in the civil courts, though this is soon to change as a consequence of the Trade Union Reform and Employment Rights Act 1993.

Proceedings for a tribunal hearing are begun by the applicant sending an application to the Office of Industrial Tribunals and Fair Employment Tribunal (see the sample in Appendix 4). Many applications will then be automatically referred to the Labour Relations Agency (see 8.3) to see if the matter can be resolved with the help of one of its conciliation officers. If a tribunal hearing does eventually take place the evidence will be presented through the testimony of witnesses or the production of documents; written representations may also be made. The tribunal is expressly authorised to regulate procedure in whatever way is deemed best. The chairperson, who is legally qualified and sits with two lay persons with industrial relations experience, has considerable control over the strictness or otherwise of the procedure to be adopted. Proceedings are meant to be informal, but since some hearings are conducted in county court rooms the atmosphere of informality is not always easy to engender.

The two sides can be legally represented at tribunal hearings but cannot obtain legal aid for this purpose. They will have to bear the cost themselves unless their representative is, for instance, a volunteer or appointed by a trade union. Legal advice and assistance, however, is still available to those who are financially eligible (see 3.3). Only in exceptional circumstances, as where one party has asked for a postponement of the proceedings or has been vexatious, will one of the parties be made to bear the other's costs. The Police Authority, for example, had to pay the costs of female reservists who successfully brought a sex discrimination claim against the Chief Constable during the 1980s (*Johnston* v *Chief Constable of the RUC:* see 2.6). The costs, however, will not normally be anything like as high as in a court case.

Decision and challenge

The tribunal's decision may be given at the end of the hearing or reached later and notified to the parties. Written reasons must be given. If the tribunal decides that the applicant is in the right the particular remedy afforded will depend on the nature of the application. For example, if the claim is in respect of redundancy or maternity pay the tribunal may assess the amount of payments due; if it concerns a claim of unfair dismissal the tribunal can order the reinstatement of the employee, or compensation, or both; if the complaint relates to discrimination an order can be issued requiring the discrimination to be stopped. A register of all decisions is open for general public inspection at the Office of Industrial Tribunals and Fair Employment Tribunal.

There are three ways of challenging an industrial tribunal's decision: there can be a review by the tribunal itself, a judicial review by the High Court (see 7.1), or an appeal to the Court of Appeal by way of case stated on a point of law (see 4.6). In each of these cases care has to be taken to make the challenge within the specified time limit. There is no appeal, as there is in social security cases, to a higher tribunal or to a Commissioner. There is no Employment Appeal Tribunal in Northern Ireland such as exists in England. If an industrial tribunal makes an award of money to one of the parties, and that party proves unwilling to pay, the award may be enforced through an application first to a county court, and then, if necessary, to the Enforcement of Judgments Office (see 5.7). In general the maximum compensation which an industrial tribunal can award for, say, unfair dismissal is £11,000 but in 1993 the European Court of Justice ruled that this limit cannot be applied in cases of sex discrimination alleged against public sector bodies.

In 1992 there were 3,012 applications to industrial tribunals in Northern Ireland; many applications are of course resolved with the help of the

Labour Relations Agency, so in 1992 there were only 525 industrial tribunal hearings.

The Fair Employment Tribunal

This tribunal was set up by the Fair Employment (NI) Act 1989 to adjudicate upon individual complaints of discrimination on grounds of religious belief or political opinion and to enforce against employers affirmative action plans directed by the Fair Employment Commission. Shortly after its inception a difficulty arose with regard to section 30 of the 1989 Act, which in some situations criminalised the disclosure of information concerning a person's religious background. It was only after this section was repealed by the Fair Employment (Amendment) (NI) Order 1991 that the Fair Employment Tribunal was able to resume hearing cases. In 1992 there were 251 applications to the Fair Employment Tribunal and 108 actual hearings. Hearings are conducted in public, although some categories of evidence, such as information originally provided in confidence, can be presented in private.

The Fair Employment Tribunal can request an employer to take action to eliminate the effects of discrimination and can award damages up to £30,000 to individual complainants. The compensation can include an amount for injured feelings but not for unintentional indirect discrimination. If an employer refuses to implement an affirmative action plan directed by the Fair Employment Commission the Tribunal can impose a fine up to £30,000. As with industrial tribunals, all decisions of the Tribunal are subject to an appeal on a point of law to the Court of Appeal.

Many of the cases dealt with by the Tribunal are financially supported by the Fair Employment Commission, just as the Equal Opportunities Commission supports many claims of gender discrimination dealt with by the industrial trinuals. The work of each of these Commissions is described in more detail in Chapter 8.

The Industrial Court

The Industrial Court for Northern Ireland, which is the counterpart of the Central Arbitration Committee in Great Britain, was provided for by the Industrial Courts Act 1919 but was not actually constituted until 1964, when it was required to give effect to the Terms and Conditions of Employment Act (NI) 1963. As in the case of tribunals, a sitting of the Court comprises one independent chairman (the President of the Court) plus two lay members selected from panels representing both sides of industry. The President of the Court is currently the same person as the President of Industrial Tribunals.

The jurisdiction of the Industrial Court is fairly limited. Until recently it dealt with failure to comply with a recommendation made by the Labour Relations Agency for trade union recognition (see 8.3). Under the Equal Pay Act (NI) 1970 it can amend collective agreements, pay structures or wages orders whenever they contain discriminatory provisions applicable to men only or women only. Certain of the Court's decisions, while not in themselves enforceable in ordinary courts, lead to the incorporation of new terms into individual contracts of employment.

7.4 The Mental Health Review Tribunal

The Mental Health Review Tribunal (MHRT) has existed in Northern Ireland since 1962 and at present operates under the Mental Health (NI) Order 1986 (Part V and Schedule 3). The total membership of the MHRT consists of legal members (appointed by the Lord Chancellor), medical members (appointed by the Lord Chancellor after consultation with the Head of the Department of Health and Social Services) and other persons (appointed in the same way as medical members) who have such experience in administration, such knowledge of social services or such other qualifications or experience as the Lord Chancellor considers suitable. At the moment the MHRT comprises five legal members, five medical members and five other members.

One of the legal members acts as overall chairperson (currently Mr Fraser Elliott QC). The chairperson or one of the other legal members presides over each sitting of the MHRT, which usually involves three members, one from each of the three groups of members. For the purposes of any proceedings which are of a preliminary or incidental nature the MHRT may consist of only one member.

The MHRT exists to hear applications for discharge from hospital made by or on behalf of patients who are liable to be detained in a hospital under the Mental Health (NI) Order 1986 or under a restriction order issued by a criminal court. The 1986 Order updated the law in Northern Ireland on the detention, guardianship, care and treatment of patients suffering from mental disorder and on the management of the property and affairs of such patients. The MHRT cannot itself instigate hearings about patients' cases, doing so only when applications in writing are made to it. As regards long-stay patients, Health and Social Services

Boards (or, in the case of restricted patients, the Secretary of State) are under a duty to refer cases to the MHRT at least once every two years. As regards restricted patients (those sent to hospital by order of a criminal court) the MHRT now has powers concerning their absolute or conditional discharge.

During the year ending 31st March 1993, the MHRT processed a total of 87 cases. Of these, all but 19 had been dealt with at a hearing by the end of the year. Several cases were withdrawn or adjourned at the hearing stage; of the 68 cases fully considered, 57 of the patients were directed to remain in hospital. The cost of operating the MHRT during 1992-93 was almost £38,700 (an increase of 61 per cent on the 1991-92 figure).

It should be noted that the MHRT does not concern itself with the management of the property of mental patients. Prime responsibility for this lies with the Office of Care and Protection, an office within the Family Division of the High Court (which is also responsible for wardship, guardianship and adoption proceedings). It is the Master (Care and Protection) who decides whether any step needs to be taken to deal with a patient's property; if necessary the Master will appoint a Controller to manage a patient's affairs. In 1992, 680 patients were referred to the Office of Care and Protection and 129 patients were visited. It is important to note that a patient living in a hospital or other statutory accommodation can have amounts of money up to £20,000 managed by the Health Board on his or her behalf without needing to involve the Office of Care and Protection.

Hearings

When the MHRT receives an application concerning a patient it sends a copy to the Health Board administering the hospital in which the patient is detained. The Board then forwards full information about the patient to the MHRT, which in turn sends it to the patient with the exception of those parts which the Board considers should not be disclosed in the interests of the patient or for other specific reasons. The patient's nearest relative or guardian is also notified. On the day of the hearing the MHRT may decide to release even the information not disclosed by the Board.

Procedures of the MHRT are governed by the Mental Health Review Tribunal Rules (NI) 1986. Once an application for a hearing has been received, the MHRT must give all parties concerned at least 14 days' notice of the date of the hearing. The MHRT has a discretion to exclude any person from the hearing, but it may appoint some person to act as the applicant's or patient's authorised representative. Representation under the legal advice and assistance scheme (see 3.3) has been available since 1980. Patients and other parties to the hearing may be accompanied by other persons of their choice.

Before or during the hearing the medical member of the MHRT must examine the patient to form an opinion about his or her mental condition. The MHRT may interview the patient, and is required to do so if the patient so requests. Written arguments can be presented, in addition to the oral testimony of witnesses; the attendance of witnesses or the production of documents can be compelled as in a proper court of law, but the MHRT has a discretion to receive in evidence any documents or information which would not be admissible in a court. It is an essential feature of the MHRT that its decisions are based as much on its own observations and assessments of the patient's mental condition as on the opinions expressed by the patient, the doctor in charge or other interested parties.

Decisions and appeals

Decisions of the Mental Health Review Tribunal can be by majority vote. They must be communicated in writing, with reasons, within 14 days of the hearing, unless the MHRT considers that this would adversely affect the health or welfare of the patient or other people.

The MHRT has power to recommend the continued detention of a patient or, if it is satisfied that the patient is not suffering from mental illness or severe mental impairment or that discharge would not create a substantial likelihood of serious physical harm to the patient or to other persons, the MHRT must order the patient's release (either immediately or on a future date). With a view to facilitating discharge on a future date the MHRT may recommend leave of absence for the patient or transfer to another hospital.

The only way of appealing against a decision of the MHRT is by requesting a case to be stated (see 4.6) for determination by the Court of Appeal. As only questions of law can be stated in this way, such appeals are rare. The substance of the law in this area is fairly clear: it is in its application to the facts, and in the ascertainment of those facts, that the difficulties lie. There can be no further appeal beyond the Court of Appeal. Of course, judicial review proceedings might also be available (see 7.1).

The Mental Health Commission

The Mental Health Commission (MHC) for Northern Ireland was set up under the Mental Health (NI) Order 1986, largely as a result of one of the recommendations made in the Northern Ireland Review Committee on Mental Health Legislation (the MacDermott Committee), which reported in 1981. The MHC has the duty of keeping under review not only the care and treatment of patients suffering from mental disorder but also the interests of staff concerned with the care and treatment of such patients. At present it has 14 part-time members, their period of appointment being at the discretion of the Department of Health and Social Services; the members include two lawyers, three doctors, one psychologist, two social workers, two nurses and four lay persons. The current Chairperson is a lawyer, Mr Henry Pierce.

The chief functions of the MHC are to inquire into any case where it appears to the MHC that there may be ill-treatment of any patient, to visit and interview in private patients detained under the 1986 Order, and to monitor the operation of the powers and duties placed by the 1986 Order on the Health Boards, the Department of Health and Social Services, the Secretary of State and persons running private hospitals. When it thinks fit it may refer to the Mental Health Review Tribunal the case of any patient who is liable to be detained under the 1986 Order. But the MHC's role is not confined to detained patients: it also covers voluntary patients and anyone else suffering from mental disorder. By April 1992 the MHC had referred only one patient to the MHRT.

The Mental Health Commission must publish a report on its activities in such form and at such intervals as the Head of the Department of Health and Social Services may direct. It can in turn be subject to investigation by the Commissioner for Complaints (see 8.1).

In 1992, after consulting with the MHC, the DHSS published a Code of Practice which gives guidance to medical practitioners, staff of the Health Boards, hospital staff and approved social workers concerning the admission into hospital of patients suffering from mental disorder and their treatment there. The 1986 Order does not impose a legal duty to comply with the Code but a breach of the Code could be cited as evidence in legal proceedings. One chapter of the Code is devoted to the handling of patients who are or have been involved in criminal proceedings.

7.5 Tribunals Concerning Land, Rents and Planning

The Lands Tribunal

The Lands Tribunal for Northern Ireland was set up by the Lands Tribunal and Compensation Act (NI) 1964. Its rules of procedure are laid down in the Lands Tribunal Rules (NI) 1976, as amended. Unlike the Lands Tribunal for England and Wales it is technically not a tribunal at all but a proper court, although it is not always staffed by judges and nor is it serviced by the Northern Ireland Court Service. Persons serving on it are barristers or solicitors of seven years' standing or persons experienced in the valuation of land. They are assisted by a registrar, an assistant registrar and a small clerical staff. There are at present only two members; one of these is a county court judge and serves as part-time President (Judge Peter Gibson), the other serves full-time and is a qualified surveyor.

The Lands Tribunal has its own courtroom and offices in the Royal Courts of Justice in Belfast, but it will normally sit in the county courthouse appropriate to the location of the land concerned whenever the parties prefer such a venue. Usually only one member of the Lands Tribunal will hear each case, with the President sitting in all cases involving questions of law, though occasionally both members will sit if the case involves particularly complex issues of law as well as difficult valuation issues; the President has a casting vote if the two members disagree.

The functions of the Lands Tribunal are varied, being derived from many different Acts of Parliament and touching upon more than 60 different matters. One of its most important tasks is to resolve disputes concerning the amount of compensation to be paid for the compulsory acquisition of land or for the injury caused to land by, for example, the making of roads. Another important function is the hearing of appeals and references concerning the valuation of land for rating and taxation purposes, a job which frequently entails deciding (and it is in this context that such decisions are usually made in Northern Ireland) whether a particular organisation is a charity or not. There is no public register of charities in Northern Ireland. The Lands Tribunal must also deal with the renewal of business tenancies, the buying of ground rents, the extension of leases and the modification of legal obligations, such as rights of way, which impede the enjoyment of land. Parties, moreover, can agree to ask the Lands Tribunal to sit in private as an arbitrator in order to settle any dispute concerning the value, use or development of a piece of land.

Hearings are in public and legal aid is available for them. Decisions, together with reasons, have to be given in writing, unless the Lands Tribunal is satisfied that no injustice or inconvenience would be caused by giving them orally. In 1992, 144 cases were referred to the Lands Tribunal but decisions were made in just 18 of them; the rest were settled by consent or withdrawn. Some of the written decisions are published and can be referred to in future cases as precedents; in 1993 a comprehensive Index to decisions of the Lands Tribunal was made available. Copies of any past decision are available from the registrar whenever required, on payment of a small fee. The decisions are final as regards the determination of facts; the only appeal is, within one week, by way of case stated on a point of law to the Court of Appeal (see 4.6). There are only one or two of these each year.

Rent assessment committees

Northern Ireland has a complex system for controlling the level of rents in the private housing sector. If on 1st October 1978 the dwelling was not let at a rent controlled under the Rent Restriction Acts, it still today cannot be subjected to control. But if the dwelling was so controlled it is now subject to the Rent (NI) Order 1978.

Under that Order the Department of the Environment for Northern Ireland will, upon application, register an increased rent if the net annual value of the dwelling is more than £60 or, when the NAV is less than £60, if the district council has certified that the dwelling meets certain standards. If either the landlord or the tenant disagrees with the registered rent, appeal against it can be made to a rent assessment committee.

The appeal is first of all sent to the Rent Officer, who is an official independent of the government. He or she makes the necessary arrangements for a survey of the premises and for the determination of the issue by a rent assessment committee at a hearing. The committees are composed of members drawn from a Rent Assessment Panel of about 40 people (all appointed by the Department of the Environment) and they sit in the principal town of each district council area. The Rent Officer appoints one chairperson for each committee and usually one or two other members.

At the hearing the landlord and tenant can be heard either in person or by being represented by a barrister, solicitor or any other authorised person. The proceedings resemble those at a social security appeal tribunal (see 7.2), with no state legal aid being obtainable. In determining the appropriate rent the committee will have regard to the report of its surveyor, its own inspection and the rents of comparable houses in the private sector and of those let by the Northern Ireland Housing Executive. These public sector rents in turn mostly depend at present on the age of the premises and the number of persons which they can accommodate. The committee will disregard any improvements made by the tenant.

Rent assessment committees also hear applications for the reassessment of registered rents in cases where there has been a change in circumstances relating to either the dwelling-house or the tenancy. This is in effect the only way of challenging a rent assessment committee's original assessment of rent.

In July 1993 there were 7,722 "regulated" tenancies in Northern Ireland and 595 so-called "restricted" tenancies, making a total of 8,317 registrations; approximately 5,000 of these had been appealed at one time or another to a rent assessment committee. Over half of the appeals resulted in rents being reduced, but these reductions must be set against the increases in all rents decreed by the Northern Ireland Housing Executive from time to time.

The Planning Appeals Commission

This is one of those bodies which, like rent assessment committees, does not call itself a tribunal but in fact operates in much the same way as those which do. It was first established in 1973 by the Planning (NI) Order 1972 though the relevant legislation is now the Planning (NI) Order 1991.

In Northern Ireland all applications for planning permission must be made to the Department of the Environment. Not all need to be advertised in the press: see the Planning Applications (Exemption from Publication) Order (NI) 1991, reproduced as a sample statutory rule in Appendix 3. The Department has a duty to consult with district councils and other affected bodies but the decision whether to grant planning permission is for it alone to take. If the permission is refused, or granted subject to conditions, the applicant may appeal to the Planning Appeals Commission (PAC) within six months (or such longer period as the Commission may allow).

The PAC consists of a Chief Commissioner and such number of other members as the Department of the Environment may determine. They are appointed by the Secretary of State for Northern Ireland. At present, in addition to the Chief Commissioner there are five full-time and six part-time members. An appeal is generally heard by one Commissioner appointed by the Chief Commissioner, and the hearing usually takes place at a venue near to the location of the relevant land. The actual decision on the appeal, however, is taken by the PAC as a whole.

As full reasons for the refusal of planning permission are not always given at the time when the refusal is first announced, the hearing before a Commissioner may be the applicant's earliest opportunity to discover what those reasons were. The Department consequently presents its case first at these hearings even though it is technically the respondent. No official rules have been made to govern the conduct of proceedings at a hearing but they are kept as informal as possible. Legal aid is not available. There is an alternative "written representation" procedure available to appellants; this avoids the need for a hearing and is used for some of the straightforward appeals.

In 1991-92 there were 19,485 applications for planning permission and of those which were considered during that year some 90 per cent were granted. The Planning Appeals Commission dealt with 351 appeals in the year ending 31st March 1992 and allowed about 25 per cent of these.

The PAC also has a duty to conduct public local inquiries (in order to consider objections made against development plans) as well as hearings or inquiries which may arise from planning applications which the Department of the Environment judges to be of major significance. Normally one member of the PAC will conduct such an inquiry or hearing and will report to the PAC as a whole. Having considered the matter the PAC prepares its collective recommendations and submits them to the Department of the Environment. It is the Department which makes the final decision. In 1991-92 the PAC made four recommendations to the Department concerning public inquiries.

There can be no further appeal against a decision of the Planning Appeals Commission, only an application for judicial review (see 7.1).

8

Watchdog Bodies

It would be misleading to create the impression that the Northern Ireland legal system, any more than other legal systems, comprises only courts and tribunals. On the contrary, there are a number of "para-legal" bodies which devote their time to overseeing the administration of the law in Northern Ireland (or in the United Kingdom as a whole) and to making proposals for improvements. This chapter briefly describes the modes of operation of nine such bodies or sets of bodies. Some are accountable to Parliament, others are not; some have real powers to change matters, others may only advise. All act as official watchdogs so that the general public may have greater confidence in the fairness and justness of the legal system in various fields.

Readers will perhaps be able to think of other bodies with a similar role in the Northern Ireland legal system, but there is not the space to describe them all in detail here. The role of the Lay Observer, *vis-à-vis* complaints against solicitors, was mentioned in 3.2, the Social Security Advisory Committee in 7.2 and the Mental Health Commission in 7.4. In many other spheres there are lobbying organisations which try to keep the law in step with prevailing views in society; reference to a few of them has already been made in 3.1 under the heading "pressure groups". The "supervisory" jurisdiction of the High Court, exercised through judicial review (see 7.1), must also not be forgotten.

8.1 Ombudsmen

The term "ombudsman", deriving from Scandinavia, is used to describe both official (*i.e.* government appointed) and unofficial positions. Industries such as banking, building societies and insurance, and even publishers of newspapers and suppliers of coal, have all established their own unofficial ombudsmen (see 8.8), but these tend to operate on a United Kingdom basis with no separate or special role in Northern Ireland. There is already a Legal Services Ombudsman for England Wales, but not yet for Northern Ireland (see 3.2), and demands are growing for a Prisons Ombudsman.

In Northern Ireland there are two official ombudsman posts for the independent investigation of complaints about public maladministration. One is the Parliamentary Commissioner for Administration and the other is the Commissioner for Complaints. Mrs Jill McIvor currently holds both positions. She and her staff spend about one-quarter of their time working on Parliamentary Commissioner cases and the rest on Commissioner for Complaints cases. In 1992-93 the cost of running the joint office was £479,000. An annual report on the work of each of the two posts has to be submitted to the House of Commons at Westminster, where there is a Select Committee on the Parliamentary Commissioner for Administration which from time to time issues a report on the work of the Northern Ireland official.

It should be noted that, no matter which of her two hats she is wearing, the Commissioner's job is to examine the procedures by which administrative decisions are reached, not to assess the merits of those decisions in the absence of maladministration. The term "maladministration" does not mean simply "error"; it refers to action which has been influenced by improper considerations, which is totally unreasonable or which smacks of incompetence, malice, discrimination or neglect. The Commissioner, therefore, does not usually investigate complaints in respect of which the complainant has, or had, a right to take proceedings in a court of law, or to appeal to a tribunal, and for this purpose the Fair Employment Commission (see 8.2) and the Independent Commission for Police Complaints (see 8.7) are treated as tribunals. Someone complaining about being refused unemployment benefit, for instance, must take the grievance to a Social Security Appeal Tribunal (see 7.2). Only if he or she is unhappy with the manner in which the claim was processed before or after the decision was made will a complaint to the ombudsman be permissible.

The Parliamentary Commissioner for Administration

The function of the ombudsman when acting as Parliamentary Commissioner is to investigate written complaints about maladministration within any of the Northern Ireland government departments (see 1.4). Unlike the ombudsman in Great Britain, the Commissioner in Northern Ireland also has the power to investigate complaints about personnel matters in the civil service. The role was created by the Parliamentary Commissioner Act (NI) 1969, two years after a similar post was established for United Kingdom government departments. As the Northern Ireland Court Service and the Northern Ireland Office are departments of the UK Government, complaints about them should be sent to the UK Parliamentary Commissioner for Administration, who is based in London; the same applies to complaints about national public bodies such as the Inland Revenue, the Post Office and Customs and Excise. Complaints about maladministration can be made by anyone who claims to have sustained injustice as a result of it. In the first instance the complaint should be made to a Member of Parliament who then passes it to the Commissioner, but, in practice, if the Commissioner receives a complaint which has not first been passed through an MP, she will refer it to an MP nominated by the complainant and ask the latter to act as a sponsor for the complaint.

A complaint must normally be made within 12 months of the time when the aggrieved person first had notice of the matters alleged in the complaint. The Commissioner may, however, investigate a complaint made at a later date if she thinks there is a special justification for doing so. In all cases except those which clearly fall outside her jurisdiction, or which are withdrawn, the Commissioner invites the comments of the body complained about, examines papers, and interviews persons privately. She then sends a report on her investigation to the Member of Parliament who sponsored the complaint, to the body complained about and to any person involved in the allegations made in the complaint.

If the Commissioner finds that a complaint is justified, she seeks to obtain a settlement of the grievance on the complainant's behalf; this may involve the granting of an apology, the remedying of some situation or even the payment of compensation. But if no settlement can be reached the complainant cannot take the matter any further, like all the official Ombudsmen in the United Kingdom, the Commissioner has the power to make a special report to Parliament, but this power is very rarely exercised.

Many of the complaints received by the Commissioner fall outside her jurisdiction. As Table 14 shows, in 1992 there were 200 complaints received, of which only 30 came directly via an MP. Nearly one-quarter of the complaints were about the work of newly formed agencies within government departments (such as the Rate Collection Agency and the Social Security Agency); 85 were against the Department of the Environment and 47 against the Department of Health and Social Services. All manner of maladministration was alleged but it is worth noting that there was not one allegation of religious discrimination. The number of cases concluded during the year was 213, of which 158 were cleared without the need for any further inquiry or formal investigation. Reports were completed on 27 cases, of which eight concerned the processing of agricultural and other grants and a further four the system for dealing with planning applications. Complaints of maladministration were upheld in 18 cases and in these there was an agreed financial settlement of between £100 and £14,387. The overall average time which elapsed between the receipt of a complaint and the issue of a formal report was 11 months, but 18 per cent were cleared in five months and 55 per cent in 10 months. Over the past five years just six per cent of all the complaints received by the Parliamentary Commissioner have ultimately led to a finding of maladministration.

THE CASELOAD OF THE OMBUDSMAN, 1988-92

	1988	1989	1990	1991	1992
Parliamentary Commissioner					
Complaints received	168	197	164	198	200
Complaints dealt with	166	200	165	194	213
Reports issued	35	27	24	24	27
Complaints upheld	12	8	12	6	18
Commissioner for Complaints					
Complaints received	314	296	331	349	326
Complaints dealt with	317	308	299	345	357
Reports issued	61	51	36	47	70
Complaints upheld	11	17	7	12	32

Table 14

The Commissioner for Complaints

The function of the Commissioner for Complaints is to investigate written complaints made directly to her by persons claiming to have suffered injustice through maladministration on the part of such local bodies as Education and Library Boards, Health and Social Services

Boards, district councils, the Northern Ireland Council for Nurses and Midwives, the Sports Council and many others. The office was also created in 1969 (by the Commissioner for Complaints Act (NI) 1969), and has a similar, but by no means identical, role to that of the Health Service Ombudsmen and the Local Administration Ombudsmen in Great Britain. Among the matters which cannot be investigated are the conduct of legal proceedings, the actions of doctors and dentists, the behaviour of the police, and the financial interests of district councillors.

This kind of complaint does not have to be processed through a Member of Parliament, but it usually needs to be made within two months of the complainant getting to know of the action complained of, or within six months of the action itself, whichever is the earlier. Investigations are conducted in the same way as described for the Parliamentary Commissioner, with reports made to the complainant, the body concerned and any other person involved in the complaint. An important difference between the two procedures is that if the Commissioner for Complaints upholds a grievance but is unable to obtain a satisfactory settlement the complainant can then apply to a county court for compensation. And the Commissioner for Complaints may seek an injunction or declaration in the High Court to restrain a body from persisting in action which has been found to amount to maladministration. These remedies are not available in England.

Again referring to Table 14, in 1992 there were 326 complaints against local and public bodies received by the Commissioner; 161 were cleared without any inquiry or formal investigation. A total of 70 reports were issued, with maladministration being established in 32 of these. More than half of the reports issued related to employment practices, such as delays in recruitment processes or in resolving pay problems. The most popular target for complaints is still the Northern Ireland Housing Executive (NIHE), but since the NIHE introduced its own internal complaints system in 1985, the number of cases involving housing matters which need to be examined by the Commissioner has dropped appreciably; in 1992, 110 complaints were made to the Commission about the NIHE but 62 were passed on to the NIHE to be processed internally. Also in 1992 there were 34 complaints against the Education and Library Boards and 33 against the district councils. The average time elapsing between the receipt of a complaint and the issuing of a report was, as with cases to the Parliamentary Commissioner for Administration, nearly 11 months, but 40 per cent were nevertheless completed within nine months. Only five per cent of all complaints received by the

Commissioner for Complaints over the past five years have resulted in a finding of maladministration.

8.2 The Fair Employment Commission

The predecessor to the Fair Employment Commission (FEC) was the Fair Employment Agency (FEA), which was set up by the Fair Employment (NI) Act 1976 (a Westminster statute) with the general functions of promoting equality of opportunity in Northern Ireland and eliminating unlawful discrimination on the grounds of religious belief or political opinion. For this purpose atheism and agnosticism are religious beliefs but "political opinion" does not include an opinion which involves acceptance of the use of violence for political ends connected with Northern Ireland affairs. During the 1980s the FEA was considered by many to have insufficient powers to deal effectively with religious and political discrimination and following extensive research conducted for the Standing Advisory Commission on Human Rights (see 8.6) the law in this area was reformed by the Fair Employment (NI) Act 1989. One consequence was the replacement of the FEA by the Fair Employment Commission. As well as retaining the duties to promote equality of opportunity and eliminate unlawful discrimination the FEC must also promote affirmative action to help redress existing imbalances. The government's Central Community Relations Unit is to undertake a comprehensive review of the 1989 legislation within five years of its introduction, a process which has already begun.

The FEC currently comprises a full-time Chairman (Mr Robert Cooper: he also led the FEA from its inception) and eight part-time members, including three trade unionists and three representatives of employers. Although all its members are appointed by the Secretary of State for Northern Ireland, and despite being entirely funded by the Department of Economic Development (to the tune of £1.69 million in 1991-92), the FEC is of course independent of the government. It now employs some 60 staff. An annual report is submitted to the Secretary of State and presented to Parliament as a House of Commons paper.

In carrying out its primary functions the FEC works in conjunction with the Fair Employment Tribunal, another product of the 1989 Act. Its role is explained in 7.3. As presently drafted neither the 1989 Act nor its 1976 predecessor (parts of which remain in force) make inequality of opportunity or unlawful discrimination a criminal offence, but 19 other offences relating to the operation of the Acts' provisions do exist. Certain forms of employment, such as serving as a cleric, a schoolteacher or in a private household remain exempt from control. All other employers come within the scope of the fair employment legislation. The exemption for schoolteaching is particularly controversial and the FEC keeps its desirability under constant review.

Equality of opportunity and fair participation

The Fair Employment Commission can require employers to take action to ensure that for the employees in their workforce there is both equality of opportunity and fair participation. To this end it has published a Code of Practice on Fair Employment, the contents of which it encourages employers and vocational organisations to adopt and the enforcement bodies rely upon the Code as good evidence of best practice. The FEC also keeps a register of trades, businesses and other activities in which people are employed; this describes the business in general terms and gives the name and address of the employer and the number of employees. The 1989 Act initially required all private sector employers with more than 25 employees to register with the FEC and from January 1992 this duty to register was extended to all employers with more than 10 employees. Public authorities are automatically registered. The register now has about 4,000 entries. It is a criminal offence to fail to register when required to do so.

All registered employers must "monitor" the religious make-up of their workforce and send details of this to the FEC each year. In addition all public sector employers and those private sector employers with more than 250 employees must return information on the religion of applicants for jobs. The FEC in turn publishes a research report summarising the returns. The aim of monitoring is to make it easier to identify job categories where there are fewer workers or applicants from one religious community than might otherwise be expected. Again it is a criminal offence to refuse to supply information which must be monitored or to disclose it to anyone other than the FEC; in 1991-92 six registered employers were fined up to £150 for refusing to submit a monitoring return. A registered employer must also review the employment practices within the firm at least once every three years (this is known as the "section 31 review"). It should be stressed, moreover, that even if an employer employs too few people to have to register or monitor the workforce, he or she is still bound by the law's requirements, outlined below, not to discriminate against a person, directly or indirectly, on the basis of his or her religious or political belief.

In 1991-92 the Fair Employment Commission sought to promote affirmative action programmes with 97 employers whose workforce was less than 5 per cent Roman Catholic or Protestant. The sorts of measures recommended included the ending of informal selection methods (such as word of mouth recruitment), the establishment of a neutral working environment without any religious emblems and the setting of goals and timetables regarding improvements to the religious balance of the workforce. Of course some of these measures have to contend with the so-called "chill factor" - some people will be reluctant even to apply for jobs in an environment where they might feel threatened.

As did the FEA under the 1976 Act, the Fair Employment Commission has power under section 11 of the 1989 Act to investigate the employment practices of particular employers to see what action ought to be taken to promote equality of opportunity. Under this power dozens of investigations have already been undertaken into private sector companies as well as several public bodies such as district councils and Education and Library Boards. If the FEC finds a failure to afford equality of opportunity it can determine what steps should be taken to secure it and can ask for undertakings from employers or give them directions. If such directions are not complied with within a resonable period the FEC can apply to the Fair Employment Tribunal (FET) for an enforcement order. If this in turn is not complied with the FET can fine the employer up to £30,000 and can disqualify the employer from eligibility for government grants and contracts (this is the notion of "contract compliance"). It can even refer the employer's case to the High Court, which has greater powers to fine and can even imprison for contempt of court.

Unlawful discrimination

To help eliminate unlawful discrimination the Fair Employment Commission can receive complaints from any person claiming to be a victim and can investigate the matter. Even positive or reverse discrimination can be unlawful under the Acts, though affirmative action programmes will generally not be.The 1989 Act made indirect discrimination just as unlawful as direct discrimination, though no compensation is payable for the former unless it was intentional.

A complaint of unlawful discrimination must be made to the Fair Employment Tribunal within three months of the discrimination occurring. The FET will refer the complaint to the Labour Relations Agency (see 8.3) to see if an amicable settlement can be reached. If it cannot then a hearing will in due course take place before the FET, where the procedures are essentially the same as in the industrial tribunals (see 7.3). As in cases of alleged sex discrimination (see 8.5), the burden of proof on the complainant is relatively easy to discharge. No legal aid is available but the applicant can ask the Fair Employment Commission for initial advice and for free legal representation before the Fair Employment Tribunal. The FET can order compensation of up to £30,000 in such cases, much more than can currently be awarded by an industrial tribunal in sex discrimination cases. The sum can include an award for injured feelings, something not usually allowable in employment disputes cases heard by industrial tribunals. The FET can also specify what other remedial action needs to be taken to correct the discrimination. An appeal lies on a point of law to the Court of Appeal.

Shortly after the 1989 Act came into force a difficulty arose with section 30, which seemed to criminalise the disclosure of information which was vital for the successful pursuit of a claim before the Fair Employment Tribunal. No further hearings could take place before the FET until the offending section was repealed by the Fair Employment (Amendment) (NI) Order 1991 (see 7.3). By the end of March 1992, therefore, only three complaints of discrimination assisted by the FEC had been upheld by the FET. But the FEC continued to defend successfully some appeals which had been taken to the county courts by employers who had been sued by employees under the 1976 Act prior to the coming into force of the 1989 legislation. Cases must still be taken under the 1976 Act procedures (whereby the FEC determines whether there has been discrimination and an appeal can then go to a county court) if the alleged discrimination occurred before the 1989 Act came into force.

Under section 42 of the 1976 Act investigations into individual complaints have to be curtailed if the Secretary of State for Northern Ireland issues a certificate that an allegedly discriminatory act was done for the purpose of safeguarding national security or protecting public safety or public order. The Fair Employment Commission, as was the FEA, is opposed to this provision and has expressed concern at its possible misuse. It has taken to the Court of Appeal a decision of the High Court in one case upholding the validity of a section 42 certificate issued in favour of Northern Ireland Electricty

Promotional work and the future

As well as dealing with the matters above, the Fair Employment Commission has a significant educational and research role. It sees itself as the guardian of fair practice, emphasising to employers the economic, social and industrial advantages which flow from fair and lawful practices in recruitment and promotion, etc. It visits employers to give training courses and advice on employment practices; it conducts seminars, shows videos and runs publicity campaigns. In the year ending March 1992 it visited 533 employers, received 3,035 telephone calls and 1,129 letters requesting advice and carried out 190 speaking engagements in schools, colleges and community groups. From April 1991 a Small Firms Fair Employment Scheme has been in place. Funded by the government and administered by the FEC, it pays for consultancy advice on registration, monitoring and good equal opportunity practices. In the scheme's first year of operation no fewer than 548 employers applied for help under it.

The Fair Employment Commission has the additional task of looking out for discriminatory advertisements. If it believes that an advertiser is likely to continue to publish such adverts it can apply to the High Court for an injunction restraining their publication.

As a whole the 1989 Act is widely viewed as the most radical fair employment law enacted anywhere in Europe, though whether it will be enough to have a meaningful impact on the unemployment differential between Roman Catholics and Protestants in Northern Ireland remains to be seen. Today the unemployment rate for male Catholics remains 2.4 times as great as that for male Protestants. According to its latest annual report the Fair Employment Commission believes that during its short existence there has already been a significant improvement concerning fair employment, but it adds that "many companies employ too few Roman Catholics and many companies employ too few Protestants. As a result there is a high degree of segregation between the two communities in employment". The monitoring report for 1991 showed a shortfall of approximately 5.6 per cent of male Catholics in employment, while the monitoring report for 1992 showed that the proportion of male Catholics in employment had increased by 0.4 per cent. The FEC concludes that if this degree of improvement were sustained it could lead to a closing of the unemployment differential between the two communities within seven years.

Dissatisfaction with the 1976 fair employment legislation led to the formulation in November 1984 of the so-called MacBride Principles, drawn up by a group of civil rights activists led by Sean MacBride, a Nobel Peace Prize laureate. The Principles were inspired by the Sullivan Principles, which were designed to encourage responsible employment practices by American firms operating in South Africa. Several state legislatures in America have endorsed the MacBride Principles by threatening to disinvest from American companies which refuse to abide by them. The British government and the Fair Employment Commission have strongly condemned the Principles, claiming that several of them actually require conduct which is illegal even under the 1989 Act. The Principles are supported, on the other hand, by the Fair Employment Trust, an unofficial body not to be confused with the FEC.

It should be noted that the Race Relations Acts which are in force in Great Britain do not apply in Northern Ireland, and the Commission for Racial Equality has no role in the province. It is, consequently, quite lawful for an employer to discriminate here on the basis of ethnic or national origins, just as there is no protection for discrimination against disabled persons, homosexuals or the elderly. In 1992, however, the government issued a consultative document setting out the options for reforming Northern Ireland's law in this respect. It would appear that the choice is between adding responsibility for dealing with racial discrimination to the tasks already allotted to the Fair Employment Commission or setting up a new Northern Ireland body with a remit similar to that of the Commission for Racial Equality in Great Britain.

8.3 The Labour Relations Agency

The Labour Relations Agency (LRA) was first created by the Industrial Relations (NI) Order 1976 (now the Industrial Relations (NI) Order 1992). Like the Advisory, Conciliation and Arbitration Service (ACAS) in England, it is a body independent of government and operating under the direction of a Board comprising representatives of employers, employees and others. There are at present nine part-time members together with a full-time Chairperson and Chief Executive (Mr F A Mackle), all appointed, after consultations, by the Department of Economic Development. A report on the Agency's activities is presented each year to the Department and can be obtained free of charge from the Agency's head office in Belfast. There are about 50 full-time members of staff employed there, with a small additional group based in Londonderry. The annual cost of running the LRA is approximately £1.3 million, which is granted by the government.

The LRA's chief tasks are to promote good industrial relations and to improve collective bargaining machinery. In fulfilment of these functions it involves itself in employment disputes in several different ways:

(1)   If the dispute involves groups of employers or employees the LRA
      can attempt collective conciliation; one of its conciliation officers
      meets with the parties and attempts to narrow their differences to
      vanishing point. During 1992-93 the LRA dealt with 87 disputes in
      this way and conciliated settlements were reached in 78 of these;
      industrial action was avoided altogether in 85 out of the 91 new cases
      received, with a stoppage of work occurring in only five cases.

(2)   If the dispute involves an individual's employment rights the matter
      will be referred to the Labour Relations Agency by the Office of
      Industrial Tribunals and the Fair Employment Tribunal (see 7.3),
      unless it relates to a claim for redundancy payment or for written
      particulars of a contract of employment. Again, a conciliation
      officer tries to arrive at a mutually agreed settlement, a service which
      is free and confidential; if a settlement cannot be reached the dispute
      can then go to an industrial tribunal. During 1992-93, 2,539 indi-
      vidual employment disputes were referred to the LRA (a decrease
      of one third on the previous year's figure) and 76 per cent were
      determined without the need for a tribunal hearing; the most popular
      kinds of claim related to unfair dismissal and unlawful deductions
      from wages. The LRA received 248 complaints of religious and/or
      political discrimination.

(3)   If the conciliation process is unattractive or unsuccessful the LRA
      can try to resolve industrial disputes by referring them to inde-
      pendent arbitration; alternatively it can hold a formal inquiry into
      the issue, this being a particular way of examining a dispute where
      there may be considerable public interest or concern in its outcome.
      A formal inquiry does not require the consent of the parties but
      occurs very rarely (only once in 1991-92 and not at all in 1992-93).
      During 1992-93 there were 25 arbitration hearings arranged by the
      LRA, with a few further hearings being held privately but with LRA
      assistance. No fewer than 18 of the arbitrations arose out of disputes
      within the education sector.

(4)   Until recently, if problems arose as to the non-recognition of a trade
      union by an employer the LRA could try to help by providing advice
      or conciliation or by issuing a report after making its own enquiries.
      During 1991-92, 15 such disputes were referred to the LRA by nine
      different trade unions, one-quarter of the cases relating to the private
      health sector. The cases dealt with were mostly settled by concili-
      ation or withdrawn, but in four of them the LRA issued a report
      following an inquiry; in three of these it recommended full recog-

nition of the union and in the fourth it recommended recognition only for disciplinary and grievance matters. As from 1st July 1992 the role of the LRA in trade union recognition disputes has been removed under the Industrial Relations (NI) Order 1992; this Order consolidated the existing law governing trade unions and brought collective labour law in Northern Ireland broadly into line with that which already applied in the rest of the United Kingdom.

(5) The introduction of legislation on equal pay for work of equal value (see the Equal Pay (Amendment) Regulations (NI) 1984) has provided industrial tribunals with great problems in assessing whether different forms of work are indeed of equal value. The Labour Relations Agency assists the tribunals by maintaining a list of independent experts available to examine such claims. There are currently seven names on this list. In 1992-93 there were five cases on equal pay; these involved 20 applications. Two "bulk" cases within the National Health Service were carried over from the previous year.

(6) To help nip industrial relations problems in the bud, the LRA provides expert advice on all aspects of employment relationships. At present, depending on the nature and complexity of each problem it faces, it divides its specialist advisory assistance into a General Inquiry Service, a Short Term Advisory Service and a Preventative Mediation Service. The assistance provided is confidential and free. In 1992-93, for example, advisory officers visited 633 organisations in response to requests for advice and assistance; preventative mediation advisory assistance was supplied to 15 different projects. Most related to the private sector.

In addition to all this the Labour Relations Agency conducts reviews of industrial relations throughout whole industries, encourages industrial relations training, sponsors research and occasional papers, gives educational talks and issues Codes of Practice. Four Codes of Practice have so far been published on disclosure of information to trade unions for collective bargaining purposes, on disciplinary practice and procedures, on time off for trade union activities and on redundancy procedures. The Codes have no actual legal force but are taken into account by industrial tribunals when deciding disputes (see 2.3). The LRA issues a twice-yearly newsletter and a series of very useful Information Notes; it also produces a regularly updated three-volume *Encyclopedia of Northern Ireland Labour Law and Practice.*

The Commissioner for the Rights of Trade Union Members

In this context it is also worth noting that the Industrial Relations (NI) Order 1992 created the post of Commissioner for the Rights of Trade Union Members, a person who may give advice and assistance to a trade union member when he or she wishes to take legal proceedings against a union. The person currently occupying the post is Mrs M-A. Dinsmore

8.4. The Health and Safety Agency

The Health and Safety at Work (NI) Order 1978 extended the protection of the health and safety legislation to all persons at work (except domestic servants in private households) and placed new basic duties regarding safety on employers, the self-employed, employees, and those manufacturing and supplying articles and substances for use at work. It protects not just persons at work but also the general public outside places of work. By virtue of the Reporting of Injuries, Diseases and Dangerous Occurrences Regulations (NI) 1986, new duties have been imposed concerning the reporting of accidents.

Northern Ireland has always had a much better industrial accident record than Great Britain, but to help with the implementation of the 1978 Order a Health and Safety Agency (HSA) was established. The HSA is similar to the Health and Safety Commission in Great Britain but its role and functions differ in some important respects. Rather than having direct executive control over authorities responsible for enforcing health and safety legislation, the HSA has mainly advisory functions. It comprises 10 part-time members including its Chairman (Mr R Thompson) and has a supporting staff of six. The members represent district councils and both sides of industry and are appointed by the Department of Economic Development. The cost of running the HSA in 1992 was approximately £146,000.

The HSA's general task is to promote health and safety at work. It fulfils this by making recommendations to appropriate government departments, by arranging for research, training and the provision of information, and by issuing and approving Codes of Practice. The recommendations made to government departments usually relate to regulations proposed by those departments or by the HSA itself for health and safety at work. The HSA cannot actually issue such regulations, but it must be consulted about their content. Its Codes of Practice have a semi-legal status in that a breach of them is some evidence of dubious practices but no offence in itself (see 2.3). One Code covers the appointment of safety representatives, who are appointed by recognised trade unions and have a long list of specific functions in their place of work.

Responsibility for enforcement of the 1978 Order rests with the government departments which happen to be concerned with the particular work in question. Work on farms, for instance, is the responsibility of the Farm Safety Inspectorate of the Department of Agriculture, while work in factories, or in offices in the public sector, is the responsibility of the Health and Safety Inspectorate of the Department of Economic Development. The Agriculture Inspectorate issued 300 enforcement notices in 1992; the Department of Economic Development inquired into 15 fatalities.

Health and safety in shops, and in offices in the private sector, remains a matter for the environmental health officers of district councils. The recent rise in the number of small businesses in Northern Ireland has made this responsibility a heavy one. The Health and Safety Agency comments on the annual reports of these local enforcement agencies in its own annual reports, which are made to the Department of Economic Development and published.

Where prosecutions have to be brought for breach of safety regulations the HSA monitors the fines imposed to see if they are of real deterrent value. The HSA has called for an increase in the maximum penalty and a Belfast magistrate commented in a case during 1992 that this should be £30,000. As awareness of the importance of safety at work increases, it is likely that the average fine will rise significantly in due course.

The HSA can recommend investigations and inquiries but cannot compel them or conduct them itself. It has commissioned research into some occupational diseases and has encouraged employers and trade unions to train personnel in good safety practices, though the HSA itself does not provide training. It has tried to promote safety at work through broadcasting short films on commercial television, as well as through publishing leaflets, conducting seminars, running competitions and issuing a bulletin (called *Health, Safety and You*) describing recent developments in health and safety at work. It publishes guides to new legislation and a *Construction Handbook* (now in its third edition).

More particular advice about occupational health problems can be sought from the Employment Medical Advisory Service, a branch of the Department of Economic Development.

8.5 The Equal Opportunities Commission

The Equal Opportunities Commission for Northern Ireland (EOC) was set up under the Sex Discrimination (NI) Order 1976 to work for the elimination of discrimination on the grounds of sex or marriage and to promote equality of opportunity between men and women generally. It consists of a full-time Chairperson and Chief Executive (currently Mrs Joan Smyth) and nine other commissioners; all are appointed by the Department of Economic Development. There are approximately 30 staff. The EOC issues an annual report to the Secretary of State, which is then published as a House of Commons paper. The EOC is funded by the Department of Economic Development; in 1993-94 the grant was just over £1.3 million.

A particular duty of the EOC is to keep under review the workings of the Equal Pay Act (NI) 1970, the Sex Discrimination (NI) Order 1976, the Equal Pay (Amendment) Regulations (NI) 1984 and such parts of the health and safety legislation which require men and women to be treated differently. In this context discrimination can refer to one of two practices: treating a person of one sex less favourably than a person of the other sex solely because of the first person's sex, or treating a married person less favourably than a single person solely because the first person is married. It does not encompass less favourable treatment of single persons or homosexuals. Indirect discrimination, if intentional, is covered.

Research and education

As well as having power to submit proposals to the government for amending the legislation which it reviews, the EOC has extensive powers covering education and research. In campaigning for fairer treatment of women it is not satisfied with pious statements of intent concerning equal opportunities policies: it requires them to be matched with affirmative action, something which is not unlawful under the legislation. Employers, for instance, can legally train more women than men for occupations in which women have previously been under-represented. The conditions of work of part-time employees are a particular concern of the EOC, since 40 per cent of women are employed on a part-time basis in Northern Ireland. Furthermore, although women constitute almost one-half of the entire full-time and part-time workforce, women's average earnings (when payments for overtime are included) are still only 68 per cent of those of men.

The EOC conducts some research projects itself and helps to finance some external projects. Recent reports include a longitudinal study of the circumstances of carers in Northern Ireland, an examination of the position of women's voluntary organisations, a study of the clothing industry, a review of the Northern Ireland curriculum in schools and a survey of the lives of 1,000 women of working age. Research is on-going into women in the media, equal opportunity practices in public service and women and citizenship.

In performing its functions the Equal Opportunities Commission publishes leaflets, posters, booklets and reports, many of which are available free. In 1992 it issued *Gateways*, a new edition of the EOC's guide to education and training for women and in 1993 the latest version of a statistical booklet entitled *Where Do Women Figure* was published, as well as a legal manual on sexual harassment at places of work. During 1992-93 no fewer than 3,762 individuals approached the EOC with a request for advice or information.

Enforcement

To fulfil its role as an enforcement body the EOC may initiate its own formal investigations into suspected instances of discrimination and may serve non-discrimination notices, which require the provisions of the Equal Pay Act (NI) 1970 and the Sex Discrimination (NI) Order 1976, as amended, to be complied with; they are eventually enforceable in a county court. A register of non-discrimination notices is available for public inspection at the EOC's offices in Belfast but none are currently in existence because in recent years the EOC has chosen not to carry out any formal investigations. The EOC also has the sole right to initiate action in relation to persistent discrimination, discriminatory advertisements and instructions, or pressure to discriminate.

In the 12 months up to April 1993 the Equal Opportunities Commission received 1,166 complaints of discrimination; 84 per cent of these related to employment issues such as discrimination in the appointment or promotion processes or because a woman is having a baby; 52 complaints concerned the equal pay legislation and 50 concerned advertising. All but about 5 per cent of the complaints it receives are dealt with internally by EOC staff, the remainder are referred to outside solicitors. In 1992-93, 116 cases were dealt with by a court or tribunal (discrimination in the field of employment is dealt with by industrial tribunals, while other cases are heard by county courts); 84 of these were settled. Of the

32 cases fought to a conclusion, 13 were dismissed and 19 resulted in an award being made.

Under article 75 of the 1976 Order the Equal Opportunities Commission can provide personal and financial assistance to complainants in cases which are complex or involve a question of principle. This can be particularly valuable in employment cases, as the civil legal aid and legal advice and assistance schemes (see 3.3) do not provide for state-funded representation in industrial tribunals. In 1992-93 the EOC assisted 140 complainants in this manner; well over half of the discrimination cases dealt with by a court or tribunal were Commission-assisted. In those assisted cases which were settled without recourse to a court or tribunal over £340,000 was paid to applicants by respondent employers.

In the 1980s the Commission assisted 31 female police reservists who were complaining that the Chief Constable of the RUC had discriminated against them by not renewing their contracts. The industrial tribunal dealing with this case referred it to the European Court of Justice, which delivered its judgment in 1986 (*Johnston* v *Chief Constable of the RUC*); the decision led to a settlement payment of £1.2 million and resulted in the Sex Discrimination (Amendment) Order 1988, which changed the 1976 Order (and the equivalent English Act) so as not to allow a claim of national security automatically to prevent a future legal action based on sex discrimination (see also 2.6). The Chief Constable, most unusually for a tribunal case, was ordered to pay the applicants' legal costs. Another significant victory was won by the EOC when it successfully challenged the Department of Education's arrangements for the selection of pupils after the 11-plus; these were held to be discriminatory against girls (*In re EOC for Northern Ireland*, 1988) and extra places in grammar schools had accordingly to be made available.

Given the fact that the EOC's caseload has grown steadily since the first year of its existence, and that the law on sex discrimination is becoming ever more complex, the case for retaining a separate watchdog body for this field seems unanswerable. Northern Ireland's Commission has a high reputation not just in the United Kingdom but throughout the European Community for the pro-active and determined stand it has taken on gender discrimination issues. European Community law is becoming ever more important in this area and the EOC seeks to ensure that it is fully implemented in Northern Ireland.

8.6 The Standing Advisory Commission on Human Rights

The Standing Advisory Commission on Human Rights (SACHR), set up under the Northern Ireland Constitution Act 1973, comprises 12 part-time members appointed by the Secretary of State for Northern Ireland. The current Chairman is Mr Charles Hill QC. The Parliamentary Commissioner for Administration and the Chairman of the Fair Employment Commission are *ex officio* members. The Secretariat contains a secretary plus four supporting staff. The SACHR's annual budget is now about £250,000, but resources, it says, are stretched to the utmost. A report is presented to the Secretary of State every year and is published as a House of Commons paper; this now includes, in a series of Annexes, a variety of reports commissioned by the SACHR during the course of the year.

The current statutory function of the SACHR is to advise the Secretary of State on the adequacy and effectiveness of the law in preventing discrimination based on religious belief or political opinion, a less wide-ranging role than was originally envisaged in the White Paper preceding the enactment of the 1973 Act. The SACHR has frequently pressed for its statutory remit to be officially widened so that it can examine and comment upon any aspect of the law affecting Northern Ireland and oversee other bodies or agencies whose activities impinge upon human rights. In 1984 the then Secretary of State gave a written undertaking that the SACHR's statutory terms of reference would be amended so as to reflect more clearly its broad concerns, but to date no action has been taken on this.

In practice, however, there is no constraint upon the SACHR if it wishes to examine the emergency laws in Northern Ireland or any other related topic. Indeed the SACHR has been encouraged by successive Secretaries of Sate to review the operation of the special legislation enacted as a result of the civil unrest in Northern Ireland (see 4.9). An analysis has been made of matters such as the length of time persons charged with scheduled offences have been kept in custody between arrest and trial, and the length of periods spent on remand during a trial. The SACHR has recommended the introduction of silent video-recording for police interrogations in the holding centres and papers have been published on the use of "supergrasses" as a method of prosecution and on the introduction of three-judge courts to try scheduled offences. Much to its disappointment, however, the SACHR was not consulted about the right to silence legislation introduced in 1988 or on the government proposals issued in 1993 on dealing with terrorist exploitation of the construction industry.

Since its inception the SACHR has regularly reviewed the operation of the law concerning public order and elections. Secretaries of State have specifically referred to it the topics of sex discrimination, homosexual law reform and family law. It played a significant role in getting the Fair Employment (NI) Acts enacted in 1976 and 1989. Most recently it has looked closely at the law on the use of lethal force by police officers and soldiers, the system for handling complaints against the police, the rights of prisoners, arrangements for supporting the victims of crime, plans for improving community relations, access to education, legal aid, inquests, abortion, race relations and the rights of disabled persons. It pays particular attention, of course, to the the law on criminal justice.

The SACHR has encouraged public discussion of whether a Bill of Rights is needed in Northern Ireland; its report on the subject in 1977 remains one of the best studies of the topic. Originally its view was that a Bill for the United Kingdom as a whole, based on the Council of Europe's Convention on Human Rights and Fundamental Freedoms (see 2.6), should be introduced as a matter of urgency; in 1992 it changed its position so as to advocate a Bill of Rights for Northern Ireland alone, again based on the European Convention. Advice is also given to the government as to the implications of other international agreements such as the European Social Charter and the European and United Nations Conventions on Torture. The SACHR intends to undertake a study of the human rights implications of European integration and the effects in Northern Ireland of the United Kingdom's opt-out from the social chapter of the Maastricht Treaty.

8.7 Bodies Overseeing the Police

The Police Authority

The organisation of the police service in Northern Ireland has been briefly outlined in 1.6. We are here concerned with the accountability of the police. Up to 1970 the Royal Ulster Constabulary was exclusively accountable to the Minister of Home Affairs in the Northern Ireland Government, but following the civil disturbances in 1969 an Advisory Committee under the chairmanship of Lord Hunt recommended the establishment of a Police Authority, free of direct political influence and with the task of monitoring the RUC's activities. This was duly brought about by the Police Act (NI) 1970.

The Police Authority for Northern Ireland is composed of a Chairman (currently Mr T. Rainey), a vice-chairman, and a maximum of 20 other persons (their identity is kept secret for security reasons). All are appointed by the Secretary of State. The membership is meant, as far as practicable, to be representative of the whole community in Northern Ireland, and in particular there should be members representing the interests of district councils, public bodies (such as institutions of higher education), the legal profession, trade unions, agriculture, industry, commerce, and voluntary organisations concerned with the welfare of young persons. The members serve in a part-time capacity and hold office for three years, though their terms can be renewed. In England and Wales, the police authorities are currently made up of local councillors (two-thirds) and justices of the peace (one-third), though the government has plans to alter this. In Northern Ireland the feeling is that if elected representatives were appointed to the Authority it might quickly become partisan in its activities.

Functions

The main function of the Police Authority, according to the 1970 Act, is "to secure the maintenance of an adequate and efficient police force in Northern Ireland". This means that the Authority is ultimately responsible for providing buildings and equipment for the police and controlling expenditure on the service. The total expenditure on the police for the year ending 31st March 1992 was £523.1 million. Of this huge sum, 83.4 per cent went on salaries to the force's 11,600 full-time officers, the 1,700 part-time reservists and the 3,000 civilian staff (telecommunication workers, vehicle maintenance officers, clerks, searchers, etc.). The rest paid for the maintenance of police stations and for equipment, such as the fleet of 2,500 police vehicles. The Police Authority must also, subject to the Secretary of States's approval, determine the maximum number of persons of each rank in the force. In addition, it employs all of Northern Ireland's traffic wardens.

The Authority appoints the senior officers in the RUC, that is, the 14 officers above the rank of chief superintendent (the Chief Constable, two Deputy Chief Constables, two Senior Assistant Chief Constables and nine Assistant Chief Constables). It is also the disciplinary authority for such senior officers and can call upon any of them to retire in the interests of efficiency. In 1988 it considered the position of senior officers involved in the shooting incidents investigated in the Stalker-Sampson report, but found none of them deserving of being disciplined. If the police are held liable to pay compensation in any legal proceedings (*e.g.* in a civil action for false imprisonment), it is the Police Authority which pays the money. In 1992-93 there were 304 of these cases dealt with, including 44 arising out of detention in the three holding centres used for persons arrested under the emergency laws: see 4.9. A total of £356,720 was paid out as compensation to claimants, making the average payment per case £1,783 (a 14 per cent rise on the 1991-92 figure). The Authority may also pay rewards to police officers for exceptional diligence or other specially meritorious conduct.

Under the Police (NI) Order 1987, the Authority has the duty to keep itself informed as to the manner in which complaints from members of the public against police officers are dealt with by the Chief Constable. Prior to 1987, if a complaint appeared to affect the public interest, the Authority could require the Chief Constable to refer it to a tribunal for consideration and report, but this was done on only one occasion (in the *Rafferty* case, 1980). Now, by virtue of article 8(2) of the 1987 Order, which has no equivalent in England and Wales, the Authority has the power to refer a matter which is not the subject of a complaint to the Independent Commission for Police Complaints (see below), provided it appears to the Authority that it is in the public interest that the Commission should supervise the investigation of the matter. Under the 1970 Act the Authority can still require the Chief Constable to submit reports in writing on such matters as may be specified, but it is thought that this power has very rarely, if ever, been exercised.

It is vital to realise that the Police Authority is not meant to interfere with the way in which the police actually do their job. This is often put by saying that sole responsibility for operational matters within the force lies with the Chief Constable; section 6(2) of the 1970 Act states that the force shall be under his "direction and control". Needless to say, it is sometimes difficult to decide whether a matter relates to "direction or control" or to "adequacy and efficiency"; it is up to the Authority and the Chief Constable to agree where the dividing line should fall.

The Authority carries out most of its functions on a committee basis, which report to the monthly meetings of the Authority. The Community Relations Committee, for instance, meets regularly with a Deputy Chief Constable to monitor the way in which complaints against the RUC are handled. The Consultative Committee on Public Order has to be consulted by the Secretary of State whenever he is considering whether to make an order under the Public Order (NI) Order 1987 prohibiting the holding of public processions or meetings. Under the Police and Criminal Evidence (NI) Order 1989 the Authority is under a duty to make arrangements for obtaining the views of the community on policing. This places on a more formal footing the contacts which the Community Relations Committee has tried to develop through the Community and Police Liaison Committees in each district council area.

It is to the Police Authority that the Chief Constable submits his annual report, but the Authority itself does not issue one. Instead it publishes a review of its activities every few years. The most recent survey covers the period 1988 to 1991.

Visitors to police stations

The Police Authority also organises a non-statutory "lay visiting" scheme in Northern Ireland. This allows for the appointment of about 50 people who, in their spare time and for no payment except expenses, are entitled to visit any of the 20 stations where people can be detained for more than six hours under the Police and Criminal Evidence (NI) Order 1989. They visit in pairs and can call at any time of the day or night. Their job is to ensure that the detainees are being properly looked after in accordance with a Code of Practice issued under the 1989 Order. To that end they can speak with the detainees and examine their custody records (if the detainee consents). After each visit a report is submitted both to the Police Authority and to the Chief Constable. To date the visitors have consistently reported that detention under the PACE Order 1989 is operating well; no major complaints have been made by any of the detainees visited. In the year to the end of March 1993 the visitors carried out 277 visits to police stations; 211 persons were detained at the time and 97 of these agreed to be seen.

Lay visitors cannot, however, visit detainees who are being detained under the anti-terrorism laws, of whom there are currently about 1,400 in Northern Ireland each year (see 4.9). These people are initially confined in one of three "holding centres" in Northern Ireland - Castlereagh in Belfast, Gough in Armagh and Strand Road in Derry. Both the Police Authority and the lay visitors themselves have tried to persuade the government to extend the remit of the visitors so that the holding centres *can* be inspected but instead the government appointed, in December 1992, an Independent Commissioner for the Holding Centres (Sir Louis Blom-Cooper QC). The Commissioner actually has greater powers than the lay visitors in that he can not only visit the holding centres whenever he wishes but also interrupt police interrogation sessions to make sure that the detainee is being properly treated. The holding centres also have closed cicuit television systems which allow the interrogation sessions to be monitored; as yet, though, the monitoring is not recorded, either in sound or in pictures.

The Independent Commission for Police Complaints

The Independent Commission for Police Complaints for Northern Ireland (ICPC) was established by the Police (NI) Order 1987 and has been operating since March 1988. It replaced the Police Complaints Board, which had existed since 1977 and which many observers felt was not effective enough. The equivalent English body is the Police Complaints Authority, created under the Police and Criminal Evidence Act 1984. The ICPC consists of a chairperson, two deputy chairpersons and five other members, all appointed by the Secretary of Sate. The present Chairman of the ICPC is Mr James Grew; all but one of the Commissioners are part-time and several of them have legal qualifications. They are appointed for a term of up to three years and must not be present or former members of a police force in Britain or Ireland. There is a staff of approximately 20 people in the ICPC and the annual cost of running it is now close to £700,000.

The ICPC's leaflet *Do you have a complaint against the police?* explains how to make a complaint and how the procedures operate in practice. It is available at Citizens' Advice Bureaux, public libraries, the Belfast Law Centre, some social security offices and police stations.

Junior officers

All complaints made by members of the public against RUC officers below the rank of Assistant Chief Constable must be recorded by the Chief Constable. Those which he feels are suitable for informal resolution may be dealt with accordingly; the remainder must be investigated formally by a member of the RUC or of another United Kingdom police force appointed by the Chief Constable, and the complaint must be referred to the ICPC. The ICPC has a duty to supervise the investigation of serious complaints (*e.g.* those alleging that a police officer caused death or serious injury) and may supervise any other investigation if it considers this desirable in the public interest. The ICPC must also supervise the investigation of any matter not the subject of a complaint provided that the Secretary of State or the Police Authority require it to do so, that the matter involves the alleged commission of a criminal offence or an offence against discipline by a police officer, and that supervision is desirable in the public interest. It *may* also supervise the investigation of a matter referred to it by the Chief Constable or the Police Authority. No matter has yet been referred by the Secretary of State or the Police Authority under these powers, but the Chief Constable has recently referred incidents involving death or injury caused by the use of police firearms.

The right to supervise investigations is one that the old Police Complaints Board did not have. It means that the ICPC can veto the appointment of any particular investigator and impose requirements on how an investigation is to be conducted (who is to be interviewed, what forensic evidence is to be collected, etc). The investigator's report must be submitted to the ICPC, which will then tell the Chief Constable whether the investigation was or was not conducted to the ICPC's satisfaction.

Until the ICPC has issued a statement on a supervised investigator's report, no disciplinary charge or criminal proceedings can be brought against the officer involved in the complaint. The Chief Constable must send a copy of the investigator's report to the Director of Public Prosecutions if he thinks that the report indicates that an officer ought to be charged with committing a criminal offence; the DPP can bring proceedings of his own motion, but this is rare. If the officer is not to be charged, or once the DPP has dealt with the question of criminal proceedings, the Chief Constable must decide whether to prefer disciplinary charges and inform the ICPC accordingly. He must also send to the ICPC the investigator's report, and his decision about disciplinary charges, in cases where the investigation was not supervised. In all cases, after it has received the relevant information from the Chief Constable, the ICPC can itself direct the Chief Constable to refer a case to the DPP and can recommend or, if need be, *direct* the preferment of disciplinary charges.

Police discipline is regulated by the RUC (Discipline and Disciplinary Appeals) Regulations 1988. Normally it is a purely internal matter, but when the Independent Commission for Police Complaints directs that it is desirable by reason of exceptional circumstances affecting the case, a tribunal may be set up to decide whether the accused officer is guilty of the charge or not. Usually the tribunal will comprise the Chief Constable as chairperson and two members of the ICPC. The standard of proof required for a finding of guilt is the same as in criminal proceedings, namely beyond all reasonable doubt, though various bodies, including the Standing Advisory Commission on Human Rights (see 8.6) have argued that the civil standard should apply instead (proof "on the balance of probablities"). In August 1993 the Northern Ireland Office issued a consultation paper suggesting fundamental reform of the police discipline system.

Senior officers

Complaints against senior RUC officers (those above the rank of chief superintendent) are the responsibility of the Police Authority rather than the Chief Constable, but the ICPC's right of supervision is just the same. Once the Authority has received a statement from the ICPC about the investigation, it must decide whether to refer the case to the DPP. Disciplinary charges will be heard by a tribunal consisting of a single person, assisted by one or more assessors, appointed by the Police Authority. In this context the ICPC does not have any power to direct referrals to the DPP or the bringing of disciplinary charges.

Reports and statistcs

The ICPC must make an annual report to the Secretary of State and a report at least once every three years reviewing the working of the complaints system. The Secretary of State can require the ICPC to report on matters relating generally to its functions or the ICPC itself can report to him on any matters which are grave or exceptional, but neither of these processes has yet been activated.

Table 15 presents the figures on complaints against the RUC during the past four years, as presented in the annual reports of the ICPC (the figures in the Chief Constable's annual reports tend to be different). When the total number of criminal prosecutions and disciplinary actions is set against the number of complaints presented, the "success rate" over the period is just under 4 per cent. What stands out most glaringly is the fact that although there have been 1,554 complaints made by persons arrested under the emergency laws (involving 1,126 allegations of assault during the course of a police interview) not a single one has been substantiated. This may have something to do with the fact that the investigations into such allegations are always carried out by the police themselves; many bodies believe that public confidence in the impartiality of the complaints system will only be assured when the power to investigate (as opposed to the power merely to supervise an investigation) is vested in a body which is entirely independent of the RUC.

COMPLAINTS AGAINST THE RUC, 1989-92

	1989	1990	1991	1992
Complaints received	2,057	2,010	2,527	2,547
Number fully considered	803	888	971	1,105
Prosecutions by the DPP	8	16	9	8
Disciplinary actions	65	106	68	79
Cases of complaints by persons arrested under the emergency laws	319	407	433	395
Allegations of assault during interview	246	328	281	271
"Emergency" complaints substantiated	0	0	0	0

Table 15

8.8 Consumer Protection Bodies

There are several bodies whose job it is to look after the interests of consumers. Some of these are branches of government at the central or local level; others are independent of government but receive government funding; a third group operates on an entirely voluntary basis.

The Office of Fair Trading

Of government bodies the most important is the Office of Fair Trading. This was established by the Fair Trading Act 1973 and is the office in London from which the Director-General of Fair Trading (currently Sir Bryan Carsberg) carries out his various statutory responsibilities for the whole of the United Kingdom. These have been extended by the Consumer Protection Act 1987 and the Consumer Protection (NI) Order 1987. They include the collection of evidence relating to business practices which may adversely affect the economic, health, safety or other interests of consumers. He may refer such practices to the Consumer Protection Advisory Committee, which in turn can make recommendations to the Secretary of State for Trade and Industry on proposed regulation of these practices (*e.g.* the banning of "no refund" notices). The Director-General also encourages trade associations to issue voluntary codes of practice to safeguard consumers' interests. He does not deal individually with complaints received directly from the public, except in so far as these alert him to a course of conduct detrimental to consumers as a whole, which he can then try to have altered, if necessary through court proceedings. In addition, most organisations giving credit to consumers can only do so if licensed by the Office of Fair Trading.

The Office of Fair Trading receives a lot of information from the local agencies which enforce legislation dealing with hygiene and with weights and measures (now called trading standards). In Northern Ireland the responsibility for supervising and enforcing trading standards (including trade descriptions) rests with the Department of Economic Development, while the control of food hygiene is part of the duties of the local district councils. These are the bodies which instigate prosecutions under the relevant legislation. The Office of Fair Trading publishes information concerning these responsibilities and provides general advice for consumers. Its pamphlets are available in advice centres and public libraries.

Local government is also responsible for the establishment of consumer advice centres. In Northern Ireland there is at present only one such centre, in Belfast. Its job is to advise consumers rather than represent them or enforce consumer protection laws. Its work is supplemented, of course, by that of the Citzens' Advice Bureaux (see 3.1).

The Monopolies and Mergers Commission

The Monopolies and Mergers Commission (MMC), also a government body, has existed in some form or other since 1948; it comprises between 10 and 27 members appointed by the Secretary of State for Trade and Industry and has its headquarters in London. The Chairperson at the moment is Sir Sydney Lipworth. The cost of running the MMC is borne by the Department of Trade and Industry and amounts to more than £5 million annually. The MMC investigates and reports on proposed or actual trade practices and structures which are referred to it by the Secretary of State or, more commonly, by the Director-General of Fair Trading. The aim may simply be to examine the facts, or it may be to assess whether the action in question will operate against the public interest. In the latter event the MMC will have to take into account, amongst other things, the interests of consumers, the need to reduce costs and the importance of developing new manufacturing techniques.

The MMC's reports usually take several months to prepare as its investigations are thorough. It holds formal confidential hearings at which witnesses will be examined and interested parties represented by barristers. The reports are laid before Parliament and published but the government is not obliged to heed the recommendations. Among the practices condemned within the field of legal services have been the restrictions placed by the Law Society on advertising by solicitors and the rule whereby a Queen's Counsel cannot work in court without the assistance of a junior barrister; some changes in these practices were made as a result. The Competition Act of 1980 extended the MMC's role by enabling it to examine the costs and general efficiency of nationalised industries, provided that such matters are officially referred to it.

In 1991 the MMC recorded a total of 1,690 complaints about anti-competitive practices or monopolies and it examined 285 merger cases. Subjects covered by recent reports include the supply within the United Kingdom of razor blades, soft drinks, matches, new cars and car parts. It has also examined the service provided by the Atomic Energy Authority.

The General Consumer Council for Northern Ireland

This body, functioning under the General Consumer Council (NI) Order 1984 came into full operation in April 1985. It replaced the Northern Ireland Consumer Council, the Northern Ireland Electricity Consumers' Council and the Transport Users' Committee. It is independent of central or local government, although its members are appointed by the Department of Economic Development and it is funded by the Department. In 1991-92 the grant was £377,000.

The General Consumer Council consists of a part-time Chairperson (Lady Anne McCollum), a deputy chairperson and up to 16 other members. There is a supporting staff of nine employees. The members represent a wide range of organisations and interests, such as the trade union movement, advice centres, local authorities and women's groups. Together these representatives make up a central body of consumer opinion, watching over consumer interests and speaking on the consumer's behalf to government, nationalised and private industries, and commercial enterprises of all sorts. The Council liaises closely with the National Consumer Council (of which its chairperson is a member) as well as with the Consumer Councils for Scotland and Wales.

The Council has a general duty to promote the consumer interest. To this end it has powers to carry out research, provide information and investigate matters of consumer concern. As it has particular responsibilities in the realms of transport, energy and food it maintains special groups working in those areas; transport matters, however, are the only ones on which it will deal with individual complaints (of which there were 31 in 1991-92). Until April 1992 it was also involved in handling complaints about the electricity service. If consumers contact the Council to complain about areas for which it has no responsibility it will give basic advice or redirect them to other bodies (see 3.1).

In recent years the Consumer Council has commissioned and published incisive reports on such matters as food safety, small claims courts (see 5.3), motor insurance costs in Northern Ireland and ferry services to and from Northern Ireland. It has also published a guide to fundamental consumer protection measures in Northern Ireland (entitled *Buying, Selling and Borrowing*) and a booklet called *Patients' Rights*. (The National Health Service has its own statutory scheme to deal with complaints about the services of a general medical or dental practitioner, as well as established procedures for handling complaints about the services or treatment in hospitals).

Unfortunately the General Consumer Council does not possess the power to compel other bodies to act on its views. It seeks to influence rather than to enforce. Through developing its consumer education service and publishing a full annual report (submitted to the Department of Economic Development) it makes consumers aware of their legal rights. The need for easily accessible consumer advice agencies in Northern Ireland is great; an official survey published in 1986 showed that the province had proportionally more consumer complaints than any other region in Britain; of those consumers who took some action on their complaint, Northern Ireland had the highest level of residual dissatisfaction.

Not within the remit of the Consumer Council are issues concerning postal and telecommunication services. Consumers' grievances in these fields should be directed respectively to the Post Office Users' Council for Northern Ireland and the regional office of OFTEL (the Office of Telecommunications), the body set up in 1984 to monitor the privatised telecommunications industry. The resolution of complaints about the electricity service is now the responsibility of the Office of Electricity Regulation (OFFER).

Co-operatives and trade unions

The Registrar of Friendly Societies operates within the government's Department of Economic Development and has the job, under a variety of statutes, of supervising the activities of Northern Ireland's industrial and provident societies (such as co-operatives and housing associations), credit unions and friendly societies. He visits these bodies and inspects their annual reports, publishing an annual report himself on what he finds. Members of the public can search the registers maintained by the Registrar for relevant information and his office answers day-to-day inquiries. The current Registrar is Mr S. McElrea.

Until the coming into force of the Industrial Relations (NI) Order 1992 the Registrar of Friendly Societies also had the duty of supervising the activities of those trade unions which were registered with him. But the 1992 Order took away that duty and vested it instead in a new post, the Certification Officer, who must in addition supervise employers' associations. The new officer is Mr A H McAlister. As well as maintaining lists of trade unions and employers' associations in Northern Ireland (and receiving their annual financial returns) he deals with trade union members' complaints about political funds and amalgamations; from January 1994 he will also be able to deal with complaints about trade union elections. He reimburses unions for certain costs incurred in conducting secret ballots. In his first year of operation the Certification Officer has received well over 100 annual returns from various trade unions and employers' associations. He is at present considering seven applications from unions to be granted certificates of independence and one application for a merger. Decisions of the Certification Officer can be appealed to the High Court and from there to the Court of Appeal.

Voluntary bodies

Of the purely voluntary organisations which act as watchdog bodies for all consumers the best known are probably the Consumers' Association and the National Federation of Consumer Groups. Both of these have members, though no groups, in Northern Ireland. The former publishes *Which?*, the magazine providing information about the range of products and services available to consumers. The National Federation of Consumer Groups is a body representing groups of consumers as well as individuals throughout the United Kingdom; it too provides information to its members concerning all aspects of consumer affairs.

Many private bodies exist to help consumers in relation to particular industries or professions. Trade associations, such as those for jewellers or manufacturers of electrical appliances, often run their own complaints machinery. The insurance industry, eager to polish up its tarnished image, has established an Insurance Ombudsman Bureau, described below. The Press Complaints Commission can deal with complaints about the accuracy or intrusiveness of newspaper articles, including those printed by local and provincial newspapers in Northern Ireland, though someone who complains to it must give a written undertaking that he or she will not begin a legal action against the newspaper at some later date, and the Commission is powerless to award any effective remedy to the complainant. People who believe they have been unfairly treated in television or radio programmes can write to the Broadcasting Complaints Commision. Complaints about advertisements in newspapers or the cinema can be made to the Advertising Standards Authority while the Independent Television Commission handles complaints about radio or TV commercials. Again, however, neither of these bodies can grant remedies.

The Insurance, Banking and Building Societies Ombudsmen

The Insurance Ombudsman's Bureau was set up in 1981 for the United Kingdom as a whole by a group of large insurance companies. It is not a statutory body and has nothing to do with the ombudsmen offices described in 8.1. There are now more than 250 members. If you are insured with one of these companies and have a complaint which is not dealt with satisfactorily by the company's own complaints procedure you can send your complaint, within six months, to the Insurance Ombudsman. He will look into the matter, if necessary ordering the firm to produce all the inter-office memos and files relating to your case. If some settlement cannot be arrived at, a formal adjudication will be made by the Insurance Ombudsman and the member firms have agreed to abide by his decisions in cases involving less than £100,000. There can be no recourse against any of the Insurance Ombudsman's decisions to the courts, but legal rights are otherwise unaffected by the scheme. The Bureau also deals with complaints about unit trusts.

The office of the Banking Ombudsman was established in 1986. It deals with complaints against any member bank, provided not more than six months have elapsed since the last word on the subject by the bank involved. The Ombudsman can award up to £50,000, and if you accept the offer of compensation you cannot later take the matter to court. The building societies set up a similar scheme in 1987; membership of it is compulsory, therefore all the United Kingdom societies are covered. The Building Societies Ombudsman will investigate complaints about mortgages and other loans, savings accounts, cheques, direct debits, etc. Neither he nor the Insurance or Banking Ombudsmen, however, can look into complaints about an institution's commercial judgment, nor can the Building Societies Ombudsman deal with complaints about surveys carried out before a mortgage is granted.

A Pensions Ombudsman also exists to deal with complaints about the administration of private pension schemes. In his first year he received more than 2,000 complaints but he upheld only 22 of these in whole or in part.

8.9 Law Reform Agencies

As explained in Chapters 1 and 2, the two main sources of law in Northern Ireland are legislation and case law. Case law is obviously an unsatisfactory medium for introducing changes in the law because it comes into being only when persons choose to take matters to court, and judges have neither the time nor the authority to expound parts of the law which are not the precise subject of the litigation before them. Legislation is therefore the preferred medium for law reform and to help Parliament and the government in designing new legislation there exist various law reform agencies.

The Office of Law Reform

The most important such body for Northern Ireland is the Office of Law Reform. This was originally constituted in 1965 as a separate branch of the Office of the Parliamentary Draftsman in Northern Ireland (now the Office of Legislative Counsel), that also being the year when the Law Commissions for England and Scotland, described below, were established. The remit of the Office of Law Reform was then to consider matters within the legislative powers of the Stormont Parliament, while bodies such as the English Law Commission retained power to consider matters falling outside Stormont's legislative capacity. The Office initiated a survey of land law in Northern Ireland, and during its first five years was instrumental in having legislation enacted on, amongst other things, theft, compensation for criminal injuries, preliminary enquiries in committal proceedings, misrepresentations, the age of majority and the enforcement of judgments.

During the short existence of the first Northern Ireland Assembly in 1974, the Office of Law Reform in effect became a separate department of the Executive, with a Minister at its head, but since the Assembly's demise the Office has functioned as a branch of what is now the Department of Finance and Personnel in the Northern Ireland Office. It has a director (Mr Piers Tweedale) and one or two other members of staff.

The Office of Law Reform no longer publishes regular reports on its activities, but its role is to consider what changes should be made in any part of the law affecting Northern Ireland. The province is still a separate legal jurisdiction within the United Kingdom, so that whenever changes in the law of England are being considered, thought has always to be given to whether similar changes should apply to Northern Ireland. The Office of Law Reform therefore devotes much of its time to examining the reports of other law reform bodies such as the English Law Commission. It also looks at suggestions for reform emanating from other common law jurisdictions, especially Canada, Australia and the Republic of Ireland. It reacts as well to proposals for reform put forward by pressure groups or dissatisfied individuals: the Law Society, for instance, has a parliamentary and law reform committee, which frequently submits ideas for change. The Office of Law Reform must inevitably work closely with the Office of Legislative Counsel (see 2.2), commenting on draft legislation and making specific recommendations for new legislation. It is also involved in preparing consolidating Orders in Council, that is, Orders which bring together in one enactment the various provisions already relating to a certain topic without making any changes in the substance of the law. At the moment the Office of Law Reform is engaged in another major review of Northern Ireland land law (which remains significantly different from that in England).

The Law Reform Advisory Committee

The absence of an independent law reform body specifically for Northern Ireland was widely lamented for many years. In April 1989, however, the government appointed a non-statutory Law Reform Advisory Committee for Northern Ireland, under the chairmanship of Mr Justice Carswell and with up to eight other members each appointed for three years and serving part-time. The Advisory Committee's secretary is provided by the Office of Law Reform.

The Advisory Committee's remit is to scrutinise the civil law of Northern Ireland, except for those matters which are "excepted" or "reserved" under the Northern Ireland Constitution Act 1973 (see 1.2), and to put forward proposals for reform. It must also consider any aspect of the civil law referred to it by the Secretary of State, although no such referral has yet occurred. Responsibility for considering reforms to the criminal law remains with the Northern Ireland Office. To date the

Advisory Committee has undertaken work on the law relating to evidence in civil proceedings, business tenancies, legal actions arising out of insidious diseases such as asbestosis, arbitration and injuries on unadopted roads. It has published three discussion papers and considered reports issued by the English Law Commission, but so far no changes to Northern Ireland's law have ensued from the Committee's work.

The Law Commission for England and Wales

Of the English law reform agencies which may have some impact on the law in Northern Ireland the most important is the Law Commission, created under the Law Commissions Act 1965. This has offices in London and is chaired by a High Court judge (currently Mr Justice Henry Brooke) with four full-time Commissioners appointed by the Lord Chancellor. It runs at a cost of over £3.25 million per year.

The Law Commission considers topics referred to it by the Lord Chancellor's Department or adjudged by itself to require attention. It is now working mainly on criminal law, family law, property law, landlord and tenant law and trust law. It normally issues consultation papers for general discussion before publishing final reports. The latter often include draft bills designed to show how the proposed changes in the law might be enacted. Since its establishment in 1965 the Law Commission (by mid-1993), had produced 126 consultation papers and 208 reports (including 27 annual reports). The majority of reports, especially the early ones, have resulted in reforming legislation within two or three years. Increasingly, though, the Law Commission is having to rely on Private Members' Bills or Private Peers' Bills to get their recommendations turned into law; a recent example is the Carriage of Goods by Sea Act 1992, introduced in Parliament by Lord Goff, a Lord of Appeal. The House of Lords now has special standing committee procedures to deal with Bills which are not contentious in a party political sense and this may facilitate the enactment of Law Commission Bills. The Scottish Law Commission, which functions in a similar way to the Law Commission for England and Wales, has also been very active; some reports are issued jointly by the two Commissions.

In addition to proposing reforms the Law Commission makes suggestions for tidying up the statute book and codifying the law. It drafts Statute Law (Repeals) Bills and undertakes consolidation work (see 2.2). It was responsible, for example, for the Income and Corporation Taxes Act 1988 which, at over 1,000 pages is the largest statute ever enacted in the United Kingdom. In 1992 it produced the Trade Union and Labour

Relations (Consolidation) Act 1992 and in 1993 it has helped with the Charities Act. In 1989 the Law Commission produced a Criminal Code Report, the culmination of its long-standing project to put into one code all of the important criminal law. Although this Report contained a draft Bill, no legislation has yet ensued. Supplementary reports aimed at codifying the criminal law are to be published soon; they will deal with offences against the person, intoxication, conspiracy to defraud and giving assistance or encouragement to crimes.

A core of 15 civil service lawyers are employed at the Law Commission, together with four draftsmen serving on secondment from the Office of Parliamentary Counsel. From time to time university academics and research assistants are also engaged. The Law Commission's librarian issues a quarterly bulletin called *Law Under Review*, which gives up-to-date summaries of all government law reform projects. In 1985, to underline further the Law Commission's commitment to practical law reform, a Standing Committee on Conveyancing was set up; this has focused its attention on procedural reforms which would be of benefit to ordinary house buyers and sellers.

The Law Commission has no direct responsibility for law reform in Northern Ireland, but many of the changes which it succeeds in getting introduced in England are later made in Northern Ireland as a matter of course.

Other review bodies for the United Kingdom

Two other committees still exist to review particular aspects of the law which are from time to time referred to them, though in recent years their services have not been called upon. They are the Law Reform Committee and the Criminal Law Revision Committee. The Law Reform Committee was appointed in 1952 as the successor to the Law Revision Committee, set up in 1934; it considers matters specifically assigned to it by the Lord Chancellor, assignments which in recent years have produced reports on, for example, rules of evidence in civil proceedings and the making, interpreting and revoking of wills. In all 24 reports have so far been produced, the last as far back as 1984 on the topic of suing for latent damage. Since then the Committee has been in abeyance.

The Criminal Law Revision Committee was created in 1959 and has issued 17 reports, some of which have taken the form of very detailed examinations of large areas of the criminal law (such as theft and evidence). The last, on prostitution, was published in 1985. The Criminal

Law Revision Committee is accountable to the Home Secretary rather than the Lord Chancellor. Like the Law Reform Committee, when it is sitting it uses part-time members and a full-time secretariat; like the Law Commission both Committees issue working papers or consultative documents.

On occasions a body is appointed by the government of the day to look into matters of specific or of general concern. The best example of the latter type are Royal Commissions, which conduct large-scale inquiries into affairs with wide-ranging social and legal implications. They are usually chaired by judges or high-ranking public servants. Recent Royal Commissions have included the Pearson Commission on Civil Liability and Compensation for Personal Injury (1978), the Benson Commission on Legal Services (1979), the Philips Commission on Criminal Procedure (1981) and the Runciman Commission on Criminal Justice (1993) (see 4.3). Their reports extend to hundreds of pages and are based on considerable empirical research. An example of a less formal investigation is that known as the Civil Justice Review, conducted under the auspices of the Lord Chancellor's Department between 1985 and 1988; it looked into ways of improving the administration of the civil courts in England and Wales (see 5.1). Other government departments, or interdepartmental working parties, frequently issue green or white papers suggesting reforms. The Northern Ireland Office, for example, issued a discussion paper entitled *Crime and the Community* in March 1993.

APPENDIX 1

WHERE TO FIND MORE INFORMATION

There are two ways to look for further information concerning any of the topics dealt with in this book. You can consult the published literature, or you can try to contact a relevant person or body connected with the inquiry. In a small place like Northern Ireland, where it is often not economically feasible to publish information or commentaries on aspects of the legal system but where personal contacts are easy to establish, the second method of seeking information will usually be the more fruitful. Appendix 2 sets out the addresses and telephone numbers of a variety of bodies which will usually be very willing to help you with any such query.

As regards the published literature there are rather few books readily available on specific aspects of the legal system in Northern Ireland and there is no other book at all on the legal system as a whole. Information is more commonly to be found in academic journals, official reports or pamphlets issued by public bodies. These are often difficult to track down. In such circumstances the most reliable source for information is the actual legal text governing the point in issue. Chapter 2 of this book explains how to search for these original legal sources, while Appendix 3 provides some samples of them. In most situations, unfortunately, you will require a legally qualified person to make sense of these sources.

Listed below are the published works relevant to each chapter in this book. Some items are relevant to more than one chapter. The more official the document, the more likely it is to be available only in a public or academic library, or on application to the body originally publishing it. Some of the books mentioned are primarily concerned with the English legal system but they contain some information relevant also to Northern Ireland. Items marked with an asterisk are available from SLS Legal Publications (NI), School of Law, Queen's University, Belfast BT7 1NN (tel: 245133 ext. 3597).

Chapter 1. The History and Administration of the Legal System

Annual Reports of the Chief Constable of the Royal Ulster Constabulary.
Annual Reports of the Prison Service of Northern Ireland.
Annual Reports of the Northern Ireland Association for the Care and
    Resettlement of Offenders and of the Extern Organisation.
D. Birrell and A. Murie, *Policy and Government in Northern Ireland:*
    Lessons of Devolution (1980; Gill and Macmillan).
K. Boyle, T. Hadden and P. Hillyard, *Law and State: The Case of Northern*
    Ireland (1974; Martin Robertson), updated by the same authors in *Ten*
    Years on in Northern Ireland: The Legal Control of Political Violence

(1980; The Cobden Trust).

*B. Hadfield, *The Constitution of Northern Ireland* (1989).

B. Hadfield (ed.), *Northern Ireland: Politics and the Constitution* (1992; Open University Press).

*J. Hayes and P. O'Higgins (eds.), *Lessons From Northern Ireland* (1990).

F. Kelly, *A Guide to Early Irish Law* (1988; Dublin Institute for Advanced Studies).

L. O'Dowd, B. Rolston and M. Tomlinson, *Northern Ireland: Between Civil Rights and Civil War* (1980; CSE Books).

C. O'Leary, S. Elliott and R. Wilford, *The Northern Ireland Assembly 1982-1986: A Constitutional Experiment* (1988; C. Hurst & Co).

C. Ryder, *The RUC: A Force Under Fire* (1989; Methuen).

S. de Smith and R. Brazier, *Constitutional and Administrative Law* (6th ed., 1989; Penguin), especially pp. 50-57.

J. Whyte, *Interpreting Northern Ireland* (1990; Clarendon Press).

D. Birrell, "The Westminster Parliament and Northern Ireland Business" (1990) Parliamentary Affairs, 43(4), 435-447.

*B. Dickson, "Northern Ireland's Legal System - An Evaluation" (1992) 43 Northern Ireland Legal Quarterly (hereinafter NILQ) 315-329.

*B. Hadfield, "Committees of the House of Commons and Northern Ireland Affairs" (1981) 32 NILQ 199.

*F. Newark, "The Bringing of English Law to Ireland" (1972) 23 NILQ 3, and "Notes on Irish Legal History" (1947) 7 NILQ 121. Both of these articles are reprinted in *Elegantia Juris: Selected Writings of F. H. Newark*.

J. Whyte, "How much discrimination was there under the Unionist régime, 1921-68?" in T. Gallagher and J. O'Connell (eds.), *Contemporary Irish Studies* (1983; Manchester University Press).

Chapter 2. The Branches and Sources of Northern Ireland Law

R. Beddard, *Human Rights and Europe* (3rd ed., 1993; Grotius Publications).

J. Bell and Sir G. Engle, *Cross on Statutory Interpretation* (2nd ed., 1987; Butterworths).

N. Brown, Sir J. Jacobs and T. Kennedy, *The Court of Justice of the European Communities* (4th ed., 1993; Butterworths).

P. Clinch, *Using a Law Library* (1992; Blackstone Press).

R. Cross and J. Harris, *Precedent in English Law* (4th ed., 1991; Clarendon Press).

J. Dane and P. Thomas, *How to Use a Law Library* (2nd ed., 1987; Sweet & Maxwell), especially Chapter 9 on Northern Ireland.

J. Farrar and A. Dugdale, *Introduction to Legal Method* (3rd ed., 1990; Sweet & Maxwell).

J. Griffith, *The Politics of the Judiciary* (4th ed., 1991; Fontana).

P. Harris, *An Introduction to Law* (4th ed., 1993; Weidenfeld & Nicolson).

G. Holborn, *Butterworths Legal Research Guide* (1993; Butterworths).

J. Holland and J. Webb, *Learning Legal Rules* (2nd ed., 1993; Blackstone Press).

P. Kenny, *Studying Law* (2nd ed., 1990; Butterworths).

S. Lee, *Judging Judges* (1988; Faber & Faber).

S. Lee and M. Fox, *Learning Legal Skills* (1991; Blackstone Press).

D. Miers and A Page, *Legislation* (2nd ed., 1990; Sweet & Maxwell).

*S. Paisley, *A Guide to EEC Law in Northern Ireland* (1986).

V. Tunkel, *Legal Research: Law-Finding and Problem-Solving* (1992; Blackstone Press).

W. Twining and D. Miers, *How To Do Things With Rules* (3rd ed., 1991; Weidenfeld & Nicolson).

M. Zander, *The Law-Making Process* (3rd ed., 1989; Weidenfeld & Nicolson).

Chapter 3. Legal Services

Report of the Royal Commission on Legal Services (Chairman: Sir Henry Benson) (1979; Cmnd. 7648); Chapters 40-42.

Report of the Review Body on Civil Justice (Chairman: Sir Maurice Hodgson) (1988; Cm. 394).

Annual Reports of the Law Society of Northern Ireland on the Civil and Criminal Legal Aid Schemes.

Annual Report of the Lord Chancellor's Advisory Committee on Legal Aid in Northern Ireland.

A. Bradney and Others, *How to Study Law* (2nd ed., 1991; Sweet & Maxwell).

Law Society of Northern Ireland, *A Guide to Legal Aid in Northern Ireland* (1993) (a pamphlet).

Legal Action Group, *A Strategy for Justice: Publicly funded legal services in the 1990s* (1992; Legal Action Group).

J. Morison and P. Leith, *The Barrister's World and the Nature of Law* (1992; Open University Press).

Chapter 4. Proceedings in Criminal Courts

Annual Report of the Lord Chancellor's Department, *Judicial Statistics for England and Wales.*

Northern Ireland Court Service, *Northern Ireland Judicial Statistics* (annual).

Northern Ireland Office, *A Commentary on Northern Ireland Crime Statistics* (annual).

Northern Ireland Office, *Northern Ireland Annual Abstract of Statistics*, Chapter 3 (Law and Order).

Report of the Commission to consider legal procedures to deal with terrorist activities in Northern Ireland (Chairman: Lord Diplock) (1972; Cmnd. 5185).

Report of a Committee to consider, in the context of civil liberties and human rights, measures to deal with terrorism in Northern Ireland (Chairman: Lord

Gardiner) (1975; Cmnd. 5847).

Report of a Committee of Inquiry into Police Interrogation Procedures in Northern Ireland (Chairman: Judge Bennett) (1979; Cmnd. 7947).

Report of the Royal Commission on Criminal Procedure (Chairman: Sir Cyril Phillips) (1979; Cmnd. 8092).

Report of the Royal Commission on Criminal Justice (Chairman: Viscount Runciman) (1993; Cm. 2263).

Viscount Colville, *Reviews of the Prevention of Terrorism Act and of the Northern Ireland (Emergency Provisions) Act* (annual).

Northern Ireland Information Service, *Quarterly Statistics on the Prevention of Terrorism Act and the Northern Ireland (Emergency Provisions) Act.*

V. Bevan and K. Lidstone, *The Investigation of Crime: A Guide to Police Powers* (1991; Butterworths).

*K. Boyle and M. Allen, *Sentencing Law and Practice in Northern Ireland* (2nd ed., 1990).

B. Dickson (ed.), *Civil Liberties in Northern Ireland: The CAJ Handbook* (2nd ed., 1993; Committee on the Administration of Justice, Belfast).

*S. Doran, *Criminal Procedure in Northern Ireland*, Chapter 5 of *The Digest of Northern Ireland Law* (1988).

Hegarty A. (ed.), *The Rights Guide* (1990; NIACRO, Belfast).

Helsinki Watch, *Human Rights in Northern Ireland* (1991; Helsinki Watch).

*J. Jackson, R. Kilpatrick and C. Harvey, *Called to Court: A Public Review of Criminal Justice in Northern Ireland* (1991).

A. Jennings (ed.), *Justice under Fire: The Abuse of Civil Liberties in Northern Ireland* (2nd ed., 1990; Pluto Press).

*D. Lavery, *Road Traffic Law in Northern Ireland* (1989 and 1993 Supplement).

J. Sprack, *Emmins on Criminal Procedure* (5th ed., 1992; Blackstone Press).

B. Valentine, *Criminal Offences in Northern Ireland* (1992; Institute of Professional Legal Studies, Belfast).

*B. Valentine and A. Hart, *Criminal Procedure in Northern Ireland* (1989 and 1990 Supplement).

C. Walker, *The Prevention of Terrorism in British Law* (2nd ed., 1992; Manchester University Press).

B. Dickson, "Northern Ireland's Emergency Legislation - The Wrong Medicine?" [1992] Public Law 592-624.

*C. Walker, "Police and the Community in Northern Ireland" (1990) 41 NILQ 105-142.

Chapter 5. Proceedings in Civil Courts

Annual Reports of the Lord Chancellor's Department, *Judicial Statistics for England and Wales.*

Northern Ireland Court Service, *Northern Ireland Judicial Statistics* (annual).

*D. Greer, *Small Claims: The New Procedure in Northern Ireland* (3rd. ed.,

1988).

*D. Greer, *Compensation for Criminal Injury* (1990).

*D. Greer and V. Mitchell, *Compensation for Criminal Damage to Property* (1989).

General Consumer Council for Northern Ireland, *How to Make Small More Beautiful: The Small Claims Procedure in Northern Ireland* (1992).

*B. Valentine, *County Court Procedure in Northern Ireland* (1985 and 1987 Supplement).

S. Sime, *A Practical Approach to Civil Procedure* (1993; Blackstone Press).

Chapter 6. Special Courts

Report of the Children and Young Persons Review Group (Chairman: Sir Harold Black) (1979).

D. McBrien, "An Outline of British Military Law" (1983) Military Law and Law of War Review 13.

Northern Ireland Juvenile Courts Association, *Lay Panel Magazine.*

Inquests and Disputed Killings in Northern Ireland (1992; Committee on the Administration of Justice, Belfast).

Chapter 7. Tribunals

Annual Reports of the Social Security Advisory Committee, the Chief Adjudication Officer and the Social Fund Commissioner.

Annual Reports of the Council on Tribunals.

J. Baldwin, N. Wikeley and R. Young, *Judging Social Security: The Adjudication of Claims for Benefit in Britain* (1992; Clarendon Press).

*P. Bateson and J. McKee, *Industrial Tribunals in Northern Ireland* (2nd ed., 1989).

Belfast Law Centre, *Information Pack* (1993; loose-leaf).

Child Poverty Action Group, *Rights Guide to Non-Means-Tested Social Security Benefits* (16th ed., 1993).

Child Poverty Action Group, *National Welfare Benefits Handbook* (23rd ed., 1993).

Department of Health and Social Services for Northern Ireland, *The Law Relating to Social Security in Northern Ireland* (8 volumes; loose-leaf).

Department of Health and Social Services for Northern Ireland, *Adjudication Officers' Guide* (10 volumes; loose-leaf).

*E. Evason, *Social Security Benefits in Northern Ireland* (1992).

*B. Hadfield, Judicial Review in Northern Ireland, Chapter 13 of *The Digest of Northern Ireland Law* (1992).

*C. MacLynn, A. Loney, R. Steele and B. Walsh, *A Guide to Procedure: Social Security Appeals and Housing Benefit Review Boards* (1990)

*B. Walsh, *Northern Ireland Guide to Supplementary Benefit and Family*

Income Supplement Decisions (1988).

Chapter 8. Watchdog Bodies

Annual Reports of the following:
  Parliamentary Commissioner for Administration
  Commissioner for Complaints
  Fair Employment Commission
  Labour Relations Agency
  Health and Safety Agency
  Equal Opportunities Commission
  Standing Advisory Commission on Human Rights
  Independent Commission for Police Complaints
  Office of Fair Trading
  General Consumer Council
  Law Commission for England and Wales
  Law Reform Advisory Committee for Northern Ireland
The Police Authority for Northern Ireland, *People, Policing, Progress: The Work of the Police Authority 1988-1991.*
Triennial Review by the Independent Commission for Police Complaints, 1991.
D. Smith and G. Chambers, *Inequality in Northern Ireland* (1991; Clarendon Press).

In addition to the above materials, which are relevant to particular chapters in this book, there are many publications which describe the workings of the entire legal system in England and Wales and which include much information that is also applicable to Northern Ireland. However, it is unsafe to rely on such works unless the relevant passages specifically state that the position in Northern Ireland is the same as in England. Even when the position is the same, the legal basis for it (*i.e.* the relevant statute or case-law) may well be different. Perhaps the best book on the day-to-day workings of the English legal system is *The Law Machine*, by M. Berlins and C. Dyer (3rd ed.,1989; Penguin). This is based on a TV documentary series explaining how the legal system operates in practice. It is very readable, containing a lot of critical comment on the present state of affairs. Of the vast array of more technical works on the subject, suitable for law students, the best are perhaps those by T. Ingman, *The English Legal Process* (3rd ed., 1990; Financial Training Publications), P. Smith, S. Bailey and M. Gunn, *The Modern English Legal System* (2nd ed, 1991; Sweet and Maxwell). J. Spencer, *Jackson's Machinery of Justice* (8th ed., 1989; Cambridge

University Press) and R. White, *The Administration of Justice* (2nd ed., 1991; Blackwell).

There are also several books which, as well as touching upon the structure and personnel of the English legal system, concentrate on introducing the reader to different areas of substantive law. The more traditional of these works, again designed primarily for law students, dwell on topics such as the law of contract, the law of torts, criminal law and land law. They include the books by P. Harris, *An Introduction to Law* (4th ed, 1993; Weidenfeld and Nicolson), P. James, *An Introduction to English Law* (12th ed., 1989; Butterworths) and K. Smith and D. Keenan, *English Law* (10th ed., 1992; Pitman Publishing). The introductory books geared more to the lay person tend, quite naturally, to dwell on the legal topics which are most likely to be encountered in every day life. An excellent work of this kind is *The Penguin Guide to the Law*, by J. Pritchard (3rd ed., 1992; Penguin). It has sections on family law, housing law, employment law, consumer law and motoring law: there are dozens of helpful diagrams to explain various procedures. Also to be recommended are P. Redmond, *General Principles of English Law* (6th ed., 1990; Pitman Publishing), A.Dugdale and others, *'A' Level Law* (2nd ed., 1992; Butterworths) and W. Brown, *GCSE Law* (5th ed., 1993; Sweet & Maxwell).

Two compendiums on English law are useful reference books if you want to look up a particular word or phrase: the Readers' Digest's *You and Your Rights: An A to Z Guide to the Law* (10th ed., 1991) and *The Oxford Companion to Law* by D. Walker (1980). The best value legal dictionaries are probably *Mozley and Whiteley's Law Dictionary*, by H. Ivamy (11th ed., 1993; Butterworths) and *Osborn's Concise Law Dictionary*, by L. Rutherford and S. Bone (8th ed., 1993; Sweet & Maxwell).

SLS Legal Publications (NI) also publish *The Digest of Northern Ireland Law*, a loose-leaf publication of which 14 chapters had appeared by mid-1993. It provides detailed information on specific aspects of Northern Ireland law for legal advisers.

APPENDIX 2

USEFUL ADDRESSES

Advice Centres (selected)

Ashgrove Community Centre
Garvaghy Road
Portadown
Co. Armagh BT62 1ED
(tel: 0762-331650)

Ballybeen Womens Group
34 Ballybeen Square
Belfast BT16 0QE
(tel: 0232-481632)

Ballynafeigh Community
Development Association
291 Ormeau Road
Belfast BT7 3GG
(tel: 0232-491161)

Belfast Consumer
Advice Centre
6 Callender Street
Belfast BT1 5BN
(tel: 0232-328260)

Belfast Housing Aid
92 Victoria Street
Belfast BT1 3GN
(tel: 0232-245640)

Centre for the Unemployed
45-47 Donegall Street
Belfast BT1 2FG
(tel: 0232-243920)

Community Advice Centre
227 Crumlin Road
Belfast BT14 7DY
(tel:0232-351652)

Craigavon Independent Advice Centre
308 Burnside
Craigavon
Co. Armagh BT65 5DD
(tel: 0762-324945)

Cregagh Advice Centre
Cregagh Community Centre
Cappagh Gardens
Belfast BT6 0ET
(tel: 0232-795848)

Derry Advice Centre
1 Guildhall Street
Derry BT48 6BJ
(tel: 0504-362444)

Divis Community Centre
9 Ard Moulin Place
Belfast BT12 4RR
(tel: 0232-242551)

Downtown Women's Centre
19 North Street Arcade
Belfast BT1 1PA
(tel: 0232-231676)

East Belfast Community Council
198-200 Albertbridge Road
Belfast BT5 4GU
(tel: 0232-451512)

Falls Community Council
50 Kennedy Way
Belfast BT11 9AP
(tel: 0232-301410)

Gingerbread (for lone parents)
169 University Street
Belfast BT7 1HR
(tel: 0232-234568)

Glen Road Advice Centre
Glen Community Centre
Carrigart Avenue
Belfast BT11 6HU
(tel: 0232-627189)

Information Plus Centre
Sedan Avenue
Omagh
Co. Tyrone BT79 7AQ
(tel: 0662-245954)

Lower Ormeau Residents Action Group
91 Ormeau Road
Belfast BT7 1SH
(tel: 0232-231752)

Newry Welfare Rights Advice Centre
2 Bridge Street
Newry
Co. Down BT35 8AE
(tel: 0693-67631)

Oliver Plunkett Advice Centre
41 Suffolk Road
Belfast BT11 9PD
(tel: 0232-627731)

Omagh and District Advice Centre
9 Holmeview Terrace
Campsie Road
Omagh BT79 0AH
(tel: 0662-243252)

Rathcoole Advice Centre
c/o Rathcoole Self-Help Group
30a The Diamond
Rathcoole
Newtownabbey
Co. Antrim BT37 9BJ
(tel: 0232-365322)

Shankill Legal Advice Centre
Shankill Community Council
177 Shankill Road
Belfast BT13 1FD
(tel: 0232-325536)

Upper Springfield Resource Centre
195 Whiterock Road
Belfast BT12 7FW
(tel: 0232-328928)

Other Agencies

A.I.D.S. Helpline (NI)
Bryson House
28 Bedford Street
Belfast BT2 7FE
(tel: 0232-326117)

Advertising Standards Authority
Brook House
2-16 Torrington Place
London WC1E 7HN
(tel: 071-580-5555)

Age Concern
3 Lower Crescent
Belfast BT7 1NR
(tel: 0232-245729)

Alcoholics Anonymous
152 Lisburn Road
Belfast BT7 7AJ
(tel: 0232-681084)

Amnesty International
c/o Corrymeela House
8 Upper Crescent
Belfast BT7 1NT
(tel: 0232-325008)

Association of Local Authorities
6 Callender Street
Belfast BT1 5BN
(tel: 0232-249286)

Banking Ombudsman Office
Citadel House
5-11 Fetter Lane
London EC4A 1BR
(tel: 071-583-1395)

Belfast Law Centre
7 University Road
Belfast BT7 1NA
(tel: 0232-321307)

Belfast Law Centre
Northern Area Office
2 John Street
Ballymena
Co. Antrim BT43 6DU
(tel: 0266-659137)

Belfast Law Centre
Southern Area Office
13 High Street
Lurgan
Co. Armagh BT66 8AA
(tel: 0762-321555)

Belfast Law Centre
Western Area Office
9 Clarendon Street
Derry BT48 7EP
(tel: 0504-262433)

British Irish Rights Watch
c/o 95 Hillbrook Road
London SW17 8SF
(tel: 071-436-0964)

Broadcasting Complaints Commission
35 Grosvenor Gardens
SW1W 0BS
(tel: 071-630-1966)

Building Societies Ombudsman
Grosvenor Gardens House
35-37 Grosvenor Gardens
London SW1X 7AW
(tel: 071-931-0044)

Bryson House
28 Bedford Street
Belfast BT2 7FE
(tel: 0232-325825)

Cara-Friend
PO Box 44
Belfast BT1 1SH
(tel: 0232-322023)
(also in Derry, tel: 0504-363120)

Central Services Agency
25-27 Adelaide Street
Belfast BT2 7FH
(tel: 0232-324431)

Certification Officer (for trade unions and
employers' associations)
Windsor House, 16th floor
9-15 Bedford Street
Belfast BT2 7EH
(tel: 0232-237773)

Charities Unit
Parliament Buildings
Stormont
Belfast BT4 3SW
(tel: 0232-520000)

Child Poverty Action Group
1-5 Bath Street, 4th floor
London EC1V 9PY
(tel: 071-253-3406)

Children's Legal Centre
20 Crompton Terrace
London N1 2UN
(tel: 071-359-6251)

Children's Rights Development Unit
Centre for Social Research
Queen's University
105 Botanic Avenue
Belfast BT7 1NN
(tel: 0232-245133 ext. 3582)

Chinese Welfare Association
17 Eblana Street
Belfast BT7 1LD
(tel: 0232-238220)

Coal Ombudsman for Northern Ireland
Freepost BE66
Holywood
Co. Down BT18 9BR
(tel: 0232-761896)

Commissioner for Complaints
Progressive House
33 Wellington Place
Belfast BT1 6HN
(tel: 0232-233821 or freephone 0800-282036)

Commissioner for the Rights of
Trade Union Members (NI)
Canada House
22 North Street
Belfast BT1 1HA
(tel: 0232-233640)

Committee on the Administration
of Justice
45-47 Donegall Street
Belfast BT1 2FG
(tel: 0232-232394)

Community Relations Council
Glendinning House
6 Murray Street
Belfast BT1 6DN
(tel: 0232-439953)

Community Technical Aid
445-9 Ormeau Road
Belfast BT7 3GQ
(tel: 0232-642227)

Companies Registry
43-47 Chichester Street
Belfast BT1 4JD
(tel: 0232-234488)

Compensation Agency
Royston House
35 Upper Queen Street
Belfast BT1 6FD
(tel: 0232-249944)

Consumers Association
2 Marylebone Road
London NW1 4DX
(tel: 071-486-5544)

Crossroads Caring for Carers Scheme
Regional Office
38 Ormeau Road
Belfast BT7 2EA
(tel: 0232-310603)
Crown Solicitor's Office
Royal Courts of Justice
Chichester Street
Belfast BT1 3JF
(tel: 0232-235111)

Cruse (Northern Ireland) Bereavement
Care
50 University Street
Belfast BT7 1HB
(tel: 0232-232695)

Department of Agriculture
Dundonald House
Upper Newtownards Road
Belfast BT4 3SA
(tel: 0232-520000)

Department of Economic Development
Netherleigh
Massey Avenue
Belfast BT4 2JP
(tel: 0232-529900)

Department of Education
Rathgael House
Balloo Road
Bangor
Co. Down BT19 2PR
(tel: 0247-270077)

Department of the Environment
Parliament Buildings
Stormont
Belfast BT4 3SW
(tel: 0232-520000)

Department of Finance and Personnel
Parliament Buildings
Stormont
Belfast BT4 3SW
(tel: 0232-520000)

or:

Rosepark House
Upper Newtownards Road
Belfast BT4 3NR
(tel: 0232-520400)
Department of Health and Social Services
Dundonald House
Upper Newtownards Road
Belfast BT4 3SA
(tel: 0232-520000)
*(local social security agency offices are
listed in the telephone directory under 'Social Security Agency'; or ring freephone
0800-616757 for general benefits inquiries or 0800-220674 for specific information and advice on disability benefits)*

Department of Public Administration and
Legal Studies
University of Ulster at Jordanstown
Co Antrim BT37 OQB
(tel: 365131 ext. 2339)

DIAL (NI): The Disability Helpline
24-26 North Street Arcade
Belfast BT1 1PB
(tel: 0232-322690)

or:

1-3 Guildhall Street,
Derry BT48 6BJ
(tel: 0504-371030)

Director of Public Prosecutions Office
Royal Courts of Justice
Chichester Street
Belfast BT1 3JF
(tel: 0232-235111)

Disability Action
2 Annadale Avenue
Belfast BT7 3JR
(tel: 0232-491011)

Educational Guidance Service for Adults
Glendinning House
6 Murray Street
Belfast BT1 6DN
(tel: 0232-244274)

Employment Medical Advisory Service
Royston House
35 Upper Queen Street
Belfast BT1 6FD
(tel: 0232-233045)

Enforcement of Judgments Office
Bedford House
16-22 Bedford Street
Belfast BT2 7NR
(tel: 0232-245081)

Equal Opportunities Commission
Chamber of Commerce House
22 Great Victoria Street
Belfast BT2 2BA
(tel: 0232-242752)

European Commission Office
9-15 Bedford Street
Belfast BT2 7EG
(tel: 0232-240708)

European Commission of Human Rights
Palais de l'Europe
67006 Strabourg
France
(tel: 010-33-88412000)

The Extern Organisation
5-11 Verner Street
Belfast BT7 2AA
(tel: 0232-240900)

Fair Employment Commission
Andras House
60 Great Victoria Street
Belfast BT2 7BB
(tel: 0232-240020)

Family Planning Association
113 University Street
Belfast BT7 1HP
(tel: 0232-325488)

or:

14 Magazine Street
Derry BT48 6HH
(tel: 0504-260016)

Federation of Independent Advice Centres
13 Stockwell Road
London SW9 9AU
(tel: 071-274-1839)

Gamblers Anonymous
4-18 Donegall Street
Belfast BT1 2GP
(tel: 0232-249185)

General Consumer Council
Elizabeth House
116 Hollywood Road
Belfast BT4 1NY
(tel: 0232-672488)

Health and Safety Agency
Canada House
22 North Street
Belfast BT1 1NN
(tel: 0232-243249)

Her Majesty's Stationery Office (HMSO)
Government Bookshop
16 Arthur Street
Belfast BT1 4GD
(tel: 0232-238451)

Home Office
50 Queen Anne's Gate
London SW1H 9AT
(tel: 071-213-3000)

Howard League for Penal Reform
708 Holloway Road
London N19 3NL
(tel: 071-281-7722)

Independent Assessor of Military Complaints Procedures
Hampton House
47-53 High Street
Belfast BT1 2QS
(tel: 0232-237181)

Independent Commission for Police Complaints
Chamber of Commerce House
22 Great Victoria Street
Belfast BT2 7BA
(tel: 0232-244821)

Independent Commissioner for the Holding Centres
Hampton House
47-53 High Street
Belfast BT1 2QS
(tel: 0232-237181)

Independent Tribunal Service
Cleaver House, 5th floor
3 Donegall Square North
Belfast BT1 5BR
(tel: 0232-539900)

Institute of Professional Legal Studies
Queen's University of Belfast
1 Upper Crescent
Belfast BT7 1NT
(tel: 0232-245133 ext. 3498)

Insurance Ombudsman Bureau
135 Park Street
London SE1 9EA
(tel: 071-928-4488)

Irish Congress of Trade Unions
(Northern Ireland Committee)
3 Wellington Park
Belfast BT9 6DJ
(tel: 0232-681726)

Irish Council for Civil Liberties
Arran House
35-36 Arran Quay,
Dublin 7
(tel: 010-3531-873-4412)

JUSTICE
(British section of the International
Commission of Jurists)
95a Chancery Lane
London WC2A 1DT
(tel: 071-405-6018)

Labour Relations Agency
Windsor House
9-15 Bedford Street
Belfast BT2 7NL
(tel: 0232-321442)

or:

3 Foyle Street
Derry BT48 6AL
(tel: 0504-69639)

Land Registry
River House
48 High Street
Belfast BT1 2DR
(tel: 0232-233552)

Law Centres' Federation
Duchess House
18-19 Warren Street
London W1P 5DB
(tel: 071-387-8570)

Law Commission for England and Wales
Conquest House
38-39 John Street
Theobald's Road
London WC1N 2BQ
(tel: 071-242-0861)

Law Reform Commission of Ireland
Ardilaun Centre
111 St Stephen's Green
Dublin 2
(tel: 010-3531-671-5699)

Law Reform Advisory Committee for
Northern Ireland
Permanent House
21-23 Arthur Street
Belfast BT1 4JL
(tel: 0232-327661 ext. 324)

Law Society of Northern Ireland
90 Victoria Street
Belfast BT1 3GN
(tel: 0232-231614)

Lay Observer
Room 409
Clarendon House
Adelaide Street
Belfast BT2 8ND
(tel: 0232-244300 ext. 2333)

Legal Action Group
242 Pentonville Road
London N1 9UN
(tel: 071-833-2931)

Legal Aid Department
Law Society of Northern Ireland
Bedford House
16-22 Bedford Street
Belfast BT2 7FL
(tel: 0232-246441)

Legal Information Forum
c/o Bar Library
Royal Courts of Justice
Chichester Street
PO Box 414
Belfast BT1 3JP
(tel: 0232-241523)

Legal Services Ombudsman's Office
22 Oxford Court
Oxford Street
Manchester M2 3WQ
(tel: 061-236-9532)

Legislative Counsel's Office
Department of Finance and Personnel
Stormont
Belfast BT4 3SW
(tel: 0232-520000)

Liberty
21 Tabard Street
London SE1 4LA
(tel: 071-403-3888)

MENCAP (for the mentally unwell)
Segal House
4 Annadale Avenue
Belfast BT7 3JH
(tel: 0232-691351)

Mental Health Commission
Elizabeth House
116-118 Hollywood Road
Belfast BT4 1NY
(tel: 0232-651157)

Money and Relationship Counselling
Room 59, 3rd floor
Scottish Mutual Building
16 Donegall Square South
Belfast BT1 5JH
(tel: 0232-240649)

Monopolies and Mergers Commission
New Court
48 Carey Street
London WC2A 2JT
(tel: 071-600-3333)

Motor Insurers' Bureau
152 Silbury Boulevard
Central Milton Keynes MK9 1NB
(tel: 0908-240000)

Multi-Cultural Resource Centre
Bryson House
28 Bedford Street
Belfast BT2 7FE
(tel: 0232-325835 ext. 48)

National Association of Citizens' Advice
Bureaux
115-123 Pentonville Road
London N1 9LZ
(tel: 071-833-2181)

National Consumer Council
18 Queen Anne's Gate
London SW1H 9AA
(tel: 071-222-9501)

National Federation of Consumer Groups
12 Mosley Street
Newcastle-Upon-Tyne NE1 1DE
(tel: 091-261-8259)

National House Building Council
59 Malone Road
Belfast BT9 6SA
(tel: 0232-683131)

Nexus (for complaints of rape etc)
PO Box 220
Belfast BT1 7HP
(tel: 0232-326803 or in Derry, 0504-
260566)

Northern Ireland Advisory Committee on
Telecommunications
   (OFTEL in Northern Ireland)
Chamber of Commerce House, 7th floor
22 Great Victoria Street
Belfast BT2 7QA
(tel: 0232-244113)

Northern Ireland Association for the Care
and Resettlement of Offenders
169 Ormeau Road
Belfast BT7 1SQ
(tel: 0232-320157)

Northern Ireland Association of Citizens
Advice Bureaux
11 Upper Crescent
Belfast BT7 1NT
(tel: 0232-231120)
(*Addresses of local CABx are listed in the
telephone directory under the heading
'Citizens' Advice Bureaux'.*)

Northern Ireland Association for Mental
Health
Beacon House
80 University Street
Belfast BT7 1HE
(tel: 0232-328474)

Northern Ireland Council for Integrated
Education
16 Mount Charles
Belfast BT7 1NZ
(tel: 0232-236200)

Northern Ireland Council for Voluntary
Action
127 Ormeau Road
Belfast BT7 1SH
(tel: 0232-321224)

Northern Ireland Council on Alcohol
40 Elmwood Avenue
Belfast BT9 6AZ
(tel: 0232-664434)

NICOD - The Disability Charity
31 Ulsterville Avenue
Belfast BT9 7AS
(tel: 0232-666188)

Northern Ireland Court Service
Windsor House
9-15 Bedford Street
Belfast BT2 7EH
(tel: 0232-328594)

Northern Ireland Federation of Housing
Associations
Carlisle Memorial Centre
88 Clifton Street
Belfast BT13 1AB
(tel: 0232-230446)

Northern Ireland Housing Executive
The Housing Centre
2 Adelaide Street
Belfast BT2 8PB
(tel: 0232-240588)
(*Addresses of district offices are listed in
the telephone directory under 'NIHE'*)

Northern Ireland Office
Stormont Castle
Stormont
Belfast BT4 3SW
(tel: 0232-520700 or the confidential line
freephone 0800-666999)

or:

Great George's Street
London SW1P 3AJ
(tel: 071-233-3000)

Northern Ireland Office
Criminal Justice Policy Division
Dundonald House
Belfast BT4 2SU
(tel: 0232-525228)

Northern Ireland Transport Users
Committee
55 Royal Avenue
Belfast BT1 1FX
(tel: 0232-244147)

NSPCC (Cruelty to Children)
16-20 Rosemary Street
Belfast BT1 1QD
(tel: 0232-240311)
(*Also: Child Protection Helpline, Advice
and Referrals, 24 hour service, freephone
0800-800500*)

Office of Care and Protection
Royal Courts of Justice
Chichester Street
Belfast BT1 3JP
(tel: 0232-235111)

Office of Data Protection
Springfield House
Water Lane
Wilmslow
Cheshire SK9 5AX
(tel: 0625-535777)

Office of Electricity Regulation (OFFER)
Brookmount Buildings
42 Fountain Street
Belfast BT1 5EE
(tel: 0232-311575)

Office of Fair Trading
Field House
15-28 Bream's Buildings
London EC4A 1PR
(tel: 071-242-2858)

Office of the Industrial Tribunals and
the Fair Employment Tribunal
Long Bridge House
20-24 Waring Street
Belfast BT1 2EB
(tel: 0232-327666)

Office of Law Reform
Department of Finance and Personnel
Permanent House
21-23 Arthur Street
Belfast BT1 4JL
(tel: 0232-327661)

Parents' Advice Centre
Bryson House
28 Bedford Street
Belfast BT2 7FE
(tel: 0232-238800)

Parliamentary Commissioner for
Administration (NI)
Progressive House
33 Wellington Place
Belfast BT1 6HN
(tel: 0232-233821 or freephone 0800-
282036)

Parliamentary Commissioner for
Administration (UK)
Church House
Great Smith Street
London SW1P 3BW
(tel: 071-276-3000)

Peace People
Fredheim
224 Lisburn Road
Belfast BT9 6GE
(tel: 0232-663465)

Pensions Ombudsman
11 Belgrave Road
London SW1V 1RB
(tel: 071-233-8080)

Planning Appeals Commission
Park House
107 Great Victoria Street
Belfast BT7 2AG
(tel: 0232-244710)

Police Authority for Northern Ireland
River House, 5th floor
48 High Street
Belfast BT1 2DR
(tel: 0232-230111)

Post Office Users Council for Northern
Ireland
Chamber of Commerce House
22 Great Victoria Street
Belfast BT2 7BA
(tel: 0232-244113)

Press Complaints Commission
1 Salisbury Square
London EC4Y 8AE
(tel: 071-353-1248)

Probation Board for Northern Ireland
RAC House
79 Chichester Street
Belfast BT1 4JE
(tel: 0232-242935)

Public Law Project
Institute of Advanced Legal Studies
Charles Clore House
17 Russell Square
London WC1B 5DR
(tel: 071-436-0964)

Rape Crisis Centre
41 Waring Street
Belfast BT1 2DY
(tel: 0232-249696)

Registrar General's Office
Oxford House
49-55 Chichester Street
Belfast BT1 4HL
(tel: 0232-235211)

Registrar of Friendly Societies
IDB House
64 Chichester Street
Belfast BT1 4JX
(tel: 0232-234488 ext. 2002)

Registry of Deeds
43-47 Chichester Street
Belfast BT1 4HX
(tel: 0232-241740)

Relate
76 Dublin Road
Belfast BT2 7HP
(tel: 0232-323454)

Royal Courts of Justice
Chichester Street
Belfast BT1 3JE
(tel: 0232-235111)

(*The telephone numbers of the Crown,
county court and petty sessions offices are
listed in the telephone directory under
'Government'; inquiries concerning small
claims should be made to county court
offices.*)

Royal Ulster Constabulary (RUC)
(Headquarters)
Brooklyn
Knock
Belfast BT5 6LE
(tel: 0232-650222)
(*The numbers for local police stations are
listed in the telephone directory, under
'Police'.*)

St Vincent de Paul Society
Eia House
244 Antrim Road
Belfast BT15 2AR
(tel: 0232-351561)

Samaritans
5 Wellesley Avenue
Belfast BT9 6DG
(tel: 0232-664422)

School of Law
Queen's University of Belfast
21 University Square
Belfast BT7 1NN
(tel: 0232-245133 ext. 3452)

Shelter (Northern Ireland)
165 University Road
Belfast BT7 1HR
(tel: 0232-247752)

Social Fund Commissioner's Office
11 Donegall Square South
Belfast BT1 5JE
(tel: 0232-247202)

Social Security Advisory Committee
New Court
Carey Street
London WC2A 2LS
(tel: 071-831-6111)

Social Security Commissioners
Lancashire House
5 Linenhall Street
Belfast BT2 8AA
(tel: 0232-332344)

Standing Advisory Commission on Human Rights
55 Royal Avenue
Belfast BT1 1FX
(tel: 0232-243987)

Taxing Master Offices
Bedford House
16-22 Bedford Street
Belfast BT2 7DS
(tel: 0232-245091)

Trading Standards Branch
Department of Economic Development
176 Newtownbreda Road
Belfast BT8 4QS
(tel: 0232-647151)

United Kingdom Immigrants' Advisory Service
Elliot House
2 Jackson's Row
Manchester M2 5WD
(tel: 061-834-9942)

Victim Support (NI)
Annsgate House
70-74 Ann Street
Belfast BT1 4EH
(tel: 0232-244039)

Wages Councils Office
83 Ladas Drive
Belfast BT6 9FJ
(tel: 0232-401520)

Women's Information Centre
115a Ormeau Road
Belfast BT7 1SH
(tel: 0232-246378)

Workers' Educational Association
(Northern Ireland District)
1 Fitzwilliam Street
Belfast BT9 6AW
(tel: 0232-329718)

APPENDIX 3

SAMPLE SOURCES OF LAW

(1) An Act of Parliament

Ch. 18   Fatal Accidents Act   1959.

1959. Chapter 18

An Act to amend the Fatal Accidents Act, 1846, by enlarging the class of persons for whose benefits an action may be brought thereunder; to provide for certain benefits to be left out of account in assessing damages in such an action; and for purposes connected with those matters.

[15th December. 1959]

Be it enacted by the Queen's most Excellent Majesty, and the Senate and the House of Commons of Northern Ireland in this present Parliament assembled, and by the authority of the same as follows:-

Extension of asses of pendants. & 10 Vict., 3

1. - (1) The persons for whose benefit or by whom an action may be brought under the Fatal Accidents Act, 1846, shall include any person who is, or is the issue of, a brother, sister, uncle or aunt of the deceased person.

(2) In deducing any relationship for the purposes of the said Act and this Act-

(a) an adopted person shall be treated as the child of the person or persons by whom he was adopted and not as the child of any other person; and subject thereto,

(b) any relationship by affinity shall be treated as a relationship by consanguinity, any relationship of the half blood as a relationship of the whole blood, and the stepchild of any person as his child; and

(c) an illegitimate person shall be treated as the legitimate child of his mother and reputed father.

(3) In this section "adopted" means adopted in pursuance of an adoption order made under the Adoption of Children Act (Northern Ireland), 1950, or any previous enactment relating to the adoption of children, or any corresponding enactment of the Parliament of the United Kingdom; and for the purpose of any proceedings under the Fatal Accidents Act, 1846, an adoption authorised by any such order made in England or Scotland may be proved by the production of any document receivable as evidence thereof in that country.

1950. c. 6.

(4) In section sixteen of the Law Reform (Miscellaneous Provisions) Act (Northern Ireland), 1937, there shall be substituted, for the words "wife, husband, parent or child" in paragraph (b) of sub-section (1), the word "dependants", and for paragraph (a) of sub-section (3) the following paragraph-

1 Edw. 8 &
1 Geo. 6.
c.9.

"(a) the expression "dependants" means the persons for whose benefit actions may be brought under the Fatal Accidents Acts (Northern Ireland), 1846 to 1959; and".

2. - (1) In assessing damages in respect of a person's death in any action under the Fatal Accidents Act, 1846, there shall not be taken into account any insurance money, benefit, pension or gratuity which has been or will or may be paid as a result of the death.

Exclusion
certain bene
assessment
damages

(2) In this section -

"benefit" means benefit under the National Insurance Acts (Northern Ireland), 1946, or any corresponding enactment of the Parliament of the United Kingdom and any payment by a friendly society or trade union for the relief or maintenance of a member's dependants;

1946. c.21.
1946. c.23

"insurance money" includes a return or premiums; and

"pension" includes a return of contributions and any payment of a lump sum in respect of a person's employment.

3. - (1) This Act may be cited as the Fatal Accidents Act (Northern Ireland), 1959; and the Fatal Accidents Act, 1846, and this Act may be cited together as the Fatal Accidents Acts (Northern Ireland), 1846 to 1959.

Short title, e
27 & 28 Vict
c.95

(2) References in this Act to the Fatal Accidents Act, 1846, are references thereto as amended by and read together with the Fatal Accidents Act, 1864.

(3) The enactments set out in the Schedule are hereby repealed to the extent specified in the third column of that Schedule.

(4) This Act shall apply only to actions brought in respect of deaths occurring after the passing of this Act.

SCHEDULE

ENACTMENTS REPEALED

Session or Year and Chapter	Short Title	Extent of Repeal
9 & 10 Vict., c.93	The Fatal Accidents Act, 1846	In section five the words "and stepfather and stepmother" and "and stepson and stepdaughter".
8 Edw. 7, c. 7.	The Fatal Accidents (Damages) Act, 1908	The whole Act.
1 Edw. 8 & 1 Geo. 6, c. 9	The Law Reform (Misellaneous Provisions) Act (Northern Ireland), 1937	In section fifteen, sub-sections (1), (2) and (4).
1948,c..232	The Law Reform (Miscellaneous Provisions) Act (Northern Ireland), 1948	In section three, in sub-section (5), paragraph (a).

(2) An Order in Council

1987 No. 1280 (N.I. 15)

NORTHERN IRELAND
The Occupiers' Liability (Northern Ireland) Order 1987

Made	*21st July* 1987
Coming into Operation	*22nd September 1987*

At the Court at Buckingham Palace, the 21st day of July 1987

Present,

The Queen's Most Excellent Majesty in Council

Whereas a draft of this Order has been approved by a resolution of each House of Parliament:

Now, therefore, Her Majesty, in exercise of the powers conferred by paragraph 1 of Schedule 1 to the Northern Ireland Act 1974 and of 1974 c. 28 all other powers enabling Her in that behalf, is pleased, by and with the advice of Her Privy Council, to order, and it is hereby ordered, as follows:-

*Title and commence*ment
   1. This Order may be cited as the Occupiers' Liability (Northern Ireland) Order 1987 and shall come into operation on the expiration of two months from the day on which it is made.

Interpretation
   2. The Interpretation Act (Northern Ireland) 1954 shall apply to   1954 c. 33. (N.I.) Article 1 and the following provisions of this Order as it applies to a Measure of the Northern Ireland Assembly.

Duty of occupier to person other than his visitors
   3.-(1) The rules enacted by this Article shall have effect, in place of the rules of the common law, to determine-
       (a) whether any duty is owed by a person as occupier of premises to persons other than his visitors in respect of any risk of their suffering injury on the premises by reason of any danger due to the state of the premises or to things done or omitted to be done on them; and

THE OCCUPIER'S LIABILITY (NI) ORDER 1987

(b) if so, what that duty is.

(2) For the purposes of this Article, the persons who are to be treated respectively as an occupier of any premises (which, for those purposes, include any fixed or movable structure) and as his visitors are-

1957 c. 25 (N.I.)

(a) any person who owes in relation to the premises the duty referred to in section 2 of the Occupiers' Liability Act (Northern Ireland) 1957 (the common duty of care), and
(b) those who are his visitors for the purposes of that duty.

(3) An occupier of premises owes a duty to another (not being his visitor) in respect of any such risk as is referred to in paragraph (1) if-

(a) he is aware of the danger or has reasonable grounds to believe that it exists;
(b) he knows or has reasonable grounds to believe that the other is in the vicinity of the danger concerned or that he may come into the vicinity of the danger, (in either case, whether the other has lawful authority for being in that vicinity or not); and
(c) the risk is one against which, in all the circumstances of the case, he may reasonably be expected to offer the other some protection.

(4) Where, by virtue of this Article, an occupier of premises owes a duty to another in respect of such a risk, the duty is to take such care as is reasonable in all the circumstances of the case to see that he does not suffer injury on the premises by reason of the danger concerned.

(5) Any duty owed by virtue of this Article in respect of a risk may, in an appropriate case, be discharged by taking such steps as are reasonable in all the circumstances of the case to give warning of the danger concerned or to discourage persons from incurring the risk.

(6) No duty is owed by virtue of this Article to any person in respect of risks willingly accepted as his by that person (the question whether a risk was so accepted to be decided on the same principles as in other cases in which one person owes a duty of care to another)

(7) No duty is owed by virtue of this Article to persons using a road and this Article does not affect any duty owed to such persons.

(8) Where a person owes a duty by virtue of this Article, he does not, by reason of any breach of the duty, incur any liability in respect of any loss of or damage to property.

(9) In this Article -
"road" means-

1980 NI 11

(a) a road as defined in Article 2(2) of the Roads (Northern Ireland) Order 1980, and

THE OCCUPIER'S LIABILITY (NI) ORDER 1987

(b) any other road or way over which there exists a public right of way;

'injury" means anything resulting in death or personal injury, including any disease and any impairment of physical or mental condition and

"movable structure" includes any vessel, vehicle or aircraft.

Visitors using premises for recreation etc.; modification of Unfair Contract Terns Act 1977

4.. At the end of section 1(3) of the Unfair Contract Terms Act 1977 (which defines the liability, called "business liability", the exclusion or restriction of which is controlled by virtue of that Act) there is added-

> "but liability of an occupier of premises for breach of an obligation or duty towards, a person obtaining access to the premises for recreational or educational purposes, being liability for loss or damage suffered by reason of the danger ous state of the premises, is not a business liability of the occupier unless granting that person such access for the purposes concerned falls within the business "purposes of the occupier".

1977 c. 50

Application to Crown

5. Article 3 shall bind the Crown, but as regards the Crown's liability in tort shall not bind the Crown further than the Crown is made liable in tort by the Crown Proceedings Act 1947.

1947 c. 44

G. I. de Deney
Clerk of the Privy Council

EXPLANATORY NOTE

(This note is not part of the Order)

This Order makes further provision with respect to the civil liability under the law of Nonhern Ireland of an occupier to persons on his land.

Article 3 replaces the rules of common law governing the duty of an occupier as to the safety of persons who are on his land without his permission. Article 4 amends the definition of the term "business liability" for the purposes of Part I of the Unfair Contract Terms Act 1977. hereby enabling the occupier of business premises. such as farmland. who permits visits for recreational or educational purposes. such as rock climbing, to include terms in the permission which restrict or exclude his liability to such visitors in respect of the dangerous state of the premises.

(3) A statutory rule

Planning   *No. 473*

1991 No. 473

PLANNING

Planning Applications (Exemption from Publication) Order (Northern Ireland) 1991

Made	*24th October 1991*
Coming into operation	*2nd December 1991*

The Department of the Environment, in exercise of the powers conferred on it by Articles 2(2)(**a**) and 21(2) of the Planning (Northem Ireland) Order 1991(**b**) and of all other powers enabling it in that behalf, makes the following Order:

Citation and commencement

1. This Order may be cited as the Planning Applications (Exemption from Publication) Order (Northem Ireland) 1991 and shall come into operation on 2nd December 1991.

Exempted applications

2. The provisions of Article 21(11) of the Planning (Northem Ireland) Order 1991 (publication of notices of planning applications) shall not apply **to** development of any class specified in the Schedule except where the development is in a conservation area.

Sealed with the Official Seal of the Department of the Environment on 24th October 1991.

(L.S.)   *E. Hayes*
                                  Assistant   Secretary

(**a**) See deftinitions of "the Department" and "development" order"
(**b**) S.I. *1991/1220* (N.I. 11)

No. 4 73   Planning
                         SCHEDULE   Article 2
    Class A
    The enlargement, improvement or alteration of a dwelling house.

Class B
The provision within the curtilage of a dwelling house of any building
or enclosure for a purpose incidental to the enjoyment of the dwelling
house or the enlargement, improvement or alteration of such a building
or enclosure.

EXPLANATORY NOTE
(This note is not part of the Order.)

Article 21(2) of the Planrnng (Northem Ireland) Order 1991 allows
the Department to specify classes of development for which notice of
application for planning permission need not be published in the press.

Article 2 and the Schedule to this Order specify classes of development which need not be published so long as the development is not
in a conservation area.

(4) A reported case

CAMPBELL v. ARMSTRONG AND OTHERS[1]

Highway - Negligence - Vehicle struck large stones on verge of road - Whether highway out of repair - Whether duty of care arises - Road (Liability of Road Authorities for Neglect) Act (Northern Ireland) 1966 (c.11), ss.1,2.

The plaintiff's son was killed while a passenger in a motor car driven by the defendant which crashed when it struck a large stone or stones which had fallen on to the grass verge bordering the road from a stone wall which marched alongside it. The defendant joined the Department of the Environment, the road authority as a third party. In a preliminary issue to determine if the Department is liable to indemnify the defendant against the plaintiff's claim or make contribution to it,

Held that a highway is not out of repair because stones lie on its grass verge and the operation of removing such stones does not amount to repairing it. Accordingly there is no liability on the roads authority arising from the Roads (Liability of Road Authorities for Neglect) Act (Northern Ireland) 1966. There is also no liability on the roads authority under the neighbour principle in *Donoghue v Stevenson* [1932] A.C.562 as that principle does not extend the liability of a highway authority for non-feasance beyond the 1966 Act.

The following cases are referred to in the judgment:

Donoghue v. *Stevenson* [1932] A.C.562.

Forsythe v. *Evans* [1980] N.I. 230

Haydon v. *Kent County Council* [1978] Q.B. 343;[1978] 2 W.L.R. 485; [1978] 2 All E.R.97

Hedley Byrne and Co. v. *Heller & Partners* [1964] A.C. 465; [1963] 3 W.L.R. 101; [1963] 2 All E.R.575.

Hereford and Worcester County Council v. *Newsman* [1975] 1 W.L.R. 901; [1975] 2 All E.R. 673.

Home Office v. *Dorset Yacht Co.* [1970] A.C. 1004; [1970] 2 W.L.R. 1140; [1970] 2 All E.R. 294.

Lagan v. *Department of the Environment* [1978] N.I. 120.

PRELIMINARY ISSUE. The facts appear sufficiently from the judgment of Kelly J.

R.L. McCartney Q.C. and *M.A. Morrow* for the defendant *R.D. Carswell Q.C.* and *B.F. Kerr* for the Department of the Environment.

---

1. In the Queen's Bench Division before Kelly J; January 22, March 13, 1981

N.I.   **Campbell v. Armstrong & Ors. (Q.B.D.)**   **Kelly J.**

Cur.adv.vult.

KELLY J. The pleadings in this action raise a point of law for determination as a preliminary issue. It concerns the civil liability of a highway authority for injury loss and damage caused by obstructions on the grass verge of a road maintainable by the authority.

The facts out of which the action arises can be stated shortly. On the 21 October 1977 the plaintiff's son was killed while a passenger in a motor car driven by the defendant which crashed when overtaking another car on a straight stretch of the Aughnacloy-Castlecaulfield road, County Tyrone. While overtaking the other car, part of the defendant's vehicle went on to the grass verge bordering the road and one or more of its wheels struck there a large stone or stones which had fallen on to the verge from a stone wall which marched alongside it.

The plaintiff as administratrix of her son's estate sues the defendant for damages under the Fatal Accident Order 1976 (sic) and the Law Reform (Miscellaneous Provisions) Act (Northern Ireland) 1937 alleging negligent driving. The defendant denies negligence and brings in as third parties to the action claiming indemnity or contribution against them, the Department of the Environment for Northern Ireland (hereinafter called "the Department") who is admittedly the road authority responsible for maintaining the roadway and grass verge in question and William Montgomery Buchanan who is the owner of the stone wall. This preliminary issue does not, however, concern the second-named third party.

It is the Department who disputes in law the defendant's claim that being the body responsible for the inspection maintenance repair and control of the grass verge and negligent in that duty in failing to keep it free of the stone or stones the Department is liable to indemnify the defendant against the plaintiff's claim or make contribution to it. The submission of the Department is that they cannot be made liable in damages.

I consider first their possible liability in damages for a breach of statutory duty. In this, one is drawn at once to the statutory duty of a highway authority in respect of obstructions on its roads contained in section 2 of the Roads (Liability of Road Authorities for Neglect) Act (Northern Ireland) 1966 which reads:

"2. (1) If an obstruction occurs in a road from accumulation of snow or from the falling down of banks on the side of the road, or from any other cause, the road authority by whom the road is maintainable shall remove the obstruction.

(2) If a road authority fail to remove an obstruction which it is their duty under this section to remove, a court of summary jurisdiction may, on a complaint made by any person, by order require the authority to remove the obstruction within such period (not being less than twenty-four hours) from the making of the order as the court thinks reasonable having regard to all the circumstances of the case."

But anyone who has suffered loss and damage from a breach of this section is stopped from embarking on a civil claim for damages by the clear prohibition of sub-section 6 of the section, which states;

"(6) it is hereby declared that nothing in this section shall operate to confer on any person a right of action in tort against a road authority for failing to carry out any duty imposed on them under this section."

A civil remedy in damages against a road authority is of course earlier given by section 1 of the same Act, which states:

"1. (1) Any rule of law which operates to exempt a road authority from liability for non-repair of roads is hereby abrogated."

but the language of section 1 has been held to confine the remedy to cases of strict non-repair of the highway (see *Lagan v. Department of Environment* [1978] N.I. 120, 124). Following this, it seems to me that it cannot be seriously argued that a highway is out of repair because stones lie on its grass verge or that the operation of removing a stone or stones from it amounts to repairing it.

This view is reinforced by dicta of Cairns L.J. in *Hereford and Worcester County Council v. Newman* [1975] 1 W.L.R. 901 and of Lord Denning M.R. in *Haydon V Kent County Council* [1978] 2 W.L.R. 485. Cairns L.J. said at page 910:

"In relation to a highway I am of opinion that in ordinary speech nobody would speak of the mere removal of an obstruction from the highway as being in itself a repair. I respectfully agree with Lord Widgery C.J. in saying that if a builder chose to dump tons of rubble on a footpath thus rendering it impassable, it would be an abuse of language to say that the highway authority had allowed the footpath to become out of repair.

It is I think striking that in all the Highway Acts from 1835 to 1959 repair and removal of obstructions are separately dealt with ...

I consider that a highway can only be said to be out of repair if the surface of it is defective or disturbed in some way."

Lord Denning M.R. in *Haydon's* case said at page 491:

" 'Repair' means making good defects in the surface of the highway itself ..."

and at page 492:

"An 'obstruction' to a highway occurs when it is rendered impassable, or more difficult to pass along it by reason of some physical obstacle. It may be obstructed without it being out of repair at all. If a tree falls across a road, it may not injure the surface at all, it may even straddle it without touching the surface, the road is then 'obstructed' but it is not out of repair ...

'Maintain' does not, however, include the removal of obstructions, except when the obstruction damages the surfaces of the highway and makes it necessary to remove the obstruction so as to execute the repairs."

The Act of 1966 does not therefore by any of its provisions give a civil remedy in

N.I.   **Campbell v. Armstrong & Ors. (Q.B.D.)**   **Kelly J.**

the circumstances of this case and that appears to exhaust any possible remedy under statute.

Has the Department also immunity from civil liability at common law? It seems to me it has. Misfeasance cannot arise on the facts, but the defendant sought to apply the neighbour principle of *Donoghue* v. *Stevenson* [1932] A.C. 562 as a means of relief, encouraged no doubt by such well-known dicta as:

> "The criterion of judgment must adjust and adapt itself to the changing circumstances of life; the categories of negligence are never closed." (Lord MacMillan in *Donoghue* v. *Stevenson* (supra) at page 619) and
> "English law is wide enough to embrace any new category or proposition that exemplifies the principle of proximity." (Lord Devlin in *Hedley Byrne & Co. Ltd.* v. *Heller & Partners Ltd.* [1964] A.C. 465, at page 531).

But I think it is wise before any new application or expansion of the neighbour principle is attempted to heed the caution expressed by Lord Diplock in *Home Office* v. *Dorset Yacht Co. Ltd.* [1970] A.C. 1004. At page 1060 in a reference to Lord Atkin's neighbour principle, he said:

> "Used as a guide to characteristics which will be found to exist in conduct and relationships which give rise to a legal duty of care this aphorism marks a milestone in the modern development of the law of negligence. But misused as a universal, it is manifestly false.

> The branch of English law which deals with civil wrongs abounds with instances of acts and more particularly, of omissions which give rise to no legal liability in the doer or omitter for loss and damage sustained by others as a consequence of the act of omission, however reasonably or probably that loss or damage might have anticipated."

Immunity from civil liability for non-repair of highways continued after the decision in *Donoghue* v. *Stevenson* in 1932. There is no reported decision that I know of, thereafter, to show that the neighbour principle was successfully applied in a case of non- repair, up to the time when statutory exemption from liability for non-repair was cancelled in England by the Highways (Miscellaneous Provisions) Act 1961 and by the Act of 1966 here. And since the passing of the 1966 Act, despite the comparatively confined meanings given to "non-repair" and "failure to maintain" in section 1 (see *Lagan* v. *Department of the Environment* (supra)) no reported case has applied the neighbour principle to extend the liability of a highway authority for non-feasance outside that section. Therefore the acts of omission on the part of a highway authority would seem not to give rise to a cause of action for damages if they fall outside the highway authority's duty under section 1 on the principle, presumably, that where there is no duty to act, an omission to act gives no remedy.

And there may be sound reasons of public policy for refusing to expand the statutory duty of a road authority outside strict repair. I have stated possible considerations in a judgment in *Forsythe* v. *Evans, Charges Brand & Co. Ltd.,* v. *The Department of the Environment* [1980] N.I. 230 (an issue concerning the civil liability of a road authority in respect of injury caused by icy roads) some of which I think are in point here. In the instant case it seems to me quite unreasonable that a duty of care should arise that obliges a road authority to inspect grass verges and free them from obstructions for the unnimpeded passage of traffic, vehicular or pedestrian.

I hold that the defendant's statement of claim does not disclose a cause of action by the defendant against the Department. I give judgment for the first Third Party, the Department, against the defendant, with costs.

Order accordingly

Solicitors for the defendant: *Wilson & Simms*
Solicitors for the Department of the Environment: *Crown Solicitor*

W.D.T.

APPENDIX 4

SPECIMEN LEGAL FORMS

Rep. 5
GREEN FORM

THE LAW SOCIETY OF NORTHERN IRELAND

LEGAL AID
NORTHERN IRELAND

SOLICITOR'S REPORT ON LEGAL ADVICE AND ASSISTANCE GIVEN UNDER
THE LEGAL AID, ADVICE & ASSISTANCE (NORTHERN IRELAND) ORDER, 1981

Key Card

PLEASE USE BLOCK CAPITALS

Surname   Forenames   Mr./Mrs./Miss

Address

CAPITAL   CLIENT   £
TOTAL SAVINGS and OTHER CAPITAL   SPOUSE   £
                                               TOTAL
                                                          £   Ⓐ

INCOME
State whether in receipt of Family Credit/Income Support.
YES/NO   If answer is YES ignore the rest of this Section.   Ⓑ

Total weekly Gross Income

   Client   £
   Spouse   £
   TOTAL   £

Allowances and Deductions from Income

   Income tax   £
   National Health Contributions, etc.   £   Ⓒ
   Spouse   £   Ⓓ
                                                      Ⓔ

Dependent children and/or
   other dependants   Number   Ⓕ

   Under 11   £

   11 but under 16   £

   16 "   " 18   £

   18 and over   £

LESS TOTAL DEDUCTIONS   ➡

TOTAL WEEKLY DISPOSABLE INCOME   £

TO BE COMPLETED AND SIGNED BY CLIENT

I am over the compulsory school-leaving age.

I have/have not previously received help from a solicitor about this matter under the Legal Aid and Advice Schemes.

I am liable to pay a contribution not exceeding.
                                                      £   Ⓖ

   I understand that any money or property which is recovered or preserved for me may be subject to a deduction if my
contribution (if any) is less than my Solicitor's charges.

   The information on this page is to the best of my knowledge correct and complete. I understand that dishonesty in providing
such information may lead to a prosecution.

Date ....   Signature ....

3F 4627

STATEMENT OF MEANS OF AN APPLICANT FOR LEGAL AID IN A CRIMINAL CASE UNDER PART III OF THE LEGAL AID, ADVICE AND ASSISTANCE (NORTHERN IRELAND) ORDER 1981

If you wish to obtain legal aid in a criminal case you must first complete this form which will be used to determine whether you are entitled to legal aid.

WARNING. IF, IN COMPLETING THIS STATEMENT, YOU KNOWINGLY MAKE ANY FALSE STATEMENT OR FALSE REPRESENTATION YOU WILL BE LIABLE TO PROSECUTION AND IF FOUND GUILTY COULD BE FINED £100 OR IMPRISONED FOR UP TO 3 MONTHS OR BOTH.

PLEASE COMPLETE IN BLOCK CAPITALS.

1. Surname (Mr Mrs Miss Ms)

2. Other names

3. (a) Date of Birth _____ (b) National Insurance No (if known)

4. Permanent address

5. If staying at temporary accommodation state address

6. Name and address of solicitor requested (if known)

7. State whether married married, living apart single widowed divorced *(delete as appropriate)*

8. Are you currently receiving

    (a) Supplementary benefit?   (Yes No)

    (b) Family Income Supplement?   (Yes No)

NOTE—
IF YOU ARE RECEIVING SUPPLEMENTARY BENEFIT OR FAMILY INCOME SUPPLEMENT YOU NEED NOT ANSWER ANY FURTHER QUESTIONS ON THIS FORM. YOU MUST, HOWEVER, READ AND SIGN THE DECLARATION AT THE END.

9. State occupation or profession

10. State whether you are employed self employed/unemployed *(delete as appropriate)*

11. If you are employed state

    (a) Whether full-time or part-time and

    (b) Name and address of your employer (a) _____ (b)

12. What is your average weekly take-home pay (ie earnings after deductions of Income Tax and National Insurance? £ _____

13. If self-employed state annual net income £ _____

14. Is your spouse employed? (Yes/No) _____ or self-employed? (Yes/No) _____
    If either answer is Yes state his/her

    (a) Occupation

                                                                        P T O

(b) Name and address of employer _____

_____

(c) Approximate weekly earnings £ _____

15. Do you or your spouse have any other income? (eg interest from investments or rents received)

(Yes/No) _____

If the answer is Yes give details and amounts (including names of banks, Building Societies, etc from which interest is received, and state type of benefit, pensions etc received).

_____

_____

_____

16. Do you or your spouse have any savings, money, property or other goods of value? (Yes/No) _____

If Yes give details _____

_____

_____

17. Have you any dependants? (Yes/No) _____

If Yes give details (including names, ages and addresses if different from your own).

_____

_____

_____

18. State the amount you pay per week for

(a) Rent   £ _____

(b) Rates   £ _____

(c) Mortgage   £ _____

(d) Board and lodging charge or contribution for keep £ _____

19. Do you have any other exceptional expenses which you feel should be taken into account?

(Yes/No) _____

If the answer is Yes give details _____

_____

_____

20. If you are under 18 state the name and address of your parent or guardian

_____

_____

21. If you are under 18 are your parents willing to assist you financially in providing you with legal aid?

(Yes/No) _____

DECLARATION

I declare that to the best of my knowledge and belief the above particulars are true and I understand that the Court may require the Department of Health and Social Services to enquire into my means before or after the granting of a Criminal Aid Certificate.

Signature _____   Date _____

MAGISTRATES' COURTS (NORTHERN IRELAND) ORDER 1981
(Article 20(1), (2) and (3); Rule 8)

Summons to Defendant to answer Complaint

[Title as in Form 1]

WHEREAS a complaint has been made before me that on the (date)
at (place)
in the said petty sessions district and county court division, you, the said
defendant

THIS IS TO COMMAND YOU to appear as a defendant on the hearing of the
said complaint at (place)   on (date)
, at (time)
before a magistrates' court for the said county court division.

This   day of   19

                                        Justice of the Peace
                                        [Clerk of Petty Sessions]

To the said Defendant

MAGISTRATES' COURTS (NORTHERN IRELAND) ORDER 1981
(Articles 20 and 45; Rules 8 and 44(1))

Summons to Defendant to answer Complaint charging an Indictable Offence specified in Schedule 2 to the Order

[*Title as in Form 1*]

WHEREAS a complaint has been made before me that on (date)
at (place)
in the said petty sessions district and county court division you, the said defendant,

THIS IS TO COMMAND YOU to appear in person as a defendant on the hearing of the said complaint at (place)   , on (date)
at (time)   before a magistrates' court of the said county court division.

This   day of   19   .

Justice of the Peace
[Clerk of Petty Sessions]

Notice under Article 45 of the said Order of 1981

The [following] offence(s) [that is to say—]

for which you are hereby summoned to appear before the court [is] [are] [an] indictable offence(s) specified in Schedule 2 to the said Order which may be dealt with summarily by a resident magistrate in accordance with Article 45 of that Order.

The purpose of this notice is to inform you that the above offence(s) [is] [are] [an] offence(s) for which you have a right to be tried by jury and which may be dealt with summarily by a resident magistrate only with your consent, and if you do so consent, only where the prosecutor also consents.

The resident magistrate may, however, even if you consent and the prosecutor also consents to the summary trial of [any of] the above-mentioned offence(s), decide that for any of the reasons specified in Article 45(1) of the said Order, it is inexpedient to deal with any such offence(s) summarily.

FORM OF INDICTMENT

THE QUEEN v.

Court of Trial:

Date:

CHARGE(S)

charged with the following offence(s):—

FIRST COUNT

STATEMENT OF OFFENCE

PARTICULARS OF OFFENCE

SECOND COUNT

STATEMENT OF OFFENCE

PARTICULARS OF OFFENCE

FORM 125

Claim No.

Application for Arbitration (Small Claims)

Order 26, Rule 3

Applicant: Full name and postal address in BLOCK CAPITALS   *Respondent:* Full name and postal address in BLOCK CAPITALS

(put your full name and address here)	*(the full name and address of the person you are claiming against goes here)*

Take notice that I the above named Applicant intend to apply to the Circuit Registrar

at   *(put name of court – see list on page 60)*   for arbitration in respect

of my claim for £

(insert particulars of claim)

> *(here insert the amount claimed and short details of your claim – see examples given on page 12)*

Date:

Signed: ....
                       Applicant

FOR OFFICE USE ONLY

NOTICE OF HEARING

This Application will be dealt with by the Circuit Registrar when he sits

at

on

The Circuit Registrar's sitting will start at

                                Chief Clerk

SC1   Date:

ORDINARY CIVIL BILL

No.

In the County Court for the Division

of

Between

of

in the County of

Plaintiff

and

of

in the County of

and Division of

Defendant

By The County Court Judge Recorder

The sittings at which this civil bill is intended to be dealt with will commence on the   day of   19 and will be held at

The defendant therefore is hereby required to appear at the aforesaid Court at the hour of   on the   day of   19 to answer the plaintiff's claim for

Costs and outlay if paid within fourteen days from date of service £

NOTE—Costs and outlay if paid after fourteen days from service will be payable at a higher scale.

Dated this   day of   19

Signed ....
Solicitor for the Plaintiff

Address ....

A & S DONALDSON (N I) LTD. Law Stationers, Lisburn

19 . No. 12345

In The High Court of Justice in Northern Ireland

QUEEN'S BENCH DIVISION

ALBERT MOUSEPARTNER

v.

PERCY VERE and JOSEPH SMITH

WRIT OF SUMMONS

GENERAL FORM

We accept service hereof on behalf of Percy Vere, one of the within named Defendants.

Dated the   day of   19

Signed:

   Holbrook, Willoughby & Griffiths,
   1 Snob Lane,
   Belfast 1.

      Lowe, Snow & Co.,
      Solicitors,
      7 Donegall Square East,
      Belfast 1.

A. & S. Donaldson (N.I.) Ltd. Law Stationers, Lisburn

<u>WRIT OF SUMMONS</u>

In the High Court of Justice in Northern Ireland

DIVISION

19   No. 12345

Between

ALBERT MOUSEPARTNER

Plaintiff

and

PERCY VERE and JOSEPH SMITH

Defendants

ELIZABETH THE SECOND, by the Grace of God, of the United Kingdom of Great Britain and Northern Ireland and of Our other realms and territories Queen, Head of the Commonwealth, Defender of the Faith:

To   Percy Vere, of "The Beeches", Weyford, and
            Joseph Smith

of   "Fag End", 1 Butt Lane, Weyford, both

in the County of Down

We command you, that within 14 days after the service of this writ on you, inclusive of the day of service, you do cause an appearance to be entered for you in an action at the suit of

ALBERT MOUSEPARTNER

and take notice that in default of your so doing, the plaintiff may proceed therein, and judgment may be given in your absence.

    WITNESS, The Right Honourable ROBERT LYND ERSKINE, BARON LOWRY, Lord Chief Justice of Northern Ireland, the   day of

19

Note:—This writ may not be served later than 12 calendar months beginning with the above date unless renewed by order of the Court.

DIRECTIONS FOR ENTERING APPEARANCE

The defendant may enter an appearance in person or by a solicitor either (1) by handing in the appropriate forms, duly completed, at the Central Office or Chancery Office (as appropriate), Royal Courts of Justice, Chichester Street, Belfast BT1 3JF, or (2) by sending them to that Office by post. The appropriate forms may be obtained at H.M. Stationery Office, Chichester House, Chichester Street, Belfast BT1 1PS.

The Plaintiff's claim is for damages for personal injuries, loss and damage sustained by him by reason of the negligence of the first Defendant and/or the second Defendant in or about the driving, management and control of motor vehicles.

If the Plaintiff sues, or the defendant is sued, in a representative capacity, this must be stated in the endorsement of claim.

G. Bull

(Signed) ....

And £   (or such sum as may be allowed on taxation) for costs, and also, if the plaintiff obtains an order for substituted service, the further sum of £ (or such sum as may be allowed on taxation). If the amount claimed and costs be paid to the plaintiff or his solicitor within 14 days after service hereof (inclusive of the day of service), further proceedings will be stayed.

This paragraph should be deleted if the plaintiff's claim is not for a debt or liquidated demand only.

This writ was issued by Lowe, Snow & Co.,

of 7, Donegall Square East, in the City of Belfast,

Solicitor for the said plaintiff whose address is

5, Council Flats, Weyford, in the County of Down

OR

This writ was issued by the said plaintiff who resides at

and (*if the plaintiff does not reside within the jurisdiction*)
whose address for service is

*IN THE HIGH COURT OF JUSTICE IN NORTHERN IRELAND

FAMILY DIVISION   *Delete as appro|

*IN THE COUNTY COURT FOR THE DIVISION OF

THE PETITION OF

1. On the   day of   19

the petitioner

was lawfully married to

(hereinafter called ''the respondent'') at

2. The petitioner and respondent last lived together as husband and wife at

3. The petitioner/respondent is domiciled in Northern Ireland.

4. The petitioner is by occupation a

and resides at

  The respondent is by occupation a

and resides at

5. There are no children of the family, now living, **except**

6. No other child, now living, has been born to the petitioner/respondent during the marriage
(so far as is known to the petitioner) **except**

7. No periodical payment order or secured periodical payments order is sought for any child of the family **except for**
on the grounds that;

There are or have been no other proceedings in any court in Northern Ireland or elsewhere with reference to the marriage (or any child of the family) or between the petitioner and respondent with reference to any property of either or both of them except

No application in respect of any child of the family has been made to the Child Support Agency for a maintenance assessment under the Child Support (Northern Ireland) Order 1991 **except**

There are no proceedings continuing in any country outside Northern Ireland which are in respect of the marriage are capable of affecting its validity or subsistence **except**

No agreement or arrangement has been made or is proposed to be made between the parties for the support of the petitioner/respondent (and any child of the family) except

The said marriage has broken down irretrievably.

PARTICULARS

PRAYER

The petitioner therefore prays:

(1) That the said marriage be dissolved.

(2) That the petitioner may be granted custody of

(3) That the   may be ordered to pay the costs of this suit.

(4) That the petitioner may be granted the following ancillary relief:

    (a) an order for maintenance pending suit and thereafter

        a periodical payments order

        a secured provision order

        a lump sum order

    (b) a periodical payments order

        a secured provision order   } for the children

        a lump sum order

    (c) a property adjustment order in relation to

Signed _____

The names and addresses of the persons to be served with this petition are:

Respondent:

Co-Respondent (adultery case only):

The Petitioner's address for service

Dated this   day of   19

Address all communications for the court to:

The Master (Probate and Matrimonial)
Royal Courts of Justice
Chichester Street
Belfast BT1 3JF

NOTICE OF INTENT TO ENFORCE A MONEY JUDGMENT
JUDGMENTS ENFORCEMENT (NORTHERN IRELAND) ORDER 1981

BETWEEN:

                                                        Plaintiff/Applicant

                                                        Defendant/Respondent
To: [1]

of [2]

TAKE NOTICE that you owe [3]
the sum of £ [4]   together with interest at the rate of [5]   per cent per
annum which is the amount due on foot of a judgment given against you in the above matter
and a copy of which is attached.

YOU HAVE 10 DAYS from the date of this notice within which to pay that amount at the
*address given below. If you do not pay proceedings will be taken to enforce the judgment
against you.

Dated [6]   day of   19

Signed   ....

                Applicant/Duly Authorised Person/
                Applicant's Solicitor

*Address   ....

                ....

                ....

REQUISITION
The Chief Enforcement Officer, Enforcement of Judgments Office.
      Please issue and serve the above Notice of Intention to Proceed on
[1]
at [2]
which is the present address of the said [1]
to the best of my/our knowledge, information and belief.

Signed ....
            Creditor/Solicitor(s) for Creditor

Dated ....

NOTES
[1] Full name of debtor.
[2] Full postal address of debtor.
[3] Full name of creditor.
[4] This figure should represent the balance of all monies due and payable under the
    judgment at the date of signing.
[5] Insert the rate of interest prescribed by the relevant rule of court. Interest is not
    chargeable where the sum due and payable under the judgment does not exceed £200 or
    the judgment is for a penal sum for securing principal and interest.
[6] Leave blank.

ORIGINATING APPLICATION TO AN INDUSTRIAL TRIBUNAL

<u>**UNDER ONE OR MORE OF THE FOLLOWING ACTS OR ORDERS**</u>

CONTRACTS OF EMPLOYMENT AND REDUNDANCY PAYMENTS (NI) 1965

EQUAL PAY ACT (NI) 1970

SEX DISCRIMINATION (NI) ORDER 1976

INDUSTRIAL RELATIONS (NI) ORDERS 1976 TO 1982

For Official Use	
Case	
Number	

CONTRACTS OF EMPLOYMENT AND REDUNDANCY PAYMENTS ACT (NI) 1965

EQUAL PAY ACT (NI) 1970

SEX DISCRIMINATION (NI) ORDER 1976

INDUSTRIAL RELATIONS (NI) ORDERS 1976

IMPORTANT: DO NOT FILL IN THIS FORM UNTIL YOU HAVE READ EXPLANATORY LEAFLET 1TL 1(NI) ALL QUESTIONS MUST BE ANSWERED.

To:- The Secretary of the Tribunals
Central Office of the Industrial Tribunals
2nd Floor, Bedford House, Bedford Street
Belfast BT2 7NR

Telephone: 227666

1. I hereby apply for a decision of a tribunal on the following question (State here question to be decided by the tribunal and the Act(s) and/or Order(s) appropriate to your case).

....

....

....

(The grounds of your application should be stated in paragraph 14 overleaf)

2. My name (Surname in block captials first) is Mr/Mrs/Miss ....

Address and telephone number ....

OR title (if company or organisation) is ....

3. Date of Birth ....   National Insurance No...........................

4. If your employment has ended have you claimed unemployment/supplementary benefit? ....

5. If you are a member of a trade union please state name of organisation ....
....

6. If a representative has agreed to act for you in this case please give his name and address below:-

Name ....

Address and telephone number ....

7. (a) Name of respondent(s) (in block capitals) ie the employer, person or body against whom a decision is sought ....

Address(es) and telephone number(s) ....

....

IT1(NI) (Rev)

7. (b) Respondent's relationship to you for the purpose of the application (eg employer, trade union, employment agency, employer recognising the union making application, etc)

....

8. Place of employment to which this application relates or place where act complained about took place.

....

Occupation or position held/applied for, or other relationship to the respondent named above (eg user of a service supplied by him) ....

10. Employment began on.........................and (if appropriate) ended on ....

11. Basic nett wage................Basic gross wage..............Other pay or remuneration ....

12. Normal basic weekly hours of work:- ....

13. (In an application under the Sex Discrimination (NI) Order 1976) Date on which action complained of took place or first came to my knowledge ....

....

14. The grounds of this application are as follows:-

15. (If dismissed) If you wish to state what in your opinion was the reason for your dismissal, please do so here.

....

....

16. If dismissed and the tribunal decides that you were unfairly dismissed, what remedy would you prefer? (Before answering this question please consult leaflet 1TL 1 (NI) for the remedies available and then write ONE only of the following in answer to this question: reinstatement, re-engagement or compensation)

....

Signature .... Date........................

FOR OFFICIAL USE

Issuing Office	Received at COIT	Initials

INDEX